The Limits of Government

The Limits of Government

Policy Competence & Economic Growth

Gunnar Eliasson
&
Nils Karlson
editors

Transaction Publishers
New Brunswick (U.S.A.) and London (U.K.)

2001 edition published by Transaction Publishers, New Brunswick, New Jersey. Originally published in 1998 by City University Press, Stockholm.

Library of Congress Catalog Number: 99-049820
ISBN: 1-56000-437-1
Printed in the United States of America

Library of Congress Cataloging-in-Publication Data

The limits of government : on policy competence and economic growth : papers from the sixth conference of the International Joseph A. Schumpeter Society in Stockholm / editors, Gunnar Eliasson & Nils Karlson.
    p. cm.
Selected papers from the sixth biennial conference held June 2-5, 1996.
Originally published: Stockholm : City University Press, 1998.
Includes bibliographical references and index.
ISBN 1-56000-437-1 (alk. paper)
1. Economic development—Congresses. 2. Economic policy—Congresses. 3. Industrial policy—Congresses. I. Eliasson, Gunnar. II. Karlson, Nils. III. International Schumpeter Society. Meeting (6th : Stockholm, Sweden)

HD73 .L56 1999
338.9—dc21   99-049820

Contents

PART II CONSEQUCENCES OF STATE
INTERFERENCE AND NON-INTERFERENCE

Acknowledgements

The Sixth Biennial Conference of the International Schumpeter Society was held in Stockholm, June 2–5, 1996. The Conference drew a record number of submissions and participants. In all more than 100 papers were presented. This volume, entitled *The limits of government*, is a set of nine essays drawn from some 30 papers presented at the Conference related to the role of government in economic growth. A set of 22 essays have been published seperately in another volume entitled *The microfoundations of economic growth : a Shumpeterian perspective*, by the University of Michigan Press.

The Conference was made possible by a generous grant from the Marcus Wallenberg Foundation for International Scientific Cooperation and from several Swedish corporations. Because of the generosity of the Swedish State Railways (Statens Järnvägar), some sessions were conducted on a conference train between Falun and Stora. Stora, the world's oldest corporation, a mining and forestry firm founded in 1288, hosted the society's General Assembly. We are grateful to the City of Stockholm for the magnificent reception in the City Hall on the opening day. To the members of the Scientific Committee and to the persons who handled local organizing, notably Monica Hamrén, Christina Carlsson, Staffan Laestadius, and Per Storm, we wish to say thanks for a job well done. Finally, we wish to thank Erik Kristow and Wera Nyren for editorial and secretarial services in the preparation of this volume on the role of government.

9

Foreword

There is no way to understand how an economy at large behaves without taking a close look at the actors who make it behave. There is no way to understand the agents operating in markets without placing them in the context of the institutions that determine the incentives that pull, and the competition that pushes them in different directions and together co-ordinate all actors into a fairly consistent macro-economic whole. This also means that successful policy-making, whether directed at the macro or micro levels of the economy, demands insights on the part of the policy-maker that go far beyond what mainstream economic theory is capable of providing.

The Sixth Conference of the International Joseph A Schumpeter Society, June 2–5, 1996, in Stockholm was arranged by the Royal Institute of Technology, in collaboration with the City University of Stockholm. The theme of the Conference was "The Microfoundations of Economic Growth." The number of papers submitted and accepted for presentation was larger than ever before. Two volumes from the Conference are therefore being published.[1]

Many interesting and excellent papers presented at the Conference focused on the role of institutions, notably government, in economic growth. The most interesting of these papers are collected in this volume.

Stockholm in February 1998

Gunnar Eliasson
Royal Institute of Technology
President of the Joseph A Schumpeter Society 1995/1996

Nils Karlson
President of the City University of Stockholm

---

1   One volume with the title *The microfoundations of economic growth,* edited by Gunnar Eliasson and Christopher Green with the assistance of Charles McCann, is published by the University of Michigan Press 1998.

The State as a Supporter or Disorganizer of the Market Economy

Gunnar Eliasson & Nils Karlson

The limits of government and the consequences of government interference in markets for economic growth are the central themes in this collection of papers from the Sixth Conference of the International Joseph A Schumpeter Society in Stockholm, June 2–5, 1996. Theoretical as well as case-oriented empirical studies are included. When and why does government interference in the market process succeed and when and why does it fail?

For obvious reasons the selected papers do not cover all of this field, but the authors have been asked to revise their papers to fit the overall theme. And with this introduction we are also trying to fill in missing links to the extent possible.

Actors in markets need various forms of support: legal, social and moral. Institutions or infrastructures such as these are part of all functioning market economies and are necessary for economic progress. Even though neglected for years by the economics profession and the growth theorists, their study is a must for anyone with the ambition to understand economic growth. Such institutions can be public or private, including the externalities emanating from the joint actions of all actors in the economy.

Collective infrastructures and other institutions facilitate exchange outside equilibrium (Day 1986) and as such contribute significally to the wealth of nations. But the same infrastructures can also operate as negative externalities and constrain and inhibit important market activities. In a sense all such infrastructures have emerged in response to a demand, government being only one among many market actors initiating the establishment of infrastructures or externalities in the economy. The volume includes several papers suggesting that a reduction of government would benefit the economy, notably in areas where market arbitrage exhibits clear advantages over policy control or regulation in allocating resources, and where policy-makers lack the necessary competence to contribute positively to economic development. The process of the establishment of infrastructures, their composition and the outcome of their influence on the economy, therefore, are an important area of scientific inquiry.

In particular, this volume focuses on the supporting collective institutions of the market processes, including the role of big government. The selection of papers can be seen as complementary to a first volume from the Stockholm Conference, *The microfoundations of economic growth* (Gunnar Eliasson & Christopher Green (eds), University of Michigan Press, 1998).

One question addressed in this volume is the lack of necessary institutions, and why market incentives and/or government action fail to establish them. This is typically the situation in the formerly planned East European economies. Another question concerns the overestablishment of infrastructures and institutions, notably by government origin, that hinders or even blocks economic progress, i e when the state turns into a disorganizer of the market economy. This is often the case in pronounced welfare economies (Karlson 1993, Karlson 1995, Eliasson 1998).

In the tradition of Joseph Schumpeter, notably his *Capitalism, socialism and democracy* (1942), society is composed of actors and institutions which partly reinforce and partly conflict with each other and the economy at large. This line of reasoning from a theoretical point of view dominates the chapters in Part I of the book: "Theories of state interference."

Democracy, as argued by Richard Day in Chapter I, can be a necessary and efficient institution to resolve and soften social instabilities caused by efficient market behavior. The same institutions, if not properly organized, argues Erik Moberg in Chapter II, may also lead to an excessive expansion of the public sector and long-term economic inefficiency. To make it worse, it may also cause an *institutional* (or political) *lock-in* that is almost impossible to get out of through a democratic process (also see Chapter VI by Reed, Karlson 1993, Eliasson 1986). While the first volume from the 1996 Schumpeter Conference (Eliasson & Green 1998) looked at technological lock-ins, we are here concerned with the incidence of possible parallel institutional lock-ins.

Is there a way out of such an unfortunate situation? How can institutional trimming or creative institutional destruction be organized in the welfare economies of the West? Clas Wihlborg, in Chapter III, discusses the introduction of *enabling law* as one possible institutional innovation that may help distressed welfare economies and East European economies out of their institutional lock-ins. However, it is far from clear that the necessary incentives and the relevant political competence for such a change are at hand.

While the individual actors in the market can pursue individual gains with a fair probability of success, his or her efforts in the political system (in the political market), as noted by Schumpeter (1942, p 261), are far less likely to contribute to his or her personal well-being. As "a member of an unworkable committee, the committee of the whole nation, and this is why he expends less disciplined effort on mastering a political problem than he expends on a game of bridge ... the typical citizen drops down to a lower level of mental performance as soon as he enters the political field."

In fact, it may be far more profitable for the individual to act rationally in the political market by pursuing personal rents offered by vote-seeking politicians, while at the same time optimally allocating his or her income in the real markets for goods and services. If the political system is so organized as to make these two rational individual decisions inconsistent the political process may create strong internal tensions in the economy (Eliasson 1986a,b), which are inflationary and may eventually be socially disruptive. This is in fact very likely to be the case, looking at Moberg's analysis in Chapter II.

While economic theory has conventionally conferred a supervising role of the markets to the government to minimize market failure, the theory has consistently failed to recognize that unique and scarce competence is required for that monitoring. Hence, mistaken identification of market failure and/or inconsequent policy action to correct for politically perceived market failure and/or inconsequent policy action to correct for actual market failure, may result in government failure, most likely on a grander scale than the market failure supposed to have been corrected.

Part II of the book focuses on empirical issues: "Consequences of state interference and non-interference."

Governments can act on the economy in two capacities; (1) *modestly*, by reforming the institutions and circumstances conditioning the behavior of the market actors and (2) *ambitiously* and dangerously, by attempting to influence the actual outcomes of the market processes. Most chapters address "type (1)" policy, as was the design of the Conference. Most evidence, however, is on the outcomes of "type (2)" policies, notably Gørtz (in Chapter VII) who observes the disastrous outcome of "type (2)" policies on a very small economy, and notes that little harm and much good could have been achieved, easily, with more modest "type (1)" policies directed at the micro-economic circumstances.

Both David Allen (Chapter IV) and Jean-Philipe Bonardi and Bertrand Quélin (Chapter V) address the design of market institutions directly. Looking at the fast computer and communications markets Allen shifts policy emphasis away from formal property rights towards anti-trust policy, but he asks for a much more sophisticated policy than current US practice. Bonardi & Quélin are concerned with the design of deregulation. How do you eliminate inefficient rent-seeking behavior in favor of productive, Adam Smith-type competition?

The rent-seeking and monopolizing behavior discussed by Allen and Bonardi & Quélin opens up a vast range of unproductive political activities, not in the least the destructive redistributive policies of democratic parties discussed by Moberg and—in a similar vein—vote-seeking through egalitarian policies.

In Chapter VI Andrew Reed discusses the institutional failures of government in the agricultural sector of Russia. Old, centralist and inefficient ways of doing things persist. In part this is, perhaps paradoxically, caused by Western organizations involved in technical assistance who naturally team up with the old bureaucracy. The result is that proper market institutions do not evolve, at least not at the pace required. The political as well as the market demand for change is too weak.

An example of a more, perhaps extreme, activist approach of state interference is provided, as noted, by Erik Gørtz in Chapter VII in his study of government subsidies to the fishing industry of the Faeroe Islands. The results were, to put it mildly, frightening. On a smaller scale, the same kind of negative consequences of state subsidies occurs in Fredrik Bergström's paper in Chapter IX on government support to corporations in order to increase employment. No positive effects can be identified.

A more optimistic view on this account, however, is provided by Karl Heinrich Oppenländer in Chapter VIII. In his study of equity support to new business start-ups in Germany he concludes that, yes, subsidies may in fact under certain conditions be helpful. Market failure caused by asymmetrical information in investment markets may indeed be a reason for government interference. If modesty pursued as "type (1)" policy aimed at improving micro-market conditions, the risks for significant government failure at the macro level are fairly small.

To summarize, three themes run through the papers of this book: (1) lack of policy-making competence to correct market failure turns into government failure; (2) the critical choice of institutions for good economic performance; and (3) the risk of institutional lock-in. A finger of warning is raised for ambitious "type (2)" policies attempting to control the actual outcomes of the market processes. It seems fair to say that there are strong limits to government interference in markets to successfully promote growth—and other targets as well.

It might be objected, however, that our choice of articles and examples are biased. Selections of articles in social sciences always, to some extent, become political and it may seem as if the selection to be presented here is biased by negative evidence on the role played by government.

First we can say that this is a fairly representative selection of the papers presented at three sessions on Government and institutions at the 1996 Schumpeter Conference. *Second*, there is one good reason for this seemingly negative bias. Schumpeterian-type analytical approaches of course dominated the papers. We, therefore, indirectly avoided having the traditional policy analysis based on intellectually controlled equilibrium models dominate. In such a traditional model analysis the central policy-maker is always in intellectual policy control conveying the idea that he may also be in practical policy control of the economy. In a realistic policy setting he rarely is, so in this sense our selection is both good contrast to traditional analyses and fair. In fact, it highlights the need to formulate better theory of policy analysis that explains the reasons for both policy failure and success, and removes the

18

impression of a supremely competent and fully informed policy actor in central control.

Democracy as a softener of markets

Richard Day (in Chapter I, "An evolutionary theory of democratic capitalism") provides a useful format for discussing the collection of papers presented in this volume. His analysis begins by arguing that institutions are needed to support dynamic market behavior and the efficient functioning of Adam Smith's coordinating invisible hand. Realistically, institutions evolve in response to a demand for such collective services.

Even though institutions evolve to intermediate activities out of equilibrium, the currently fashionable repertoire of economic theory provides practically no intellectual help in dealing with this important socio-economic problem.

Above all, Day argues, when out of equilibrium adjustments become too rough and/or when the existing institutions are not up to their task of softening the consequences of change for people, "the imbalances spill over into the political system." Government institutions have evolved to deal with those instabilities to preserve a politically orderly economic process. Democracy, Day emphasizes, is a cost-efficient institution to deal with social conflicts caused by economic imbalances.

Even though democracy undoubtedly is an important softener of markets, if inappropriately designed it can cause serious functional problems within the economy.

When and why democracy may run out of control

Erik Moberg (in Chapter II, "The expanding public sector—a threat to democracy?") takes a, from Day, different public-choice-oriented, approach to democracy. He develops a political decision theory of *delegation and instruction*. Constitutional environments, he argues, which favor delegation tend to be presidential ones, with a strong executive power separately elected, but also with very independent legislators, as in the US. The instruction-based, parliamentary political system, on the other hand, features strong parties canvassing the market for votes, offering to sell, through formulated programs, favors to special interest groups and minorities, at the expense of the powerless majority.

Moberg's theoretical argument is that the parliamentary-based political agenda of instructions is inherently spendthrift and oriented towards politically engineered redistribution of favors, using the tax system and the public sector as a vehicle. Therein lies an inevitable expansion of the public sector (in percent of total output) in such political regimes. When manipulated extensively parlamentarism easily turns into party dictatorship, but also, Moberg argues, winds up in an over-dimensioned public sector and economic crisis, with no democratically determined exit. The people have democratically imprisoned themselves. The inevitable economic crisis, if sufficiently deep, may resolve the situation, or people will vote with their feet physically and/or economically leaving the country, thereby undermining the tax base of the public sector and forcing economic collapse.

The Moberg view constitutes a serious catch that would make economists and political scientists alike very pessimistic. Is there no nice way out?

Enabling law may break institutional lock-in

Clas Wihlborg (in Chapter III, "The role of enabling and mandatory company law for financial systems efficiency") introduces *enabling law* as an institution that gives parties to an agreement: (1) *freedom* to design contracts to suit their local needs; and (2) *predictability* in the sense that enabling law may be made to dominate other law (old and new) in case of conflict and to guide precedent formation. The first attribute is obtained by allowing the parties to deviate from a standard contract by mutual consent. The second attribute is obtained if the constitution specifies that enabling law dominates mandatory law in case of conflict. This applies also in countries with developed legal systems where mandatory law is used to achieve other objectives than economic efficiency, for instance pursuing extreme egalitarian objectives.

At a first glance, the two dimensions of enabling law may seem to contradict one another, when they really complement each other. The second attribute was first established in Eliasson, Rybczynski & Wihlborg (1994) as a "means" to overcome the contradictory institutions in formerly planned economies when trying to introduce market regimes. Rather than taking on the impossible task of attempting to specify an entirely new institutional code for the desired market regime, a few dominant principles of enabling law could be introduced as a "constitutionally based" principle to override all earlier and new mandatory legislation that contradicted the new principles and thus enforce new precedent. Legal and institutional predictability would be established. Enabling law in this second sense, hence, offers a way out (Eliasson 1998), not only for socially and politically distressed formerly planned economies, but also for overdimensioned parliamentary welfare regimes bogged down in the marshes of rent-seeking, rational voters. (See Karlson 1993 for an alternative way to escape the lock-in.)

The recent decision (April 1998) passed down by the EU Court imposing the free trade principle in services as well on government provided health insurance and health care provision is an excellent example of enabling law as a "constitutional principle." The Court judgment overrides local (national) mandatory law that restricts the freedom of nationals to shop for health care services across the EU. It (1) raises economic efficiency through removing public monopolies in health care, and (2) introduces consumer sovereignty in a previously government controlled market and, hence, is in every respect a positive measure consistent with the EU principles of economic freedom.

The EU Court decision, Wihlborg observes, runs counter to previous precedent formation. At least in Sweden, it appears, the more detailed and prespecified mandatory law, the more it seems to take precedent over principles of enabling law in higher court decisions.

Enabling law as defined here, hence, can substitute as a constitutional principle that carries certain efficiency characteris-

tics associated with flexibility and predictability. Wihlborg
then goes on to illustrate the two laws with examples from finance. His general conclusion is that mandatory law specifying one compulsory "standard-form contract" can never be
efficient since the circumstances always vary to the extent that
customized contracts are more efficient. Excessive use of detailed mandatory contracts, therefore, typically signal that
other objectives than efficiency are pursued by the lawmak-
ers.

The significance of the design
of market supporting institutions

David Allen (in Chapter IV, "Microsoft vs Netscape—policy
for dynamic models : anti-trust and intellectual property
rights revisited") hits the core of the Schumpeter, or rather
Austrian, problem when attempting to resolve the balance between innovative activity and the economies of scale emanating from standardization, on the one hand, and to clarify the
nature of intellectual property rights in the world of rapidly
merging computing and communications industries, on the
other.

The neoclassical, and perhaps outdated, standard view is
that legal protection should be available to guarantee an incentive rent to the innovator, a standard argument rephrased
by Arrow (1962) to mean that efficiency and welfare will perhaps be maximized if R&D is socialized and the results made
available free of charge. This view, derived from the standard
Walrasian model, disregards the influence on research productivity of the organization and incentives of R&D production. It also sets the stage for R&D, the winner takes all, races.

Allen's view is different. *First*, he observes that in the rapidly changing and complex network of merging computing
and communications technology legal property rights may
get in the way of innovative change. *Second*, he says, look at
the Microsoft-Netscape fracas and Microsoft's predatory behavior as a temporary monopolist. Perhaps the best protection for the innovator Netscape, after all, is protection from
the competitor and predator monopolist imposing a standard

that kills the innovator, and locks the industry into an obsolete technology, let us say Esperanto instead of English. But (and *third*), Allen argues, antitrust legislators have little understanding of the dynamics of this industry. They use overly blunt instruments to curb monopolist behavior, and, after all, the industry needs a standard, at least temporarily during a consolidation period, after a solution has been sorted out during an earlier innovation phase. Perhaps even an inferior standard will be better than no standard at all, *provided* it is not allowed to impede innovative progress, to the extent of soon breaking itself up. What can be done? Well, let us look at Allen's argument by looking at the members of a functioning family. To make the family business work the individual members have to behave. You cannot have one family member predate on the other members. They will stop contributing and leave the family. Big is good only as long as big behaves as a member of the family. The complex and rapidly moving computing and communications innovation game requires that the players work together in order not to break up development. They have to follow the norms of well behaved team participation. The delicate team cohesion cannot take a spoiler like Microsoft, aiming for family (market) control, Allen argues. Hence, if the spoiler does not voluntarily behave, antitrust authorities have to use their very blunt second best instruments to contain him.

Can deregulation succeed?

Jean-Philippe Bonardi and **Bertrand Quélin** (in Chapter V, "Regulatory body, rent-seeking and market activities : the case of telecommunications in Europe") study what happens when a formerly regulated market, often a state monopoly, is deregulated, when the government moves out. What conditions are necessary to end the rent-seeking activities and to promote a competitive market?

Focusing on Public Telecommunications Operators in Europe, Bonardi & Quélin observe that deregulation is a slow and complex process. More than ten years after its beginning it has not been completed and rent-seeking activities are still frequent. The operators possess strong political resources which they devote to various activities aimed at influencing government policies, to get subsidies, to restrict competition etc. Moreover, they are extremely competent when it comes to achieve their ends, due to their direct access to public decisions, lengthy relations with government agencies and informational asymmetries that work to their advantage. The same phenomena can of course be observed in a number of other European industries, i e in rail and air transport, in education, television, health care, etc.

Bonardi & Quélin argue, from a comparative study of German, French and British examples, that deregulation will only be successful, at least among Public Telecommunications Operators, if a specific regulatory body is created that has the power to change the regulatory governance of the sector. Such power, in turn, must be based on (1) freedom of action, i e independence from political authorities, and (2) a clear incentive to favor the entry of competitors into the industry. If not, i e if such a body lacks the required incentives and autonomy, rent-seeking and quasi-monopolies will persist.

There is always a risk, however, they observe, that such an agency may itself turn into a rent-seeker. The way out of the institutional lock-in, hence, creates its own problem.

Institutional failure

Andrew Reed (in Chapter VI, "Russia´s agrarian dilemma : the legacy of an economy *without* innovation, entrepreneurs or market competition") provides an interesting illustration from Russian agriculture of how regulation that restricts the ways to organize production, that reduces economic incentives and that lowers competition, cripples the ability of the formerly planned economy to allocate resources efficiently for sustained long-term economic growth. Understanding this situation has been a perplexing experience for the West, notably its advisors, approaching post-Soviet Russia with the a priori textbook "understanding" that economic infrastructure is lacking. Since it appears not to be lacking in the conventional sense, the problem must lie in lacking institutions, a problem formulation unfamiliar to western advisors.

The main culprit, Reed argues, is the lingering hierarchical (Soviet) tradition of discriminating against alternative, innovative ways of doing things. Since organizations in the West involved in technical assistance typically approach their problem with a centralist, interventionist mind set, they tend to team up with the bureaucracy of the past, rather than to attempt to break it up. The traditional Soviet policy of mobilizing resources for planned growth rather than using resources in an economically efficient way has made the Russian agricultural industry deficient in acquiring new technology and utterly helpless in coping with privatization, new competition and change.

With a system that favored high-cost production of low quality products in large volumes, deregulation produced two expected outcomes; some producers were able to adjust, others not. Those who could adjust increased their profits and could afford to pay high wages. People with relatively high and rising incomes are demanding a high quality and a more varied food that Russian agricultural industry cannot supply. This demand, hence, can only be satisfied through imports. The outcome has been catastrophic for Russian agriculture. Most problematic of all, Reed notes, is the inability of the Russian mind to grasp the concept of an economy with a self-organizing structure.

The evolution of a market economy can be described as a chaotic development with feedback mechanisms that allow agents to make qualitative assessments of alternatives. The "Perestroika" jump started the feedback mechanisms, but the Soviet system had a seriously impaired ability to respond.

Reed also notes the similarities with the European, Brussels-regulated and subsidized agriculture and the Russian dilemma. While Russian agriculture underproduces with no quality variation and little appeal to customers, the West overproduces. In both cases Government has contributed to the inefficient outcome. When Government intervenes in markets with lacking insight and competence, problems are created rather than solved.

Policy failure on a grand scale in a small place

The consequences of policy action are best highlighted when policies are extreme, and the economy is small and simple (two sectors). Such an economy is not robust, and ill-conceived policies typically hit hard and fast. **Erik Gørtz'** story (in Chapter VII, "Private and public expenditures and the Faeroese business cycle") of the policy disaster of the Faeroese islands provides a perfect and very pedagogical setting for the analysis of grand-scale government failure.

During the 1980s the small Faeroese economy was excessively primed by investment subsidies. For some years the investments amounted to 40–50 percent of GDP, practically none of it being filtered by market criteria. Rates of return to investments were driven down far below market interest rates. Since most investments went into one production sector, fishing, or associated public infrastructure, the resulting expansion depleted the stock of fish. This in turn resulted, after some years, in a sudden collapse of both output and the (only) exports of the islands. 25 percent unemployment, an explosion of public debt and the emigration of ten percent of the population followed, the last consequence being already predicted in Moberg's analysis (in Chapter II).

How could such a destructive policy be politically allowed and sustained?

Well, Erik Gørtz concludes, with a fragmented political system, with self-centered rational local politicians, with the absence of political responsibility and without direct economic feed-backs a touch of public-choice analysis would predict the political system's failure.

But the Faeroese problem was not really created by policy, Gørtz continues. It would have happened anyway. It was only made worse by misdirected attempts at macro stabilization, he argues. The real problem was micro-economic and one of institutional design. And understanding that would have suggested much easier solutions.

An example of a fairly successful intervention

Markets fail for several reasons, and the government has a role to play in attempting to remedy such situations. Correcting market failure, however, requires unique competence on the part of the policy-maker, notably a thorough understanding of the dynamics of an experimentally organized market economy (Eliasson 1992). This understanding is not typically present outside the business community, and economic theory guiding policy advisors is grossly inadequate in this context. Hence, government attempts to correct market failure easily lead to significant government failure, if not cautiously and competently administered. We have one fairly successful attempt, and one failure to report on.

Karl Heinrich Oppenländer (in Chapter VIII, "Problems in assisting new business start-ups in Germany") studies the German equity assistance program for new business start-ups. He observes that market failure appears to be characteristic of the venture end of the capital markets, caused primarily by informational asymmetries. He wants to know whether this can be remedied by an equity capital assistance program implemented by the German government.

His conclusion is that, indeed, the program has been valuable in financing new firms and innovations at the micro level in a way that had positive consequences for economic growth. Because the participants had to fulfill certain requirements and provide information about themselves, the informational asymmetries were reduced and thereby also the risk to the lender/investor.

We also have to observe that the German intervention in the markets was very cautious and concerned with remedying a particular situation in the market, not with achieving certain outcomes or social policy ends. The risks for creating macroeconomic disturbances were minimal. While the German policy results appear promising, the Swedish employment-oriented support programs do not fare well in a similar analysis.

Policy failure on a small scale

Fredrik Bergström (in Chapter IX, "Do public capital subsidies to firms increase employment?") is very explicit in his empirical analysis of the two kinds of failures, market and government. Incompetent government action to correct market failure, in fact often seems to result in a much bigger government failure.

Employment support of failing firms, for instance, often results in industrial technological lock-ins. As shown already in Eliasson & Lindberg (1981), it is all right for firms to make significant investment or business mistakes. The economy at large can sustain such mistakes, which are in fact a normal cost for economic learning in a dynamic market economy (Eliasson 1992). The really large, negative macro-economic effects occur when production is allowed to go on in the failed investments. Such sustained failure could not occur in the market, only under a protective government subsidy umbrella. And a democratic political institution will, by its very political charter, be bad at correcting or terminating mistakes (Eliasson 1990, p 285). Carlsson, Bergholm & Lindberg (1981), Carlsson (1983), furthermore, show that it is normally far better for long-term employment to subsidize the most profitable firms, if you have to subsidize at all, and disregard possible direct negative employment effects. The same study also demonstrates that when subsidy support of defunct firms is pushed to the extreme, as in the case of Swedish shipyards during the 1970s, severe negative macro-economic effects can be observed. Bergström observes that the symptoms are very similar in his sample of firms, but that they only constitute a mini-example of the shipyard debacle of the 1970s.

Bergström's case is, however, clear. The Swedish Government, when subsidizing industrial firms, has in fact engaged in a significant government failure under the cover of attempting to correct market mistakes. Subsidies have tended to go to inferior, low productivity firms, reinforcing the negative effects through both creating additional negative productivity effects in the firms receiving subsidies, and holding back investment and growth in other, non supported firms.

28

In addition, Bergström observes, by engaging in life-supporting measures on obsolete firms, the Government may not only slow growth but also create lock-in effects in obsolete industries and technologies.

Bibliography

Arrow, K J (1962), "Economic welfare and the allocation of resources for invention." Ch 7 in Nelson, R (ed), *The rate and direction of inventive activity : economic and social factors*. Princeton: NBER, Princeton University Press, 1962.

Carlsson, B (1983), "Industrial subsidies in Sweden : simulations on a micro-to-macro model," in *Microeconometrics*, IUI Yearbook 1982–83. Stockholm: IUI.

Carlsson, B, Bergholm, F & Lindberg, T (1981), *Industristödspolitiken och dess inverkan på samhällsekonomin* (Industry subsidy policy and its macro-economic impact). Stockholm: IUI.

Day, R H (1986), "Disequilibrium economic dynamics : a post-Schumpeterian contribute." Ch 3 in Day, R H & Eliasson, G (eds), *The dynamics of market economies*. Stockholm: IUI & Amsterdam: North-Holland, 1986.

Day, R H & Eliasson, G (eds) (1986), *The dynamics of market economies*. Stockholm: IUI & Amsterdam: North-Holland.

Eliasson, G (1986a), "A note on the stability of economic organizational forms and the importance of human capital," in Day, R H & Eliasson, G (eds), *The dynamics of market economies*. Stockholm: IUI & Amsterdam: North-Holland, 1986.

Eliasson, G (1986b), "The economics of institutions and markets : the organization of research at IUI." Ch I in *The economics of institutions and markets*. Stockholm: IUI.

Eliasson, G (1992), "Business competence, organizational learning and economic growth : establishing the Smith-

Schumpeter-Wicksell (SSW) connection," in Scherer, F M & Perlman, M (eds), *Entrepreneurship, technological innovation and economic growth*. Ann Arbor: The University of Michigan Press, 1992.

Eliasson, G (1998), "From plan to market," in *Journal of Economic Behavior and Organization*, Vol 34, pp 49–68.

Eliasson, G & Green, C (eds) (1998), *The micro foundations of economic growth*. Ann Arbor: The University of Michigan Press.

Eliasson, G & Lindberg, T (1981), "Allocation and growth effects of corporate income taxes," in Eliasson, G & Södersten, J (eds), *Business taxation, finance and firm behavior*, Conference Reports 1981:1. Stockholm: IUI.

Eliasson, G, Rybczynski, T & Wihlborg, C (1994), *The necessary institutional framework to transform formerly planned economies : with special emphasis on the institutions needed to stimulate foreign investment in the formerly planned economies*. Stockholm: IUI.

Karlson, N (1993), *The state of state : an inquiry concerning the role of invisible hands in politics and civil society*. Stockholm: Almqvist & Wiksell International.

Karlson, N (ed) (1995), *Can the present problems of mature welfare states such as Sweden be solved?* Stockholm: City University Press.

Scherer, F M & Perlman, M (eds) (1992), *Entrepreneurship, technological innovation and economic growth*. Ann Arbor: The University of Michigan Press.

Schumpeter, J A (1942), *Capitalism, socialism and democracy*. New York: Harper & Row.

PART I

Theories of State Interference

Chapter I

An Evolutionary Theory of Democratic Capitalism

This paper contains material presented at the 1996 Schumpeter Society Conference. The present version was prepared especially for this volume.

Richard H Day

Abstract

The market process sometimes expels participants, sometimes creates monopolies. Such non-Pareto outcomes stimulate innovation in government monitoring and regulation. Such mechanisms may also introduce inefficiencies in resource allocation. The economist's fundamental role is to identify appropriate government policies that maintain access to markets and that lower the social costs of rapid change that market economies produce.

1 Backing up and starting over

The central message of Adam Smith consists of the recognition that although no one understands everything, private individuals in the pursuit of self-interest can contribute to the advantage of others, even though they may not intend to do so and even though they may not concern themselves with the economy as a whole. A system of private property and market competition is needed to make this possible: private property creates scope for discretion in coping with local situations which is what each individual knows best; market competition provides incentives for individuals to expand their potentials and exercise effective choices. In setting forth this vision of the competitive process, Smith and his followers explicitly recognized that individuals adapted their behavior to price signals which were in turn adjusted to imbalances in supply and demand.

A century after Smith, Leon Walras formalized the idea of a balance in supply and demand and specified two quite explicit mechanisms of out-of-equilibrium adjustment: consumers' tâtonnement involving price adjustments in response to discrepancies in supply and demand, and producers' tâtonnement involving quantity adjustments in response to profit opportunities. He emphasized that such a system of dynamic relationships would not converge to a general equilibrium but would oscillate around one, sometimes approaching a steady state (like a "glassy sea"), sometimes exhibiting more or less turbulent fluctuations (like an "ocean storm").

Thus, from the beginning of the discipline's "modern" era, two complementary or "dual" fundamental streams of thinking have flowed through the domain of economic theory; one stream characterizing, establishing existence conditions, and deriving properties of economic equilibrium; one stream characterizing and deriving properties of disequilibrium. Both streams are found running through all the great classical and neoclassical founding fathers and in the great economists of this century including (among many others) Wicksell, Keynes, Schumpeter, Hicks, and Hayek (albeit with differing emphasis and sometimes different policy interpretations).[1]

Far removed from this classical vision is an alternative theoretical position which argues that the only way to think about the subject is to think of individual behavior *as if* it were always based on a complete understanding of the entire system and *as if* each individual's actions were consistent with everyone else's. The leading exponents of this school recognize the facts of individual economic life as well as anyone. Their followers insist, however, that economic *theory* does not need to and should not incorporate such facts. This is, indeed, a striking departure from the dual channels of scientific reasoning which characterized economic theory through most of its development. During the last quarter century this "New Classical" school has achieved a remarkable status. The result has been to impede progress in economic science and to confuse issues of public policy.

When a line of inquiry has been pursued in one direction long enough, it seems inevitably to take off on a tangent to the curved space of experience and into a scholastic realm far removed from the world as we know it. When this happens, it serves a salutary purpose to think back to a former time, before things got out of hand, to reconsider the earlier seminal contributions, and with renewed inspiration from that starting-point to begin again the task of improving our understanding of economic life as we know and experience it. In accordance with this opinion, I intend in the remainder of these remarks to "back up and start over."

2 Modes of economizing behavior

My first step is to observe that behavior in economic choice situations is governed—in addition to conscious comparison of alternatives—by imitation, by "trial and error," and by accidental modifications of behavior that, in effect, constitute unintended "innovations." Such "innovations," if successful,

---

1 Through this discussion I have in mind a Nash equilibrium as in a Walrasian general equilibrium for a deterministic economy or in a strategy space when risk is present as, for example, defined by Hahn (1973). Note that *defining* an equilibrium does not establish *existence*, nor does the *proof of existence* constitute a mechanism for finding or approximating one—unless the proof is *constructive*.

can be selected by others through imitation in the pursuit of advantage. Less successful behavior may be culled as experience accumulates. Obviously, of course, intended innovation guided by conscious design also contributes to the process, but the central point is the impossibility of acting optimally because of informational and cognitive limits and the possibility of improving performance nonetheless. Many authors have recognized this possibility beginning, as observed above, at least with Adam Smith. Classic modern expositions of this argument will be found, for example, in Schumpeter, Simon, and Alcian.

In addition to experimentation (trial and error) and imitation, I include explicit (procedural) optimizing, following an authority or tradition, habit, unmotivated search, and following a hunch as distinguishable (but perhaps not independent) modes of economizing behavior. All of these modes—including procedural optimizing—share the characteristic that those who use them, do not know and *do not find out* what is the best thing to do. At best, they can only do their best as they are able to perceive or calculate it and this may lead them to abandon optimizing behavior and engage in trial and error search, imitation, obedience to an authority, to mindlessly repeat previous actions, or simply guess.[2]

3 The problem with disequilibrium: suboptimality, instability and inviability

Starting from this factual, behavioral foundation, intelligent individuals have good reason to seek knowledge and understanding and to modify their behavior, or more generally, their modes of behavior. These are costly activities that absorb time and other resources, thus perturbing individuals from whatever positions they are in and, as a corollary, perturbing the entire interacting system of which they are a part. Such in-

2 In his classic paper Armen Alcian (1950) observed that [in the real world] "...modes of behavior replace optimum equilibrium conditions as guiding rules of action." I have elaborated these "modes of economizing behavior" most recently in Day (1992). Pingle (1992, 1993) has shown how these modes arise in various laboratory experiments.

dividuals can strike an equilibrium, if one exists, only by chance and the chance would be vanishingly small. If an equilibrium did result, no one would know it. Further efforts to understand the situation and to improve the possibilities would perturb the system anew and kick the system out of it. For this reason alone, economic systems rarely, if ever, display the characteristics of economic equilibrium.[3]

This is an implication of bounded rationality that has not yet received adequate attention. Certainly, the neoclassical economists did not deal with these implications. Subsequent writers who emphasized realistic behavior have often been, I believe, rather too sanguine about the market's ability always to overcome the difficulties it creates through its own internal workings. After all, markets are essentially a network of firms that mediate transactions for profit and whose managers are governed by the same modes of behavior that govern producers and consumers. If producers and consumers cannot perform equilibrium miracles, then how can market mediators? Of course, they cannot. Indeed, the economy as a whole can be viewed as a vast system of simultaneous experiments undertaking trial and error search. It is in Eliasson's (1986) felicitous phrase, "an experimentally organized economy."

The consequence of disequilibrium is serious at all times for some and at some times for many. If the agents are not in equilibrium, then they are out of it; and if they are out of it, some people cannot do what they want or hope to do. In extreme but not infrequent situations, survival may be threatened for individuals and organizations. Some may not survive. In short, economic selection, like its biological counterpart, is cruel: it expels its participants; those who can't compete successfully, lose their chance to do so. Thus, the system evolves in a fundamental way, that is, by changing its constituent "parts." Sometimes technologies or activities, or, more generally, ways of life are abandoned. Sometimes they are individual firms or other organizations. These are impersonal components of the economy, but they are components made up of humans whose individual fortunes depend on the activities, ways of life, or organization of which they are a part. When

3 See note 1 above.

any of them is eliminated, the humans involved will be forced to change in ways they never intended.

When expulsion by economic selection occurs relatively slowly and involves only a few activities and organizations at any one time, the individual consequences can be absorbed without great disruption. When it occurs rapidly and involves many activities and organizations, the system, as a whole, begins to tremble.

4 Market instability, institutional innovation and government

Every now and then, economic systems are so thoroughly destabilized by disequilibrium developments that they collapse entirely as occurred in Russia in the early part of this century, in Germany in the 1930s, and more recently in the Soviet Union. Other countries, for example Great Britain and the United States, have also experienced economic crises and periods of political turmoil. They have been more fortunate, however, having successfully avoided (so far) complete collapse. Their history is characterized instead by episodes of substantial modification of market and government institutions within the same overall conceptual structure of political/economic organization. These episodes are often followed by somewhat less dramatic periods of consolidation or partial retrenchment.

A brilliant analysis of the Anglo-American interaction of market and state is to be found in John R Commons' no longer read masterpiece, *The legal foundations of capitalism* and in a somewhat more readable rendition, edited by Kenneth Parsons, *Collective action*. Commons' method was founded on the direct observation of market and government organizations in action, on a careful description of the origin and development of specific market and governmental institutions, and on a pointillist analysis of specific conflicts that arose among private and public agents in the process. He was able then to show in varied empirical examples how specific privately organized economic activities could emerge as a result of private and public innovations as new opportunities opened up, how laws were modified or re-interpreted, and how new public agencies were created to deal with conflicts that occurred when the actions of some agents led to diminished payoffs to others.

Many of the opportunities and conflicts that trigger these institutional innovations arise endogenously through the out-of-equilibrium working of the market system, as explained above. The institutional changes that occur in response then modify the economic environment of the private sector by redefining opportunities, constraints, and potential payoffs and by providing specific new mechanisms for resolving conflict and mediating transactions. To characterize this interaction, I refer to it as the "coevolution of market and state." A very similar vision, also based on historical analysis, is the grand theory of Douglass North (1990).[4]

5 The general theory of market and state

Many scholars are now rethinking economics from an evolutionary view, consciously or unwittingly backing up and starting over by taking the "other" theoretical path. This is not the place to review this growing literature. I should like instead to provide a brief outline of the theory of the coevolution of market and state that has its foundations in the "modes of economizing behavior" listed above.[5]

---

4 Armen Alcian's papers are written within this tradition. Alcian argued that until you know how the system works, you can't understand how it can work well, and that an understanding had to rest on a recognition that non-optimizing modes of behavior must play a central role, that structure of property rights and the mechanisms of market and government selection were required to explain how individual fortunes and public welfare evolve. I emphasize the coevolution of market and government because changes in one virtually always directly involve or trigger changes in the other. This brings us again to Alcian, in particular to his insight "...that there should be an evolutionary force toward the survival of larger clusters of certain types of rights in the sanctioned concept of property rights." He did not allude to John R Commons' brilliant analysis of the evolution of property as the chief medium through which the institution of government and market coevolve in response to conflicting economic interests, but his own contribution, along with Coase, was instrumental in setting off an independent, somewhat parallel line of work that has sharpened our understanding of private property and how the real economic system works.

As the system of individuals and of market and government institutions is never in equilibrium, for those whose activity is blocked, various options have to exist for economic life to go on; options to work, produce, exchange, and consume. These options include doing without, drawing from inventories, queuing, or resorting to some contingent tactic that can "keep one going" for the time being until an alternative course of action can be identified and pursued. In short, *inconsistency forces unwanted change.*

To prevent such inconsistencies and unwanted changes, "markets" fulfill two very important functions. They intervene between agents who wish to exchange but who could not possibly expend the resources necessary to find one another. For example, when we want food, we do not any more seek out the farmer but take ourselves to a market (literally the "supermarket") where what we want is available without us knowing how or who, or even why it was provided. It is there because we are willing to pay the cost of mediation provided by the merchant instead of paying a greater cost of finding the goods for ourselves. Likewise, the farmer no longer sends his milk in a pony cart, driven by his child, to dole out ladles full in crockery bowls to housewives along a route through the town, but delivers his goods to a buyer or wholesaler or processor and, without ever knowing the path by which the milk finds it way to someone's cereal bowl or who, indeed, will consume it. In addition to lowering the cost of exchange, markets buffer the discrepancies between demand and supply that follow from the aggregate of actions taken out of economic equilibrium. They do not ever bring the economy into equilibrium—no one knows where one is or how to get to it. Instead, *they produce viability for individuals in an economy too complex to be perfectly coordinated by any individual or by any system, market-oriented or otherwise.*

As the amounts and variety of goods have escalated, the role of market mediation has escalated until it is usual for marketing costs to exceed production costs and often by substantial margins. In principal, we could all be better off if we

5 The following summarizes the theory explicated in greater detail in Day (1987). I have produced numerous variations on this theme. For example, my 1992 paper.

didn't have to pay for all these people and resources expended in the marketing process, if only we could exchange costlessly in equilibrium. The resources saved could be used to produce more of the goods and services we really want, or to enjoy more leisure. Since we can't determine such a situation, we are better off paying the cost and giving up the idea that we could be better off without mediation. Thus it is that "markets" or, more generally, "market mechanisms" create viability. They make complex exchanges economically feasible and unwittingly coordinate individual decisions that would be inconsistent without them.

This, however, is not the whole story. Disequilibrium creates dynamic movements as producers, consumers, and mediators adjust prices and quantities in attempts to balance supply and demand. We know that these dynamic movements vary in magnitude, sometimes displaying modest fluctuations, sometimes substantial ones, and occasionally such great imbalances arise that the system of mediation that has evolved to date cannot continue to establish interagent viability. Enormous discrepancies in demand and supply can emerge. Among the effects at such times is the expulsion of large numbers of agents from the market; that is, participation in work, management, production, and consumption under prevailing conditions is blocked for some individuals, both business people and workers. When their numbers are large enough, they constitute a potential constituency and the imbalance spills over into the political system.

Government mechanisms have evolved to regulate private activity so as to reduce such occurrences, to lower their private and social costs, and to re-establish access to the system. These innovations in government have arisen in large measure as responses to the direct or indirect pressures created by the collective actions of individuals who have discovered common economic interests during times of duress. The mechanisms of modern democracy make such innovations possible within an evolving system of institutions and laws that can be created or redirected without overthrowing the entire system of government—or, so it has worked for more than two centuries. Democracy lowers the cost of social conflict caused by economic imbalance by providing recourse for those expelled or threatened with expulsion from the market.

This is not to say that any given governmental device or even the whole lot of such devices has been entirely successful. Indeed, there can be little doubt that many government regulations and activities have been counter-productive, moving the economy farther from desirable states than would have been the case without them. Moreover, it is correctly argued that, left to their own devices, private individuals and enterprises can and often do create sufficient new opportunities by *adjusting themselves* to aggregate imbalances, thus eliminating or drastically reducing the problems of individual inviability that disequilibrium conditions tend to cause.

But market capitalism is, if anything, an engine of rapid change. It can produce imbalances that can overwhelm its capacity for timely self-correction. When *people* are expelled from the system of *markets*, they have recourse in the system of *government*. Indeed, the mere perception of the possibility of expulsion is enough to motivate government innovations to modify the system, and once it is realized that the government not only creates but can influence or control, or even eliminate markets, the pressures to substitute the government agency for a private agency can proceed far enough to stifle the beneficial effects of market competition.

Thus, it is that in their coevolution, the institutions of market and of government have multiplied and elaborated their functions, evolving ever more complex public and private systems of mediation in response to the fluctuating imbalances among economic flows. This process does not end on a path that no one would want to change, or a set of rules that all would want to live with forever after.

I do not believe that we economists can change these basic facts. But if we understand that it is the economizing modes of behavior by individuals interacting out of equilibrium that explain market *and* state, and if we make this coevolution a central part of our thinking, then we will be empowered to illuminate the truth more than to obscure it and to contribute policy analyses that do more good than harm.

Bibliography

Alcian, A A (1950), "Uncertainty, evolution and economic theory," in *Journal of Political Economy*, Vol 58, No 3, pp 211–221.

Commons, J R (1924), *Legal foundations of capitalism*. New York: Macmillan Company. Reprinted by the University of Wisconsin Press, Madison, WI, 1959.

Commons, J R (1950), *The economics of collective action.* New York: Macmillan Company.

Day, R H (1987), "The general theory of disequilibrium economics and economic evolution." Ch 3 in Batten & Casti (eds), *Economic evolution and structural change*. Berlin & New York: Springer-Verlag.

Day, R H (1992), "Bounded rationality and the coevolution of market and state." Ch 4 in Day, R H, Eliasson, G & Wihlborg, C (eds), *The markets of innovation, ownership and control*. Amsterdam: North-Holland in cooperation with IUI-Stockholm.

Eliasson, G (1996), *Firm objectives, controls and organization*. Dordrecht: Kluwer Academic.

Hahn, F (1973), *On the notion of equilibrium in economics*. London: Cambridge University Press.

North, D C (1990), *Institutions, institutional change, and economic performance*. Cambridge: Cambridge University Press.

Pingle, M (1995), "Imitation versus rationality : an experimental perspective on decision-making," in *Journal of Socioeconomics*, Vol 24, No 2, pp 281–315.

Pingle, M (1994), "Submitting to authority : an experimental examination of its effect on decision-making." Unpublished manuscript.

Chapter II

The Expanding Public Sector–a Threat to Democracy?

Erik Moberg

Abstract

The political competition for power is considered as a main force propelling the expansion of the public sector in democracies. The character of the competition, and thereby the expansive force, is thought to depend on the type of constitution in the country concerned. The most rapid expansion will probably occur in parliamentary countries with proportional elections. Anyway, expansion seems to be an almost unavoidable side-effect of democracy. The possibility that a democracy's life is limited to the time it takes for the public sector to grow from low to impossibly high levels is therefore finally mentioned and commented on.

1 The expansion of the public sector

It is well known that the public sector has increased continuously and considerably in a lot of countries, at least in modern times. In several Western European countries the public sector is now well above 50% of GDP. Now, even if there may be some occasional exceptions to this general pattern, even if the size of the public sector differs considerably between the countries, and even if the speed of the sector's expansion differs considerably between different periods of time, the general tendency towards expansion seems nevertheless almost unavoidable and in the nature of things. It is therefore hardly surprising that this tendency is widely and since long observed and acknowledged, and that many efforts to explain it have been done.

The most well-known of these explanations is perhaps the one suggested by Adolph Wagner, who argued that increasing per capita income, and increasing standard of living, in a society, gave rise to an increasing public sector (Wagner's law). Other scholars have explained the expansion, at least in democracies, as a side-effect of the political struggle for power. Still other types of explanations have been brought forward.[1] In spite of the many explanations it is, however, widely agreed that public sector expansion is still a poorly understood phenomenon. A lot of empirical studies have made it clear that no proposed simple explanation is capable of clarifying the involved mechanisms single-handedly. Rather several explanations together carry the truth. It is, I submit, also likely that further elements, which have not so far been taken into account, can contribute to our understanding of the expansion of the public sector.

Political competition in democracies undoubtedly contributes importantly to expansion. At the same time I believe, however, that, the political competition takes different forms, and therefore also creates different effects in different democracies depending on their type of constitution. This is the theme that I am going to develop in this paper.

The theme, it should be noted, fits well into an intellectual tradition initiated by Joseph A Schumpeter. In addition to his

1 Larkey, Stolp & Winer (1981) is a survey of theories of public sector growth.

other achievements he made, as we know, a pioneering study of democracy and thereby also inspired the later emergence of public choice theory.[2] At the heart of Schumpeter's analysis lies a distinction between the motives of the political actors, and the societal effects of their activities, analogous to Adam Smith's distinction between the butcher's, baker's and brewer's profit motives, and the effects of their undertakings. In either case the effects depend on the structure of incentives facing the actors. In Smith's case the incentives are, of course, those of the market, whereas, in the political case, the incentives are those of the competition for power. In the former case the effects are, as we know, on the whole beneficial. In the political case there is no such generally accepted conclusion. On the whole the analysis still remains to be done. This paper is an effort to contribute to that task.[3]

2 Political parties and party systems

In order to study the impact of constitutions it is necessary to classify them in some relevant way. A reasonable suggestion is that the distribution of power, as determined by the constitution, should be of importance. Here, I hypothesise that the constitutional elements most likely to affect that distribution are those determining the properties of political parties and party systems. These elements, in turn, I submit, are the rules for appointing the executive, and the electoral laws.[4] When discussing the influence of these rules I am mainly interested in two clusters of properties of parties and party systems, namely:

- The cohesion and discipline of the parties, in particular of their groups in the legislature, and their stability over time.

2 Schumpeter, J A (1976), *Capitalism, socialism and democracy*. New York: Harper & Row Publishers. In particular Downs (1957) was inspired by Schumpeter.

3 To a large extent the paper is a condensed version of some main parts of a forthcoming book of mine provisionally titled *Democracy : constitutions, politics and wellfare effects.*

4 The importance of the electoral laws for the parties is widely discussed in political science but there is, to my knowledge, no corresponding interest in the effects of the rules for appointing the executive.

- The number of parties, and the distribution of the size of the parties.

There are two principal methods for appointing the executive; (1) the one used in parliamentary systems, and (2) the one in presidential systems. According to the parliamentary method the people first elect the legislature, which then, in turn, appoints the executive. In a pure parliamentary system the executive, furthermore, can remain in office only as long as it enjoys the confidence, or support, of a majority in the legislature. This requirement is therefore often referred to as the parliamentary principle. The presidential method, on the contrary, means that separate elections are held for appointing a president and thereby also the rest of the executive. In a parliamentary country there are thus, at the national level, popular elections only for electing the legislature whereas, in a presidential country, there are two main types of elections, those for electing the legislature, and those for electing the executive.

A parliamentary system depends, for its functioning, on the existence of stable, centralised and cohesive political parties in a way that a presidential system does not. The reason is that the parliamentary support, in order to be reliable and lasting, cannot be anonymous. A support expressed by an ad-hoc, transient majority of individual members of the legislature cannot, it is easy to realise, have much value. The support has to be expressed by a few stable and identifiable actors, which, in effect, means political parties.

A parliamentary system is, however, not only dependent on stable, centralised and cohesive parties; conversely it also gives strong incentives for the formation of such parties, and sometimes also for forming big parties.[5] The reason is that those properties enhance a negotiating party's credibility and reliability and thereby its chances to become a member of the executive, a membership which often is quite attractive, or

5 One advantage for a big party, as we shall see later on, is that it may impose its ideology on the rest of the society. A big party often also has the advantage of being the component by which a coalition building-process starts. Even small parties may, however, have advantages by fitting well into minimum winning coalitions in Riker's (1962) sense. The incentives related to size are thus complicated.

even lucrative. This attractiveness, in its turn, is, at least to some extent, related to the fact that, in a democracy using the majority rule, a majority can exploit the outsider minority, for example by taxing it. In a parliamentary democracy this majority power is permanently anchored to the executive.[6]

Continuing with the electoral laws used for appointing the members of the legislature it is enough to consider two main types of systems. First there is the system with single-member constituencies in which, in each constituency, the candidate who gets a plurality of the votes, is elected. Then there is the system with multi-member constituencies in which the mandates are distributed to the parties in proportion to their votes.

The electoral system affects the parties in two ways. First, the plurality system has a strong tendency to reduce the number of parties, in the extreme to two parties, whereas there are no such reductive forces operating in the proportional system.[7] Second, in contrast to the plurality system, the proportional system puts strong means for enhancing discipline, and thus for the creation of stable and cohesive parties, in the hands of the party leaderships. The main factor here is that the candidates for the legislature are largely dependent on the party leadership, both for nomination and for campaigning.

Now, by combining the methods for appointing the executive, and the electoral systems, we get four main types of democratic constitutions.[8]

6 The idea that parliamentarism is dependent on stable, cohesive parties is generally accepted in political science. The opposite idea, that parliamentarism enhances stability and cohesiveness, is however, to my knowledge, not discussed in a systematic way at all, and when the topic occasionally arises for some reason, the idea is sometimes supported, sometimes discarded. An example of the latter is given by Sartori when he writes (1994, p 95) that "... party solidification and discipline (in parliamentary voting) has never been a feedback of parliamentary government."

7 Maurice Duverger claimed (1964, p 217) that the tendency of a plurality system to enhance a two-party system came close to being "a true sociological law." This relationship, often referred to as "Duverger's law," is, however, not generally accepted in political science.

8 This fourfold classification of constitutions is not totally absent in the political science literature. It is thus clearly indicated in for example Powell (1982) and Sartori (1994), and it is explicitly emphasised in Lijphart (1991). Neither of these authors do, however, stress the importance of the classification for parties and party systems.

1) Parliamentary constitutions with proportionalism. The main examples are in Western Europe. Usually there are some five to ten disciplined, stable and cohesive parties. Some of these parties may also be substantially bigger than required by a contingent threshold rule. Parliamentarism gives the incentives to discipline and, occasionally, to size, and proportionality the means. There are, however, no strong forces reducing the number of parties.

2) Parliamentary constitutions with plurality. This system is characteristic for the United Kingdom and some other countries in the Commonwealth. Due to the plurality system the number of parties are usually few. In spite of the incentives given by parliamentarism the discipline is, however, lower than in constitutions with proportional elections, since the means are weaker.

3) Presidential constitutions with proportionalism. Several Latin American constitutions are of this type. Often there are many parties since the number-reducing forces operating in the elections for the legislature are weak. This is, however, often, to some extent, offset by a number-reducing effect of the presidential elections. The parliamentary incentives for discipline are absent, but there may be other incentives, and the means, given by proportionality, are there. Thus, in some countries the parties have a low coherence, while, in others they exhibit a considerable discipline.

4) Presidential constitutions with plurality. The main example here is the US. There we find two large parties with low internal discipline.

This fourfold classification is useful for my purpose, even if not exhaustive. In particular the constitutions which simultaneously have elements of presidentialism and parliamentarism, as for example the French constitution, are not represented—although, as we know, they are gaining popularity. Anyway, in the following, and due to lack of space, I will restrict the discussion to the first and fourth types of constitutions above. I will be comparatively detailed about the first type, and use the fourth type mainly as an illuminating contrast. Since these two types of constitutions can be looked upon as extremes in several respects this seems to be a defensible procedure.

3 The distribution of power

It is easy to see that the power distribution is very different in the two constitutional systems selected for discussion. In the parliamentary system with proportionalism the parties are so consolidated and disciplined that they can reasonably be considered as unitary actors. This does not mean, of course, that individuals are not important. It means, however, that the individuals almost exclusively play their roles within the parties. The individuals have a say in determining the party positions, and more so the higher they are in the party hierarchy. When it comes to dealings with actors outside the party, for example with other parties, or with the electorate in campaigns, or with lobbying organisations, it is usually the party as such, or the party leadership, which acts. It is in that sense that the party is a unitary actor.

In the parliamentary system with proportional elections the power is thus concentrated at the hierarchical tops of the political parties, albeit not evenly. In fact, almost all the power during the current election period is held by the constellation of parties belonging to the executive, or to the parliamentary majority supporting the executive. The power is thus very concentrated and the main actors, the important parties, are often fewer than five.

The US presidential system with plurality contrasts strikingly to this pattern. There, the party restrictions on the behaviour of the president, and on the members of the Congress, are very weak indeed, and all these individual human beings can therefore be considered as fairly independent actors. In such a system there are thus hundreds of actors in the legislature and the executive. The power is diffused, not only between the president and the Congress, but also among all the members of the Congress.

These different patterns should reasonably be of great importance. It thus seems likely, to put it that way, that the transaction costs of political processes depend critically on the number of independent actors taking part.[9][10] Considering the

9 The transaction cost concept was, as we know, introduced by Ronald H Coase (1937) in economics, and by James M Buchanan and Gordon Tullock (1962) in constitutional analysis. In economics low transaction costs is gener-

particular processes one may also say that the number of independent actors is likely to affect the possibilities to build decisive majorities or blocking minorities, the character of
lobbying-processes, and the expediency of various strategies
in the political competition.

As for lobbying the commonly held opinion, that it is more
developed and more influential in the US than in other countries, is probably wrong. This is rather an impression created
by the fact that the targets for lobbying are so many and so dispersed that the activities unavoidably become open and visible for everybody. Lobbying cannot, as in a parliamentary
system, be hidden in a few closed rooms. For the same reason
lobbying in the US is also less effective, and requires more resources, than lobbying in parliamentary countries.

4 Delegation and instruction

The character of the relation between the voters (the princi-
pals) and the political main actors (the agents), whether individuals or parties, are important and dependent on the constitution.[11] For the discussion of these matters I will differentiate
between two types of such relations, which I call delegation
and instruction.

Delegation is the simpler of the two and most people have
experience of it from everyday life. When people in typically

ally considered as desirable, but in politics, where the majority rule usually
reigns, it is not necessarily so. Low transaction costs may, for example, facilitate the formation of majorities exploiting the outsiders.

10 When talking about transaction costs here I am thinking about the transactions *between* political actors, and thus about their *outward* activities in relation
to each other. A disciplined political party, considered as a unitary actor, is
however also characterised by a lot of *inward* activities. These activities are
important since they, to a large extent, can thwart the intentions embedded in
a constitution. A system of checks and balances can, for instance, be completely put out of function if the real decisions are taken within disciplined
political parties which control the different branches of government. These
matters have been analysed by, among others, Donald Wittman (for example
1989, a and b).

11 The nature of the relationship between voters and politicians has, it should
be emphasised, been an important subject in the social sciences since long.
Early and important contributors to the discussion were for example Ed-
mund Burke and John Stuart Mill.

voluntary associations like the local sports club or charity association elect presidents, secretaries, and so on, they usually do not require more than having confidence in the persons elected. They just want to be able to rely on them to act in a way that is in accordance with common sense and the purpose of the club. Feeling such confidence they delegate the decision-making to the people elected. Mostly such a system works well but if some functionary, for some reason, starts to act in ways of which the members disapprove, there are usually provisions in the club's charter for displacing the functionary. This rather simple kind of relation occurs not only in clubs, but also in politics.

Instruction, on the other hand, prevails when the voters do not limit themselves to a simple confidence in the ones elected but rather require that they execute a certain program, which may be worked out in a rather detailed way. Therefore, when people are elected, a program, or an instruction, for the elected to realise, is also adopted. The program may very well be, and often is, formulated by the people who want to get elected. Different candidates for political positions thus offer the voters to carry through different programs if they are elected. This, however, is fully consistent with the view that the program, once a candidate is elected, can be considered as an instruction from the voters to the elected.

It is easy to see that mixtures of delegation and instruction often appear in reality. Sometimes the element of delegation dominates, sometimes the element of instruction. One may therefore ask about the conditions favouring the one or the other type of relation. My hypothesis is that the parliamentary system with proportionalism has a tendency towards instruction, whereas the US presidential system has a tendency towards delegation.

The reason is simple. In the parliamentary system a campaigner, which in that case is a party, will be able to fulfil its promises if its electoral success is big enough. If, for example, a party alone gets more than fifty percent of the seats in the legislature, it can, by itself, form an executive and effectuate all its promises immediately. In fact, as we shall see later on, even a small party has a good chance of delivering on its promises if, after the election, it manages to join the executive.

A system of the US type is, in this respect, quite different. Imagine, for instance, a person running for the presidency, or for a seat in the Congress. In both cases everybody knows that the person, after the election, and however great the electoral success, will not, without further cumbersome and yet uncertain negotiations, be in a position to deliver on his or her campaign proposals. Exactly for that reason it would not be particularly clever, and perhaps even a bit ridiculous, to let detailed proposals dominate the campaign. It seems more expedient for the candidate to emphasise his or her own personal qualities, thereby indicating a capacity for prudent action in various future situations which, at the moment of the election, are impossible to foresee. That, on the whole, is also what candidates seem to do, and the resulting relation to the voters, hence, is primarily that of delegation.

5 General and specific instructions

Having thus argued that instructions are likely to play a relatively important role in a parliamentary, proportional setting I will now discuss the possible nature of those instructions. My main distinction is between general and specific instructions.[12]

General instructions may be based on ideological ideas about the ideal character or construction of society, or they may be derived from ideas about the common, or public, interest. The implementation of general instructions will thus usually affect the society at large.

Specific instructions, on the other hand, satisfy the interests of particular groups of people, that is special interests. Specific instructions are thus independent of notions about ideal societies, or about the common good—they exist just because people want more of the goods of this world, and can use majority politics for satisfying such wants. The implementation of specific instructions usually means that some people satisfy their interests at the expense of others.

---

12 This distinction is closely related to a distinction between *generality* and *particularity* made by Buchanan (1993a).

I will now argue that, on the whole, it is easier for political parties to make deals (or logroll) about specific instructions than about general ones. If, for example, one party is committed to a particular specific instruction, and another party to another one, they can easily agree about supporting each other—if you support my instruction, I support yours. General instructions, on the contrary, are often in conflict with each other, and are therefore not easily reconciled—you cannot have socialism and capitalism at the same time. Sometimes, however, there may be deals in which a general instruction of one party is knit together with a specific instruction of another party. They may agree that the first party supports the second party's specific instruction, if the second party supports, or perhaps just tolerates, the first party's general instruction. It may also be argued that general instructions, which give a prominent and far-reaching role to the state, are easier to reconcile with specific instructions than those giving a limited role to the state. The reason, of course, is that specific instructions often are natural parts of state interventionism.

6 The competition for a place in the executive

We are now able to deal with the political competition in some detail. In a parliamentary, proportional setting there are two stages in that competition, first the competition for votes in a general election, and after that the positioning and bargaining in order get into the executive. The competitors are, as we have seen, the parties. Which strategies are most likely to lead to success in this context?

Focusing first on the second stage, the problem of getting into the executive, each of the parties knows that it is unlikely to get a majority of its own, and that it therefore must be able to make deals about a governmental program with other parties. This gives these hypotheses about the likely character of the party programs:

- Specific instructions are likely to be frequent in all parties' programs.

- All parties do not necessarily have general instructions in their programs, and when such instructions appear they are likely to be pragmatic or attenuated.

In addition to this we also get these hypotheses about the executive coalitions likely to emerge, and about their governmental programs:[13]

- A governmental program containing only specific instructions is perfectly possible.

- A small party may be committed to some general instructions, but it is not likely to get them included in a governing coalition's program.

- If a governmental program contains general instructions, and in that sense has an ideological inclination, those instructions are likely to have come directly from a big, dominating party's program. Either that party has been able to form an executive on its own, or it is the main actor in an executive involving one or a few small extra coalition members. In this latter case there may be a deal saying that the dominating party will support some specific instructions of the smaller parties, if they support, or tolerate, the dominating party's general instructions.

- Parties with articulated and conflicting general instructions on their programs are not likely to be able to make deals about specific instructions with each other.

- A small party not having any general instructions in its program is completely free in choosing its partners, irrespective of their general instructions. Such a party is often able to play a pivotal role in coalition building processes and is thus particularly likely to get its specific instructions implemented.

13 The ideas expressed here are similar to, although not identical with, those in the so-called *portfolio allocation approach*. According to this approach, which has been elaborated by, among others, Laver & Shepsle (1994, 1996), the governmental program is determined by the allocation of ministries, or portfolios. Thus, if the head of the ministry of agriculture comes from party X, the agricultural policy of the government will, more or less, be the agricultural policy proposed in the party program of party X, and so on. In that way the total policy, or program, of the governmental executive will thus be composed of the relevant elements in the participating parties' programs

- A small party with strongly held, articulated and controversial general instructions in its program, for example a party with an extreme ideological inclination, may affront most other parties. If so the party may be excluded from all possible coalitions, and thus from all influence.

- A big party may dominate the politics of its country for a long period even if it suffers occasional electoral retrogressions and, indeed, even if it never has a majority of its own. The party can stay in the executive all the time by just making deals about some specific instructions favoured by one or two small parties, and then govern together with them.

7 The competition for votes

The competition for votes is more difficult to analyse than the competition for places in the executive, and we have to be satisfied with a few hypothetical preliminary steps. One reason for the difficulties is that the process, by which a voter decides which party to support, usually is complex. The issues are not presented one by one, as in a number of consecutive referendums, but rather as parts of complete party programs. In principle the voter thus has to weigh the pros and the cons, for each of the parties, in order to arrive at a final decision. Some voters may find that simple, but others feel uncertain almost all through.

In order to get a grasp of a mechanism, which may be important in parliamentary democracies with proportionalism, we can consider a party S of modest size which, in an election campaign, tries to attract a particular group of voters by offering them some advantages at the expense of other voters. This offer, or proposal, which we can call P, is thus an example of a specific instruction. Then some members of the target group, who appreciate the proposal, vote for S, which thereby becomes somewhat bigger than it would otherwise be. After the general election S will be considered a possible executive member and, in the negotiations preceding the formation of the executive, S promises to support important points in the other prospective member parties' programs in return for their support of P. The parties reach an agreement along these lines and form an executive. P thus becomes part of the executive's program and will therefore become implemented. Is this kind of scenario, we may ask, likely, or even typical, of a parliamentary democracy with proportionalism? Since the conditions therefore are fulfilled, my answer is in the affirmative.

The main condition is that the parties have the capacity to act in the way described. What is required, basically, is that the parties have reasonably clear voices when talking to the voters, that they can make firm deals with other parties, and finally that they can fulfil their own promises to the other parties by controlling their own people in the legislature. All of these requirements are better fulfilled in a parliamentary, proportional setting, with its unitary partisan actors, than in any other type of democratic system—or, in other words, the campaigners capacity for credible commitment towards the voters is greater than in any other constitutional setting. The conclusion that the parties can act as described therefore seems reasonable.

This, however, does not settle the issue. It is obviously not sufficient for the parties to be able to act in the way described. They must also find it expedient to do so, it must pay in terms of votes. More exactly, the action must be expected to result in a net gain in votes—the number of voters attracted from other parties must be greater than the number of voters repelled.

In principle this is all practicable. The negative effects may for example be spread out so thinly, and over so many people, that those hit hardly notice. With some shrewd manoeuvring it may even be possible to allocate the negative effects mainly on voters who would not have voted for the party anyway.[14] Beside these problems about the management of the negative effects it is, however, also necessary to consider the reactions of those favoured by the proposal. Are they really likely to feel

14 The prerequisite that the campaigning politicians are able, to a sufficient extent, to recognise "their own people" is, as I will soon argue, likely to be valid. When that is so the campaigners can also afford, and perhaps even find it expedient, to offend other people. In Sweden there is even a particular term for politicians who choose to offend their opponents explicitly, namely *politicians of confrontation*. If that is taken to mean that not only opponent politicians, but also their presumptive voters, are railed at, then, I think, such politicians are hardly imaginable in a presidential setting with plurality.

attracted and thus to change their minds in favour of the proposing party? Some may perhaps do so immediately, but there may also be those in the target group who, although favoured by the particular proposal, generally dislike the system of politically distributed goods and clientelism, and therefore want to change the system rather than to take part in it.[15]

Such voters, according to the terminology used here, favour some general instruction rather than the specific instruction at issue. But perhaps there is no party committed to the general instruction which these voters endorse, or if there is such a party its chances of becoming big enough for getting the instruction into a governmental program may be slim. Such dilemmas are, in fact, as we saw in the preceding section, quite likely. Our voters may thus find it best to play safe and vote for the party offering the favours. Voting for the second best may, after all, seem more prudent since it may give a payoff even if the favoured party, after the election, is still quite small.[16]

The conclusion thus is that strategies including specific instructions about favours to particular target groups may be quite profitable, and are more likely to be profitable in the parliamentary, proportional setting than in other constitutional contexts. Although other types of strategies will certainly also be used this is an important conclusion which, as we shall see in the next section, is relevant for the expansion of the public sector. Furthermore it paves the way for the following hypotheses about parliamentary, proportional systems:

15 This requires, though, that the voters are endowed with a certain amount of idealism. If that is not so the target group, and in particular the individual voters in it, should rather, using Mancur Olson's concept, be considered as extremely narrow actors who do not care about the general effects of their behaviour at all.

16 An interesting implication of this is that the idea of rational ignorance has only limited application. The individual voter may be thought of as giving some additional weight to some instruction, which is already effectuated to some extent, and thereby, marginally, increase the advantages which are delivered according to that instruction. The returns on an individual vote are therefore greater than usually allowed for in the arguments supporting the idea of rational ignorance. This should lead to a higher turnout in general elections in parliamentary democracies with proportionalism than in other democratic systems, and seems to do so.

- Specific instructions tend to drive out general instructions.[17]

- The log-rolling processes preceding government formation easily result in exploiting majorities.

- Since the parties are likely to develop programs which favour particular groups of voters, long-lasting, mutually supportive relations between parties and voters tend to develop. The party leaderships will thus, as it was put earlier, be able to recognise their own people to a large extent.

In a presidential system with plurality, such as the US system, all of this is likely to be different. First, we remember, there is a tendency towards delegation rather than instruction. Candidates thus have an inclination to sell themselves, rather than programs. Furthermore, since strategies deliberately designed for attracting particular groups of voters do not work well the candidates must, rather, concentrate on not repelling voters.[18] Since the electorate to a large extent is not committed from the beginning this means that they must be cautious not to repel anybody. There is, in fact, no opposition in the sense that there is in a parliamentary system. To this we can, however, also add that obligations of the state, once they exist, and whatever the reasons for their existence, are probably more difficult to remove in a presidential system of the US type than in a parliamentary system. The reason is the expediency, or even the necessity, of non-offending strategies in such a country.[19]

17 This, it may be noted, is in agreement with Buchanan's contention that "Political players who might seek to further some conception of an all-encompassing general, or public, interest cannot survive" (1993a and b). Buchanan is, however, discussing democratic constitutions in general, whereas the focus here is on parliamentary constitutions with proportional elections which, I submit, are extreme in the respect considered.

18 Perhaps this explains the great importance of money and advertising in US election campaigns. There, policies do not speak for themselves to the extent that they do in systems encouraging political clientelism.

19 In his book *Demosclerosis* (1994, p 124f) Jonathan Rauch, calling it an "asymmetry," says that "(t)o create a new subsidy or anticompetitive deal is hard, but to reduce a subsidy that already exists is much harder."

8 An asymmetry favouring the public sector

This paper basically argues that the democratic competition for power propels the expansion of the public sector. Campaigners, in order to win, promise their voters, if they win, a better life at the expense of the losers. One prerequisite for this, however, is that a majority rule is used. If the unanimity rule were used there would be no outside minority for the majority to exploit. But, as we know, there is no democracy in which the unanimity rule plays an important rule; all democracies rely mainly on various kinds of majority rules.

Another important prerequisite for the expanding public sector is that the exploitation, in fact, is done by taxation. This, however, is not necessarily the case. Those exploited must not necessarily pay by increased taxes. Another possibility is that they pay by having some already existing politically decided privileges reduced. Obviously we have to consider this second possibility since, in contrast to the first, it leaves the public sector unaffected.

There is however, I submit, an asymmetry which makes the second possibility much less likely than the first, namely that the task of taxing a large part of a population evenly is, administratively, much easier than the task of reducing marginally a lot of privileges of various groups, with the same final distributional effect.

It thus seems reasonable to expect expanding public sectors in all democracies. Still, the speed of expansion may differ depending on the type of democracy. A main reason for this, as I have argued, is that exploiting majorities are more easily formed in some democracies than in other others.

9 The empirical evidence

The general expansion of public sectors is a phenomenon which is well documented. Here, we are therefore only interested in data relevant for explaining the expansion mechanisms. The data of that kind that I know of is, however, utterly sketchy and inconclusive. To a large extent each reader has to use his or her own knowledge about things, and rely on the judgements that follow from that. There are, however, a few facts worth mentioning.

- Several Western European countries with parliamentary constitutions and proportionalism exhibit exceptionally large public sectors.

- In an interesting and well-documented paper Grilli, Masciandaro & Tabellini (1991) discuss the properties of different democratic constitutions, using a classification similar to mine. Although their focus is on public deficits and debts, rather than on expenses, their empirical data lend some support to my hypotheses about public sector expansion in parliamentary democracies with proportional elections as well. Their explanation, however, differs completely from mine.

- Ståhl (1991) has made the observation that among the six democracies with the largest public sectors in the world, five are kingdoms, asking if this is merely a coincidence. The analysis presented here suggests, I think, a negative answer to that question. The Western European kingdoms we are talking about are also the most pure parliamentary systems. In them there is no democratically elected actor, president or other authority, who has any responsibility for "the common good." All elected actors represent some kind of special interest.

- I have myself shown (Moberg, 1992) that, in Sweden, in spite of rapidly expanding total public expenses, the share of those expenses used for collective goods has, over a long period, and except for the time of the second world war, been fairly constant (3–6%). The rest of the public expenses, which consequently has increased continuously, has been used for individual goods or transfers. That, I think, suggests that public means are extensively used for attracting votes. Sweden has a parliamentary constitution with proportional elections.

10 Conclusions

The discussion can now be concluded with the following two main hypotheses:

- Due to the political competition the public sector is always, and almost unavoidably, likely to expand in a democracy. The basic cause is the majority rule, which makes it possible for a majority of the electorate to exploit the minority. With the unanimity rule, which unfortunately is very unpractical, that kind of exploitation would not be possible.

- The rate of the expansion is likely to differ between different types of democracies. The highest rate will be found in parliamentary democracies with proportionalism.[20]

11 Implications

An almost unavoidable expansion of the public sector seems to imply that a democracy breaks down when the public sector gets impossibly large. If that is true, it is also true that the life of a democracy is limited to the time it takes for the public sector to grow from low to impossibly high levels. Are these conclusions really compelling, we may therefore ask, or are there ways to avoid the disastrous outcome? I will conclude by making three brief comments on this topic.

The first comment is related to the nature of the threat. Using Hirschman's (1970) well-known distinction between voice and exit democracy may be considered as rule by voice. Within that perspective the breakdown of a democracy is equivalent to an undermining of the voice option. Exit thus becomes the only remaining option for dissatisfied citizens, and a lot of different exit reactions are, I think, likely to occur. Some people may move to other countries, but many people may also exercise the exit option while staying where they are. They may, for example, turn from white to black markets, or from paying taxes to not doing so. If this happens the state,

---

20 In his book *Demosclerosis* (1994, p 124f) Jonathan Rauch, calling it an "asymmetry," says that "(t)o create a new subsidy or anticompetitive deal is hard, but to reduce a subsidy that already exists is much harder."

when it finally collapses, may be quite empty and void of authority, and it may have lost most of its tax-collecting power. Within this general framework many different specific outcomes seem possible. Some may be relatively fortunate, but it is also easy to imagine anarchical conditions with a lot of uncontrolled violence.

The second comment is related to the difficulties, in general, of undertaking preventive measures in controlled forms, in good time before the impending break-down. A main problem is that an expanding public sector automatically makes more and more people dependent on the sector, for example as receivers of transfers, or as public employees. Since these people are voters as well, and likely supporters of the public sector in that capacity, the problem of halting the growth, and contracting the sector, becomes more difficult the greater the sector is. These problems are dealt with in Eliasson (1986).

The third comment is related to the constitutional aspects of the challenge just mentioned. Above, in the section "the competition for votes," I made the point that although the public sector probably expands more slowly in normal times in a presidential democracy of the US type than in a parliamentary democracy with proportionalism, it may nevertheless be more difficult to reverse the expansion, that is to contract the public sector in an emergency situation, in the former constitutional setting. It may be easier to mobilise the power necessary for that purpose in the top-heavy parliamentary system. If this is correct it would really be a disaster to substitute a constitution of the US type for a parliamentary constitution with proportionalism in a country with a big and oppressive public sector. Rather, it would be necessary to reduce the public sector before the introduction of a new constitution. There are thus several different, difficult problems involved in the challenge, and the order in which their solutions is implemented are of critical importance. At last: Even if the expansion of the public sector is relatively slow in a presidential constitution with plurality, it is still important to design democratic constitutions which automatically contain public sector growth.

Bibliography

Buchanan, J M & Tullock, G (1962), *The calculus of consent : logical foundations of constitutional democracy*. Ann Arbor: The University of Michigan Press.

Buchanan, J M (1993a), "How can constitutions be designed so that politicians who seek to serve 'public interest' can survive and prosper?" in *Constitutional Political Economy*, Vol 4 (1993), No 1.

Buchanan, J M (1993b), "Public choice after socialism," in *Public Choice*, 1993, pp 67–74.

Coase, R H (1937), "The nature of the firm," in *Economica*, Vol 4 (1937).

Downs, A (1957), *An economic theory of democracy*. New York: Harper Collins Publishers.

Duverger, M (1964), *Political parties : their organisation and activity in the modern state*. London: Methuen.

Eliasson, G (1986), "A note on the stability of economic organizational forms and the importance of human capital : a proposition about the endogenous, market-induced disintegration of the non-market sector," in Day, R H & Eliasson, G (eds), *The dynamics of market economies*. Amsterdam: North-Holland, 1986.

Grilli, V, Masciandaro, D & Tabellini, G (1991), "Political and monetary institutions and public financial policies in the industrial countries," in *Economic Policy*, 1991 (October).

Hirschman, A O (1970), *Exit, voice and loyalty : responses to decline in firms, organizations, and states*. Cambridge, MA: Harvard University Press.

Larkey, P D, Stolp, C & Winer, M (1981), "Theorizing about the growth of government : a research assessment," in *Journal of Public Policy*, Vol 1 (1981).

Laver, M & Shepsle, K A (eds) (1994), *Cabinet ministers and parliamentary government*. Cambridge: Cambridge University Press.

Laver, M & Shepsle, K A (1996), *Making and breaking governments : cabinets and legislatures in parliamentary democracies.* Cambridge: Cambridge University Press.

Lijphart, A (1991), "Constitutional choices for new democracies," in *Journal of Democracy*, Vol 2 (1991), No 1.

Moberg, E (1992), *Offentlig produktion av individuella och kollektiva nyttigheter.* Stockholm: Näringslivets Ekonomifakta (mimeo).

Powell, G B (1982), *Contemporary democracies : participation, stability and violence.* Cambridge, MA: Harvard University Press.

Rauch, J (1994), *Demosclerosis : the silent killer of American government.* New York: Times Books.

Riker, W H (1962), *The theory of political coalitions.* New Haven: Yale University Press.

Sartori, G (1994), *Comparative constitutional engineering : an inquiry into structures, incentives and outcomes.* Basingstoke: Macmillan & New York: New York University Press.

Schumpeter, J A (1976), *Capitalism, socialism, and democracy.* New York: Harper & Row Publishers.

Ståhl, I (1991), "Hur kan de svenska skatterna sänkas? : svensk offentlig sektor i ett internationellt perspektiv," in *Den nya svenska modellen.* Stockholm: Svenska Arbetsgivareföreningen.

Wittman, D (1989a), "Why democracies produce efficient results," in *Journal of Political Economy*, Vol 97 (1989), pp 1395–1424.

Wittman, D (1989b), "The constitution as an optimal social contract : a transaction cost analysis of The Federalist Papers," in Grofman, B & Wittman, D (eds), *The Federalist Papers and the new institutionalism.* New York: Agathon Press.

Chapter III

The Role of Enabling and Mandatory Company Law for Financial Systems Efficiency

I am grateful to Gunnar Eliasson and Shubhashis Gangopadhyay for discussions of earlier versions of this paper.

Clas Wihlborg

Abstract

The main issue in this paper is how principles of company law help or hinder the efficiency of the financial system. Efficiency is here defined from a dynamic Schumpetarian perspective. A distinction is made between "enabling" and "mandatory" law. Enabling law gives great leeway for shareholders and other stakeholder to design and change corporate charters. Mandatory law, on the other hand, offers detailed binding specifications. It is argued that the relative advantage of enabling and mandatory law depends on the objectives of company law and whose interest it is intended to serve. A constitutional principle implying that law with a higher degree of generality dominates law with less generality would be consistent with enabling law dominating mandatory law in case of conflict between laws.

1 Introduction

Company law defines the rules for the governance of firms as legal entities, and the rights and obligations of shareholders relative to management, lenders, and to some extent, other stakeholders in the firms. Economists in the Anglo-Saxon countries in particular have taken an increasing interest in company law during the last decade, reflecting the increasingly widespread view that institutional structures and economic organization are important determinants of economic growth. From an economist's point of view, company law can be approached as an industrial organization issue or as a financial market issue. Markets for securities issued by firms are markets for influence and control over company affairs, as well as markets for a stream of dividend or coupon payments. Lending by financial institutions are similarly associated with a degree of control over a firm's business operations. The influence and control aspects of the financial system are often analyzed as "markets for corporate control" within the financial economics literature. It focuses on mechanisms for changes in management and ownership, and on the incentives of managers relative to financial stakeholders in particular.

Markets for corporate control vary across the countries with the legal and regulatory institutions for firms and financial markets. In the USA and the UK, the threat of hostile takeovers plays an important role, while in many European countries and in Japan changes of ownership and management are organized within industrial groups closely associated with banks. In both cases, company law determines important aspects of the relations between users and suppliers of financial resources.

In this paper company law is studied from the perspective of the financial system. The main question is how the principles of company law relate to the efficiency of the financial system. A distinction is made between "enabling" and "mandatory" law. Enabling law gives great leeway for shareholders and other stakeholders to design and change the corporate charter. Mandatory law lays down detailed standard specifications. It will be argued that the advantage of enabling law over mandatory law depends on what objectives and whose interest company law serves. It is also argued that the complexity of the relations among users and suppliers of financial resources makes it very difficult—if not impossible—for legislators and regulators to know, whether intended objectives of detailed mandatory law will be achieved.

In Section 2 the concept of an "efficient financial system" is discussed. Drawing from Wihlborg (1998), efficiency is defined for a dynamic economy where suppliers and users of financial resources, as well as policy-makers face uncertainty. Above all, the conditions are uncertain to such an extent that standard mandatory rules and contracts may distort contractual relations relative to what would be mutually agreeable. If economic growth is the policy objective, then "enabling" rules and laws are preferable.

Section 3 provides a brief description of the social role of contracts and company law. Alternative objectives with this body of law are discussed. In Section 4, arguments for enabling and mandatory law are presented. It is argued that mandatory law tend to affect specific groups and, therefore, such law would violate constitutional principles giving dominant status to laws with greater generality. Such laws are rare in modern democracies, however.

Another aspect of law discussed in Section 5 is the capacity of the legal system. This capacity may be low in many emerging market economies.

In Section 6, some aspects of company law are discussed. The difficulty of foreseeing the consequences of mandatory rules is emphasized and it is argued that enabling law is usually consistent with shareholder wealth maximization.

In the concluding Section 7 it is suggested that enabling law could be given higher constitutional status than mandatory law in order to enhance the dynamic efficiency of the financial system. A constitutional principle providing higher status for law with higher degree of generality would imply that enabling law would dominate mandatory law in case of conflict between old an new law, and between conflicting laws covering the same contractual relation.

2 Financial markets and institutions—functions and efficiency

Financial markets allow individuals facing income uncertainty to smooth consumption over time and to obtain risk-sharing by investing in a number of projects with different risk-characteristics. By traditional welfare criteria, financial system-efficiency occurs when individuals optimize with regard to their risk-return preferences and firms use financial markets returns including risk-premia to discount the expected future cash flows of alternative projects. Financial resources are then allocated to projects according to individuals' preferences with regard to return and risk.

It is by now well-accepted that efficiency as defined cannot be reached if information about project-returns is costly to obtain or if there are other transactions costs in financial markets (Grossman and Stiglitz, 1980). If all relevant information were costlessly available and reflected in prices, there would be little trading. Liquid secondary markets could not exist under these circumstances. One of the important functions of secondary markets for securities is to provide liquidity, however. Direct lending from financial investors to firms would be severely constrained in the absence of liquidity. Other institutional forms for lending would be required.

The assumption that all relevant information about projects is costlessly available is obviously unrealistic, if not absurd. The return to innovative activity for example cannot be characterized by an externally given frequency distribution. It is actually likely to depend strongly on the competence and the behavior of individual actors in markets. Since most projects contain an element of innovation information about projects must be constantly gathered and analyzed by the financial market participants for the information to be incorporated in market-prices. Thus, one important role for financial markets is to provide incentives for information gathering and processing. Information activities contribute to liquidity, as well, because trading activity increases as information becomes more differentiated among individuals.

Information activities and liquidity contribute to the efficiency of financial markets in the sense that the informational content of prices increases and transactions costs fall. On the other hand, perfect informational efficiency and liquidity cannot be achieved if there are information and transactions costs.

The existence of information and transactions costs in securities markets implies that other financial organizations could be more efficient from an information and transactions costs point of view. Considerations of such costs necessitates a dynamic view of efficiency. Hence, the rules of the economy should be such that there are incentives for pulling, and competitive forces for pushing the actors to look for new contractual and organizational solutions. A dynamically efficient system need flexible contractual organizations to cope with unexpected change.

Standard mandatory rules tend to become inefficient because possible sources of agency costs among, for example, owners, lenders, and shareholders are likely to depend on a number of technological and environmental factors that cannot easily be identified. It is never possible to say that there are not better contractual arrangements and organizational solutions available. What is thought to be best today is most likely going to change in the future. Eliasson (1987, 1991) calls such an economy experimentally organized in the sense that all business ventures can be seen as more or less well-prepared experiments, and all agents in the markets must be prepared to be mistaken and to deal with the mistakes. The uncertainty implies that the "best" contractual arrangements have to be determined through experimentation. Hence, contractual arrangements and organizations have to be flexible allowing the perceived "best" contractual arrangements to change over time. Just as competition among products is expected to lead to an efficient dynamic process for product development, competition among contractual and organizational arrangements is required for development of the arrangements that minimize expected future costs of agency, contracting and enforcement at a given level of output.

This view of the dynamics of the economy is elaborated on in Wihlborg (1998). There it is argued that dynamic efficiency must be defined in terms of the system's ability to adjust to changes in preferences and productive conditions at the lowest costs and, especially, to adjust to new conditions affecting the incentives of individuals to develop new explicit and implicit contractual arrangements. If, for example, such contractual arrangements do not develop in response to new informational conditions influencing potential agency costs, then the system lacks dynamic efficiency. Analogously, if new firms do not enter a market characterized by monopoly and low entry barriers, then there is dynamic inefficiency.

Although the evaluation of the degree of efficiency of a financial system is impossible for all practical purposes, the nature of the concept of efficiency presented here has clear policy implications. Specifically, if competition is allowed among different organizational structures, different contractual arrangements, and different financial services, then these structures, contractual arrangements, and services will develop in response to incentives to develop better and cheaper sources of information, incentives to obtain more incentive compatible contracts at lower enforcement costs, and incentives to satisfy consumer needs. However, no planner, regulator or legislator would know which are the most efficient structures, contracts and services, neither ex ante nor ex post. Thus, the task of the regulator and the legislator seeking to enhance efficiency should be to create the conditions for dynamic efficiency by making efficient contract formulation possible. In other words, legislation and regulations should make incentives work in the direction of improving informational efficiency and the incentive compatibility among market participants. Laws and regulations should enable market participants to discover the most efficient solutions to particular information problems. Competition among organizations and contractual arrangements would determine the actual trade-offs among the different functions of the financial system.[1]

Company law regulates contractual arrangements among managers and financial stakeholders in firms. This body of law is therefore of crucial importance for the efficiency of the financial system. After a brief discussion of the purposes of

1 Market failures in goods and factor markets could make the efficient financial system inefficient in a broader welfare analysis. Addressing problems caused by failures of, for example, labor markets with restrictions and rules for the financial system is bound to be costly in comparison with policies targeting the specific labor market problem.

company law, the issue of enabling law for financial system efficiency is addressed in greater detail.

3 Contract costs and company law

The firm can be seen as a *nexus of contracts* regulating the sharing of income and risk among the stakeholders (shareholders, lenders, managers, employees, customers, suppliers) as well as the obligations of these stakeholders.[2]

A *contract* regulates the conditions for the exchange of resources (property, goods, services, money, claims) in a transaction. It requires that *property rights* are defined, i e who can manage resources, access the rents and trade in the assets. Contractual rights must also be enforceable, requiring proof of ownership through, for instance, registration, unless simple possession is sufficient.

Efficient allocation and the alignment of incentives require that voluntary contracts are recognized and enforceable. Any hindrances to potentially mutually agreeable contracts imply that mutually beneficial transactions will not take place.

Simultaneous payment (delivery) of well-specified units is the simplest form of contract. Contractual costs, incentive and enforcement problems arise when complexity increases. Sources of complexity are:

a) Specification and monitoring of the quality of goods or services

b) Uncertainty about the contingencies influencing the parties' ability and willingness to fulfill the contract

c) Long time horizon

d) Asymmetry of information

Since all contingencies affecting the performance of the parties to a transaction are not known when a contract is entered, it is a difficult problem to determine when a breach of contract has occurred. All contracts are therefore incomplete in one way or another.

The fulfillment of contracts is always subject to unobserved behavior of the parties causing potential "moral hazard." In

2 Milgrom & Roberts (1992) provide a textbook treatment of this view of the firm.

other words, the contract may induce unobservable risk-taking as is well known in the field of insurance. Institutional arrangements are often designed to reduce problems caused by such asymmetric information (incentive contracts, banks as monitors, etc). Most of these arrangements and contracts are formulated in the market by people who are affected by moral hazard.

Unobserved characteristics of parties to a contract at the time it is entered are sources of "adverse selection," meaning that those with unobservable low quality characteristics may seek to take advantage of contract terms that cannot be differentiated among individuals with different characteristics.

Unobservable behavior (moral hazard) and characteristics (adverse selection) are sources of "agency-costs" in economic relations. These costs would show up as costs to information gathering, monitoring, enforcement or as a reduced volume of economic activity.

A third type of contract cost appears when one or both parties to a transaction invest "specialized assets" in an economic relation. By definition a specialized asset has a particularly high value in one economic relation. In this case, the party who commits specialized assets be they physical or human, risks being taken advantage of once the assets are committed and the party is "locked in."[3]

The consequence of this risk is that the owners of specialized assets are reluctant to commit these assets unless the other parties to transactions also put physical or human assets at risk. In the following we include costs associated with transactions involving specialized assets in the concept of agency costs.

Explicit law provides *standard-form contracts* reducing transactions costs and the agency costs of organizing a business venture. A contract between those financing a corporation and those managing the corporation is complex. The standard form specified by law helps potential financiers formulate contractual terms for a number of contingencies.

A second role of law is to aid in the enforcement of contracts of different kinds. Without enforcement possibilities contracts

3   See Klein, Crawford & Alchian (1978).

are of no value and transactions/ventures may simply not take place.

We can distinguish between three types of enforcement mechanisms:

1) Self-enforcement
2) Court-enforcement of voluntary contracts
3) Court-enforcement of standard form contracts in law

An important question in all economies and in emerging market economies in particular is how far self-enforcement in the market works, since legal expertise and experience may be lacking.

We can distinguish between three kinds of self-enforcement:[4]

1) Reputation
2) Internalization
3) Bonding arrangements (hostages)

Contractual agreements are often self-enforcing, because the parties do not want to risk their reputation in the market. Reputation is a valuable asset for an individual or a corporation and it is a standard enforcement mechanism in small matters. It is important for any firm with repeated transactions with firms and individuals. "Internalization" of transactions within firms in the form of, for example, vertical integration is another way of solving difficult contractual arrangements. For example, if contracts between suppliers and a firm cannot be made credible, then suppliers may be integrated as subsidiaries. Countertrade arrangements, such as buy-backs, are also within this category.

Company law provides standard form contracts for the relation among the owners and the management of a firm, and, to some extent, the lenders to a firm that has obtained the status of a separate legal entity. A different kind of firm is a partnership that has no legal status apart from that of the partners. Important characteristics of corporations are the limited liability of the owners, and the separation—in principle—of ownership and control. The limited liability of the owners of a corporation implies that company law defines the aspects of the contractual relation between lenders and owners. Limited liability increases the risk of the lenders to a corporation but it

4 See Rubin (1992).

78

also increases decision-making efficiency in important ways. Without limited liability few shareholders would be willing to supply financial resources without a strong say in management. Partnership offers a "standard form contract" for owners of firms which can operate efficiently with a collective of influential owners involved in management.

Company law contributes to economic efficiency if it offers standard form contracts that would have been entered voluntarily at a higher cost in terms of negotiation and enforcement regarding, for example, the liability of the owners relative to other financiers, the conditions for an owner's withdrawal, and the dissolution of the firm.[5] The law specifies in more or less detail the contents of corporate charters including the rights of the shareholders to, for example, cast votes for membership on the board of directors, and the shareholders' influence on take-over and reorganization decisions. Managers' rights and obligations are also specified in charters and law.

The absence of company law would enable founders of firms to construct the corporate charter they like. In order to be credible the corporate charter protecting outside stakeholders, defining the liability of the investors, and setting the rules for corporate governance would have to be submitted for registration and made available to the stakeholders. The main disadvantage with the lack of standard-form contracts is that the suppliers of financial resources to a firm would have to study each corporate charter in order to understand its specific conditions. With standard-form contracts lawyers in a country are able to specialize and become experts on specific types of contracts. Similarly, judges who resolve conflicts become experts on a particular set of contracts. They can interpret contracts based on common business practices. Clearly, the founders of a firm have an incentive to choose a known contractual form in order to make the firm attractive to financiers. Thus, standard-form contracts and general business practices are likely to develop "in the market place". Explicit law can reduce the costs of developing the standard form that is preferred by a large share of the market participants.

In many countries the purpose of company law goes beyond reducing transactions and agency costs among stake-

5 See Posner (1992), *Economic Analysis of Law*, Ch 14.

holders. For example, employees are assigned a specific role in the governance of firms in many European countries in order to increase the influence of employees or unions on important economic decisions. The "social responsibility" of the corporation can be influenced by law either by limitations on contributions to various causes, or by requirements to serve politically determined social causes.

Bankruptcy law or other laws referring to firms in distress are usually not considered parts of company law. The rights of different stakeholders in case of business failure is bound to be important for the stakeholders' willingness to enter contracts at the time a firm is formed, however. Thus, company law and laws for firms in distress jointly determine the standard form contracts among managers, shareholders, and other financiers.

From a transactions costs' perspective, bankruptcy law reduces the costs of reaching a mutually agreeable contract among creditors and debtors with respect to exempt assets in case of bankruptcy and with respect to the priority of various creditors relative to non-exempt assets.

Without formal procedures for liquidation and reorganization various financial stakeholders would have the incentive to "come first" to claim their assets on the firm in near distress, forcing the dissolution of a company prematurely. It is likely that banks, as primary lenders and monitors of borrowers, would be able to establish control over firms in distress by withholding financing. Thus, the major conflicts of interest would exist between banks and other stakeholders, but the banks would have the incentives to ensure that the suppliers of inputs and the workers would not withdraw their services and force liquidation prematurely. Without established procedures the costs of arriving at agreements could be high, however, and if a firm wants to gain access to direct borrowing in securities markets by-passing the banks, then well-defined bankruptcy law is necessary. Thus, the development of bankruptcy law is likely to be correlated with the development of financial arrangements. Another problem with a lack of standard procedures in law is that managers and owners would have the incentives to make side-deals securing wealth for themselves as soon as distress becomes likely.

As in the case of company law, the laws for firms in distress may serve other functions than reducing transactions and agency costs. In some countries laws specify employee rights to such an extent that laws for firms in distress become an aspect of labor market and industrial policy. I will return to this issue in Section 5.

4 Enabling vs mandatory law

4.1 Efficiency aspects of enabling and mandatory law

Legal scholars in market economies have debated the relative advantages of enabling and mandatory law especially in the area of company law. Mandatory law rules specify the exact set of contract terms that regulate the actions of the parties to a contract under different conditions. Enabling law, on the other hand, leaves the specific contract terms open to the mutual agreement of the parties. Highly enabling law can nevertheless go a long way in specifying the potential sources of conflicts that must be addressed by the contract, by providing a "standard-form contract" that is binding if the parties to the contract do not explicitly agree on other terms.

The distinction between enabling and mandatory law is of particular relevance for highly complex contracts such as corporate charters regulating the terms of agreement among several types of stakeholders in firms. It also applies to less complex transactions, however, in cases when the parties cannot immediately observe the degree of contractual fulfillment at the time of a transaction. For example, product liability law may specify in great detail whether the buyer or the seller must "beware" of different aspects of a product's quality, or it can leave the degree of buyer and seller responsibility to be agreed upon or determined in the market place.

The main argument in favor of enabling law made, for example, by Macey (1998) is that it provides flexibility of contractual terms. These terms can be varied according to the needs and preferences of individuals and firms. The investors in firms change frequently, as do products, technology, human capital requirements, etc. Some activities of firms can be easily monitored by outsiders while others are hard to observe, even in hindsight. There is not one single set of rules that will meet the needs of all investors, individuals, or firms.[6]

The argument that company law should be enabling is consistent with the conditions for financial system efficiency discussed in Section 2. There it was argued that in an efficient system the regulatory and legal structures enable alternative contractual and organizational arrangements to be developed by market participants in response to information problems, and the alternative arrangements are allowed to compete. In this view, the role of explicit law in the efficient financial system is to reduce the transactions costs of entering a contract that all parties would agree upon. Economies of scale in information seeking is achieved in the case of enabling company law. For example, transactions cost-saving is achieved by a company law that specifies a contract that covers all potential sources of conflict but allows deviations from the standard form by mutual agreement. The law helps those starting a business to identify possible sources of conflict and it reduces the need for all parties to sit down together to hammer out agreements.

Mandatory law rules cannot possibly represent the voluntarily agreed upon contract in a wide variety of circumstances across firms and over time. Many scholars argue, however, that mandatory law is necessary in order to avoid that a majority of shareholders change the terms of the contract among the owners to the disadvantage of the minority that has become owners under specific contractual terms.[7] Macey (1992) counters this argument on the grounds that the corporate charter can itself include provisions specifying requirements for changes in it while protecting minorities. Furthermore, the price of ownership shares reflects the uncertainty about future contractual arrangements that could cause price changes on ownership shares. Thus, one aspect of enabling law is that it enables the stakeholders to seek an efficient degree of permanence of contractual terms.

6 See Macey (1992), and Eliasson, Rybczynski & Wihlborg (1994).
7 Eisenberg (1989), McCheny (1989), Gordon (1989), Romano (1989).

In emerging market economies where many investors and individuals lack experience in business deals, it is particularly important that individuals have the incentive to seek out the knowledge and information that will reduce the scope for opportunistic behavior-creating agency costs.[8] Highly detailed mandatory law specifying the terms of a contract under most contingencies would have the effect of reducing the incentive of contractual parties to gain an understanding of the potentially opportunistic behavior of other parties and of the contingencies that influence the success of a business venture. Mandatory law has an insurance aspect. It is not an insurance in the common sense that future outcomes are made more certain, but nevertheless an insurance under different contingencies. Like other insurances, mandatory law influences incentives. In this case, the incentive to seek the knowledge to develop the most efficient contractual relations is reduced.

4.2 Non-efficiency objectives of mandatory law and constitutional principles

If enabling law is associated with the efficient contracting arrangements among users and suppliers of financial resources, then it also follows that, if company law has other objectives than efficiency, mandatory law will and must be used. In other words, mandatory law serves as the means to achieve contractual terms that all parties would not voluntarily enter. For example, if there is a political decision that labor unions should have a direct influence on investment decisions, then the channels of influence must be specified by mandatory law. Managers and owners would not want labor unions to have a say in investment decisions unless the labor unions accept lower wages in return for their influence. Another use of mandatory law is the pursuance of egalitarian distributive results. Laws setting maximum interest rates and rents, and minimum wages, are examples of mandatory contractual terms.[9]

8   The opposite point of view—that investors in emerging market economies must be given substantial protection and pre-set rules because they lack information and experience—is often heard. This point of view is clearly static and it ignores that institutions develop and improve by learning.

The inefficiency properties of mandatory law are further reinforced if mandatory law is allowed to guide precedent formation. This appears to be the case in Sweden and many other parliamentary democracies in the sense that the more detailed and specific mandatory law is, the more dominant it seems to become in case of conflict between laws referring to the same contractual relation. In general, laws oriented towards a specific outcome for an identifiable group tend to dominate more general law. Wihlborg (1998) argues that a constitutional principle giving general rules higher status than laws with specific objectives for identifiable groups would contribute to more enabling law. The founders of the US constitution incorporated such a constitutional principle, although the principle is not upheld strongly today.

The European Court applies some general rules that may be contrary to mandatory law. For example, the Court ruled recently (April 1998) against the Swedish National Health Insurance Authority, that has tried to stop the practice of Swedish citizens using Swedish public insurance to pay for health care services of their choice within the EU countries. The Court argued that the principle of free mobility of services was violated by the Swedish Authority.

EU law is by no means general and enabling across the board. In the area of company law current harmonization attempts often involve mandatory law. We return to this issue in Section 6.

4.3 The law of property and enabling law

It is obviously not acceptable that physical force or the threat of violence define property rights or become the primary means for contract enforcement. In a legal vacuum with no enforceable prohibitions and/or no rules regulating allowed transactions, Mafia type regulation and enforcement will develop to make socially desirable commercial transactions possible. The result is a very inefficient system with high transactions costs. A viable market economy requires that the parties

9 Tax law is, of course, the major instrument to achieve egalitarian objective. Tax law is not properly law of contract, however, because contractual terms can be adjusted based on knowledge of tax rates.

to a voluntary transaction must feel secure that traded property changes hands securely, with a minimum of transactions costs, and each party must have some recourse to corrective action, other than threat of violence, in case of non-performance by the other party to the transaction. One requirement of this security is that the buyer knows that the seller has the right to sell. For many kinds of property simple possession defines ownership, but real estate transactions require more formal proof of ownership in the form of registration and title of ownership. This area is still unsettled in many of the formerly socialist countries.

Enforcement of financial contracts requires that property of a delinquent borrower can be identified and transferred. Similarly, contractual arrangements with and among firms require that the property of the firm, and the individuals signing for the firm are identifiable. Thus, firms as legal persons must be registered with the names of the individuals acting as their agents.

Apart from these registration requirements for some property, the security of contractual relations requires that the state enforces standard-form contracts written in law as well as other voluntary and "reasonable" contracts, i e contracts that are not entered under duress. Some kind of arbitration and dispute settlement mechanism can be agreed upon in contracts, but for decisions of arbiters to be enforced it is necessary that the state acts as the "enforcer of last resort." It is also necessary that courts and enforcing authorities are able to act with some speed. If contractual enforcement is uncertain or takes many years, then the risks associated with economic activities become large.[10]

Posner (1992) distinguishes among three types of common law in a market economy. First, the "law of property" is concerned with creating and defining property rights. Second, "the law of contracts" facilitates the voluntary movement of property rights, and, third, "the law of torts" is concerned with the protection of property rights. Most of the discussion here about company law and laws for distressed firms refers

10 In, for example, Kenya the resolution of bankruptcy proceeding may take 5–10 years. As a result the borrowers' collateral for loans are almost worthless.

to the law of contracts. Enabling "law of contracts" discussed above requires that the law of property is well-developed. This body of law is enabling at a more fundamental level. In the industrialized market economies the law of property is taken for granted but in emerging market economies the definition and the enforcement of property rights cannot be taken for granted. Even if property rights are recognized ill-defined or insecure property rights imply that the enforcement of contracts becomes uncertain. Next, the effects of uncertain enforcement on the efficiency of enabling and mandatory law are discussed.

5 Insufficient legal capacity and enabling law

What demands do enabling and mandatory company law put on the enforcement capacity of the legal system? Given a lack of enforcement capacity, is the case for enabling company law weakened or strengthened?

Consider three alternative models. In the first most enabling model for the legal system courts recognize all contracts that are entered voluntarily unless duress can be shown by one party. In the second model dominated by mandatory law, "standard-form contracts" specify in detail contractual outcomes under different contingencies. The third model is also highly enabling but "standard-form contracts" specify only the different potential sources of conflict that must be dealt with in a contract. For example, company law could specify that corporate charters must include rules for permissible dividend remittances under various circumstances without specifying the exact rule.

It must be recognized that all contingencies can never be specified even in detailed mandatory law. Questions of interpretation and applicability of contract terms will therefore arise in all cases. The completely enabling model is likely to be more legally resource-using either during the process of negotiating contract terms covering a wide range of contingencies, or as a result of conflicts when contingencies are not covered. This consideration is particularly relevant for complex contractual arrangements. The third model would economize on these costs because the standard-form contract helps the parties identify potential sources of conflict. Mandatory law, however, is likely to be more legally resource-using for other reasons. Specifically, unless the mandatory rules are perfectly aligned with the rules that the contractual parties would have agreed upon voluntarily, all parties have the incentive to argue for an interpretation of rules in their favor as soon as there is some ambiguity about interpretation. Such disputes would not arise if enabling contract models were used because the contract terms would be those voluntarily agreed upon. Thus, enabling law is likely to be associated with greater transactions costs ex ante, while mandatory law would be associated with greater enforcement costs due to the greater incidence of attempts at "cheating" on the contract. If enforcement capability is a bottleneck enabling law would have less enforcement problems.

As noted, parties to contracts can agree on arbitration under a foreign legal system. Such agreements would economize on a country's legal capacity but, as noted, the domestic system must "back up" the foreign arbitration.

6 Cases of company law—in whose interest?

In the following, a few issues in company law are discussed in order to illustrate the complexity of arriving at unambiguous conclusions about welfare effects of mandatory rules. The examples show, however, that mandatory rules serve a non-efficiency objective. Furthermore, the consequences of pursuing such objectives are often extremely difficult to foresee. First, the "equal treatment rule" designed to serve the interests of non-management-shareholders is discussed. Second, arguments for insider trading-rules serving similar interests are reviewed. Third, arguments for laws against differentiated voting-rights per share are discussed. Fourth, preemptive rights and restrictions on dividend policy are discussed. Each of the issues, as well as many others discussed in Macey (1992), could be debated at length. Here, the focus will be on the main arguments for and against mandatory rules from the point of view of an efficiency objective assumed to be shareholder wealth maximization.

6.1 The equal-treatment rule

The equal treatment principle means that all shareholders should be treated the same in all corporate transactions. Unequal treatment would be if, for example, in a take-over process one group of shareholders obtain a price above the market value and above the value after the take-over is completed. Another example is "green mail," meaning that an individual buys up shares in a firm in the belief that it is undervalued and a potential take-over target. A green-mail-payment in excess of the market value is then made to buy out the buyer/greenmailer. Other shareholders will not receive a corresponding payment, however, with the implication that the greenmail-payment makes other shareholders poorer.

Empirical studies indicate that shareholders' wealth often increases as a result of greenmail, because the undervaluation is discovered in the greenmail process and management may take action in case the greenmail was based on perceived bad management.[11] Thus, permitting greenmail may obviously lead to unequal treatment but it could be consistent with shareholder wealth-maximization.

In some countries law-regulating hostile take-overs requires a bidder for a firm to notify stock-exchange authorities when five percent of a firm's shares are acquired, and at a higher percentage the bidder must make an open offer to all shareholders. Similar proposals have been put forward by The European Commission. The disclosure rule makes private information public and it reduces the scope for the bidder to make a capital gain on the purchase of the target-firm's shares. By the same token it makes investment in information gathering about potential take-over targets less profitable. The bidder's profitability of a take-over would simply evaporate if the bidder's information about the firm's post take-over value would become public knowledge. By making take-

11 See Macey (1992) for a review of arguments and empirical studies.

overs less profitable, disclosure rules reduce the possibility that value-increasing take-overs will occur.

Even if disclosure is required, the bidder could make the take-over profitable by bidding high for a fraction of all shares. Those shareholders not tendering their shares would have to accept the post take-over market value. The requirement that all shareholders must be paid the same amount for their shares prevent take-overs from becoming profitable this way. The equal treatment rule like the disclosure rule is a disincentive for hostile take-overs, and, therefore, potentially value-decreasing for all shareholders.

Enabling law with respect to equal treatment would be a "standard-form contract" specifying equal treatment and disclosure under specific conditions with the provision that the shareholders are allowed to "opt out" of this standard form.

6.2 Insider trading

Insider trading refers to trading on private information of managers and others involved, for example, in a take-over. Prohibition of insider trading is often based on a fairness argument but there are also agency cost-arguments against insider trading. For example, managers could make investment announcements and investment decisions in order to make a quick profit before resigning from a corporation.

The arguments favoring insider trading is that a firm's shares will be priced based on better information, and that insider profits are part of the return to information gathering leading up to a take-over.

The fairness issue can only be addressed by mandatory law prohibiting insider trading. The agency cost argument against insider trading does not require legal remedies, however, because the shareholders would have an incentive to address this issue in the contract with management. Thus, with enabling law the shareholders would be able to weigh the firm-specific costs and benefits of prohibiting insider trading by managers, and, thereby, to determine the efficient contract for management.[12]

It can be argued that a regulatory authority has an advantage in monitoring trading in order to discover insider deals. This objective can be pursued whether insider trading is permitted by law or not. In the former case, the authority provides valuable information to shareholder groups concerned about managers' conflicts of interest.

Another aspect of prohibiting insider trading is that only actual purchases or sales can be monitored, while decisions *not* to buy or not sell are unobservable. Thus, the effectiveness of the enforcement of insider laws is always going to be questioned.

6.3 Differentiated voting rights

In many countries it is mandated that all shares are given one vote, while company law in other countries allows substantial differentiation. Preference shares with prior claim to dividend distribution and priority relative to regular shares in bankruptcy can be issued in some countries with no voting rights attached.

From a majority owner's point of view one benefit of differentiated rights is clearly that equity capital can be raised without or with little dilution of the majority owner's control, provided willing investors can be found. One potential drawback of differentiated voting rights is that a minority shareholder with majority in votes is able to extract "private benefits" in a variety of ways. The majority of the shareholders cannot prevent that the controlling shareholder makes strategic decisions that do not maximize the shareholders' wealth. [13]The controlling shareholder is shielded from the threat of hostile take-overs. This threat provides an incentive for management to work in the interest of the majority of the shareholders in corporations with dispersed ownership.

Even if a majority of the shareholders have given up their voting rights voluntarily, it is possible that circumstances change such that the majority would prefer a return to one

12 See Posner (1992), Ch 14.
13 See Grossman & Hart (1988).

share—one vote. Once the voting rights have been given up, there is formally no return, however.

Would not shareholder maximization be served better by restrictions on voting rights? There are several reasons why differentiated voting rights are likely to be superior even from the perspective of shareholder wealth-maximization. First, without the possibility to differentiate the voting rights many firms would remain privately held with reduced capability to finance expansion. Second, the agency problem associated with separation between management and control is alleviated because managers extracting benefits at the shareholders' expense can be monitored and dismissed by controlling owners with relatively small ownership stakes. Third, the price of shares with low voting rights would be relatively low if the majority owner wishing to raise equity capital is not expected to maximize shareholder wealth. Thus, the cost of capital for the controlling shareholder suspected of extracting private benefits would be high.

What if the management's objective changes from shareholder wealth maximization at the time equity with low voting rights are issued to an objective contrary to the interests of the majority? In this case, the majority of the shareholders suffers a capital loss, and they are unable to dismiss the board of directors. However, the risk that such a change of course for the corporation would occur must have been reflected in the original price of the equity with low voting rights. Furthermore, the fall in the price of equity when the corporate objective changes has the consequence of raising the cost of capital. Thus, the competitiveness of the firms that work with objectives other than shareholder wealth maximization is relatively low with the result that such firms remain small or decline in size over time.

In summary, the costs associated with controlling the shareholders' extracting private benefits are likely to be limited even if different voting rights are permitted. The major gain associated with differentiated voting rights is that the scope for "entrenched managers" extracting private benefits without effective shareholder control is reduced.

6.4 Pre-emptive rights and restrictions on dividend policy

Pre-emptive rights imply that shareholders have the right to purchase stocks out of a new issue in order to maintain their share of the outstanding stock. A mandatory contract with these rights would on the face of it protect minority-shareholders against involuntary dilution of both their economic interests and their voice. If, as in the US, company law enables firms to "opt-out" of pre-emptive rights then the costs of recapitalization are reduced, however.[14] One reason is that investment banks selling issues of shares to the public do not have to make their sales effort contingent on the shareholders' exercise of pre-emptive rights. A second reason is that pre-emptive rights make the shareholders' strategic behavior possible. For example, the existing shareholders are able to extract side-payments from firms in distress when these firms try to issue preferred stock in order to obtain needed capital. A third reason is that under some circumstances share issues directed at a specific group of investors allow the firm to tap into new sources of funding at a lower cost benefiting old shareholders as well.

The management, and the directors of a firm, discovering that the survival of the firm is threatened have an incentive to secure as much wealth as possible for themselves, before lenders and other stake-holders become aware of the threat. Mandatory law-restricting dividend payments, when profitability is low, could in principle reduce the agency costs for the stake-holders with a higher priority than the shareholders in case of bankruptcy. On the other hand, dividend policy is an important aspect of a firm's capital structure choice serving as a signal to the stake-holders about the management's belief in the future prospects of the firm. Thus, the management may wish to keep dividend payments high in a profit-slump in order to avoid an excessive fall in the share-prices relative to the management's beliefs about the correct value of the firm. In other words, the informational role of dividend policy and capital structure choice is reduced by mandatory law about dividend policy.

14 See Macey (1993).

Restrictions on dividend policy is also unnecessary, if there are alternative means available to the lenders to prevent the shareholders from impoverishing the firm. If the lenders are aware of this possibility they can, for example, add covenants to loan-contracts specifying the conditions triggering the repayment of the loan. Banks as lenders monitor borrowing firms continuously in order to reduce the likelihood that the shareholders divert resources from the firm.

In many developing countries the incentives of banks to monitor firms' behavior are reduced by various forms of state-guarantees of the banks. In this case, the restrictions on dividend policy could possibly serve the state's interests.[15] However, as long as the state's policies reduce the banks' incentives to establish sound credit evaluation procedures, restrictions on dividend policy will not reduce the incidence of bad loans. The restrictions may only have the effect of prolonging the time before a shut-down of a money-loosing venture becomes necessary.

7 Conclusions

The laws and regulations for corporations are one important aspect of the financial system, because they determine the range of feasible contractual arrangements between many users and suppliers of financial resources. Those contractual arrangements serve to limit agency costs due to asymmetric information and they are critical for an efficient use of financial resources.

It has been argued that from an efficiency point of view enabling law is necessary, because there does not exist one efficient contractual arrangement among managers, shareholders, and other creditors. The efficient contract (corporate charter) is likely to vary substantially across firms and industries.

Mandatory law specifying a compulsory "standard form contract" cannot be the contract all firm's stakeholders would voluntarily agree upon, and over time its rigidity would cause increasing inefficiencies.

15 Indian Company Law prohibits dividend payments in excess of available profits unless prior approval is obtained from the Company Law Board.

One reason for mandatory law is that there are other policy-objectives than efficiency. Company law that is intended to serve the interests of a particular group of stakeholders must be mandatory. Efficiency losses associated with such laws can be severe, however, and usually unforeseen, as well as unforeseeable, by the legislators.

The argument in favor of enabling law is strengthened in countries where the capacity of the legal system is insufficient to credibly enforce contracts. Lack of enforcement increases the need for contracts that stakeholders in firms would voluntarily agree upon in order to reduce the likelihood of conflicts.

Enabling law can be given higher constitutional status than mandatory law, if laws with general applicability, as opposed to laws serving the interests of identifiable groups, are given higher constitutional status, as suggested in Wihlborg (1998). Under such a constitutional principle enabling law would overrule mandatory law in case of conflict between laws that apply to the same contractual relation.[16]

Bibliography

Day, R, Eliasson, G & Wihlborg, C (1993), *The markets for innovation, ownership and control*. Stockholm: IUI & Amsterdam: North Holland.

Diamond, D W (1984), "Financial intermediation and delegated monitoring," in *Review of Economic Studies*, Vol LI, pp 393–414.

Dietrich, J K & Wihlborg, C (1994), "Capital structure and universal banking with endogenous effort and monitoring." Gothenburg Studies in Financial Economics, Göteborg University.

16 See Eliasson, Rybczynski & Wihlborg (1994), and, for a more elaborate argument, Eliasson (1998).

Eisenberg, M A (1989), "The structure of corporate law," in *Columbia Law Review*, Vol 89, No 7 (Nov).

Eliasson, G (1987), "Technological competition and trade in the experimentally organized economy." Research Paper no 32, Stockholm: IUI.

– (1991), "Modeling the experimentally organized economy : complex dynamics in an empirical micro-macro model of endogenous economic growth," in *Journal of Economic Behavior and Organization*, Vol 16, No 2, pp 153–182.

– (1998), "From plan to market," in *Journal of Economic Behavior and Organization*, Vol 34.

Eliasson, G, Rybczynski, T & Wihlborg, C (1994), *The necessary institutional framework to transform formerly planned economies.* Stockholm: IUI.

Franks, J & Mayer, C (1990), "Capital markets and corporate control : a study of France, Germany and the U K," in *Economic Policy*, Vol 10 (April).

Gangopadhyay, S & Knopf, J (1998), "Dividends and conflicts between debtholders and equityholders in Indian firms," in Doukas, J, Murinde, V & Wihlborg, C (eds), *Privatization and financial sector reform in transition economies.* Amsterdam: North Holland, 1998.

Gordon, J N (1989), "The mandatory structure of corporate law," in *Columbia Law Review*, Vol 89, No 7 (Nov).

Grossman, S J & Hart, O D (1988), "One share—one vote and the market for corporate control," in *Journal of Financial Economics*, pp 175–202.

Klein, B, Crawford, R G & Alchian, A (1978), "Vertical integration, appropriable rents, and the competitive contracting process," in *Journal of Law and Economics*, Vol 21 (Oct).

Macey, J (1992), *Corporate law and governance in Sweden : a law and economics perspective.* Stockholm: SNS.

McCheney, F S (1989), "Economics, law and science in the corporate field : a critique of Eisenberg," in *Columbia Law Review*, Vol 89, No 7 (Nov).

Posner, R A (1992), *Economic analysis of law*. Chicago: Little, Brown and Scottsman.

Romano, R (1989), "Answering the wrong question : the tenuous case for mandatory corporate laws," in *Columbia Law Review*, Vol 89, No 7 (Nov).

Rubin, P (1992), *Private mechanisms for creation of efficient institutions for market economies*. Paper presented at the Arne Ryde Symposium in Rungsted Kyst, Denmark. Sweden: University of Lund.

Rybczynski, T M (1988), "Financial systems and industrial restructuring," in *National Quarterly Westminster Bank Review*, Nov.

Walter, I (1993), "The battle of the systems : control of enterprises and the global economy." Kieler Vorträge, Institute für Weltwirtschaft, Universität Kiel.

Wihlborg, C (1998), "Economic efficiency with enabling and mandatory law," in Eliasson, G & Green, C (eds), *The microfoundations of economic growth*. Michigan: The University of Michigan Press, 1998.

Wihlborg, C (1998), "The bargaining democracy : (un)democratic dynamics." Working paper, Göteborg University.

PART II

Consequences of State Interference and Non-interference

Chapter IV

Microsoft vs Netscape—Policy for Dynamic Models

Anti-trust and Intellectual Property Rights Revisited

The current version has benefited from comments by participants in a seminar at the Ecole Polytechnique, Paris, May 21, 1997, organized by Petros Kavassalis; also a session at Global Networking '97, Calgary, June 15-18, 1997. I particularly appreciate insights from three discussants, Dieter Elixmann, WIK; Laurent Caby, CNET; and Christian Licoppe, CNET. More generally, this paper is a successor to a work presented at the Schumpeter Society meeting a year earlier, Stockholm, June 2–5, 1996. I especially thank Don Lamberton and Gunnar Eliasson for exhaustive reviews, including comments from two anonymous reviewers which Don arranged.

David Allen

"And so we have people here, engineers here [at the World Wide Web Consortium/W3C], who have been forming the Web for a long time, and they keep in the back of their minds the **long-term vision**, the long-term **goals of a clean architecture**, of making decisions now which won't hamper us tomorrow for the things that we haven't even dreamed of yet, but still making sure that the Web will be able to encompass them."

"There is this enormous market, which follows from the interoperability and common standards firstly, and secondly—sort of ironically but appropriately—by the tremendous **competition** there is to try **to put extensions on top**, to produce the smartest way of **leveraging the common standards**."

Tim Berners-Lee [2]

"This is unprecedented, but we realized we need to work together [with Netscape] for the **common good**. We decided we should not propose separate standards for privacy software."

**David Fester, Microsoft,
June '97** [1]

Netscape goes back to the trenches as it revives the browser war: Remember the browser war? Well, it's back with a vengeance. ...[B]y officially reviving **hostilities with Microsoft** last week, Netscape ... [has begun] a new assault on the ... market.

**Steve Lohr, reporter,
New York Times, August '97** [3]

1 New York Times, June 12, 1997, p D1.
2 As quoted in Web Week, Vol 2 (1996), No 11 (August 5), p 45. For the purposes here, it is useful to have a record of recent industry history; Web Week [the name has subsequently changed to Internet World] serves as one excellent chronology.
3 New York Times, August 25, 1997, p D7.

Abstract

Traditional static approaches to competition policy are coming under increasing scrutiny in dynamic technology markets. Beginning with the face-off between Microsoft and Netscape, the torrent of innovation which is the 'Net and the Web yields a model to capture the essential dynamics. Simple at its core, the novel model unfolds to the natural richness of the evolving Web (with, among others, flexible industry structure, an information 'product' distinct from the industry behavior which creates it, variety and commonality as part and whole, shared protocols to guide process, and a working definition for "openness"). Inference derives from industry and technology cases, throughout. Now with a template in hand to describe the evolutionary scenario, anti-trust and intellectual property rights can begin to be retooled, to suit the dynamics of change. At stake are productivity and a society's standard of living.

The Internet and Web, in the last few years, have been party to one of the more surprising runs in the annals of innovation. Sustained innovation—and with that the prospect for long-term productivity increase—lie at the root of a society's capacity to improve its standard of living. Development of the 'Net and Web carries encapsulated within its story a model for industry organization. In this story, the borders that define industry actors shift dynamically, contrary to convention. I suggest this model is pivotal in the remarkable capacity to sustain innovation.

This paper, beginning from the intense commercial conflict particularly between Netscape and Microsoft, goes to some pains to elucidate the embedded industry model. With the model in hand, the question becomes, and the paper turns to, comparisons against prevailing theories and policy prescriptions.

101

The agenda

Since Microsoft swung its guns onto the Internet in late '95 / beginning '96, there ensued an intense and ferociously fought commercial battle, in the first instance between the upstart wunderkind Netscape and Microsoft the new Goliath. In their public profiles, the two seem to epitomize fundamentally opposed and contending styles of industry organization. Netscape, on its side, seems to carry into the private sector the novel model for industry organization which has propelled the 'Net so far. Microsoft, for its part, has seemed to embody the very extreme for the currently prevailing policy mandate: competitive behavior—to the point finally of crossing irretrievably into anti-competitive territory.

With the first and major part of this paper devoted to elucidate the novel 'Net model for industry organization, the first half of the first part delineates the two opposed approaches Netscape and Microsoft seem to offer. Others, such as Sun, also play a key role. We find this is useful introduction, but a full description of the novel model requires we turn back in time to the story of 'Net development itself. This is the second half of the first part. Here positive description begets normative prescription as well. Sub-sections focus on industry conduct and structure in the model, also on the information "product."

With the novel model in hand, the paper can turn to its briefer second part, to prepare the ground for comparing the new model against prevailing theories and policy. Anti-trust and intellectual property rights policy are both reconsidered.

Part one
A novel model for industry organization

1 Microsoft and Netscape

The Internet and now the Web have been the occasion for a remarkably rapid and sustained run of innovation, even accelerating in recent years. The pace of change is such that 'Web years' has become a common term, where a single calendar year is thought somehow to shoehorn perhaps seven Web years inside. Customers have been noted to lament, "I can't take this much innovation this quickly."[4] The ability to innovate so nimbly lies at the heart of a society's capacity to improve its lot markedly, its standard of living.

Coming upon this scene about two years ago, in late 1995, Bill Gates found that his Microsoft was caught flat-footed. The company's cash flows were tied to desktop computing, but there was a fundamental shift underway, toward networked computing. Remarkably, among many such performances by the man, he turned his leviathan virtually "on a dime" and steamed it off in relentless and vigorous pursuit of the Internet. There quickly arose a most intense opposition.

On the one side, an informal group emerged for whom "anyone but Microsoft" was the rallying cry. This could on occasion include Netscape, Sun, Oracle, Apple, or IBM, along with an entire contingent of the developer community who felt palpable antipathy to the threat of Microsoft hegemony. Microsoft has, by appearances, often seemed alone in its struggle against this opposition. Often, in a given fight, it is the bogey arrayed against one or the other of the informal sometimes-allies. In its efforts to make and keep dominance, Microsoft's behavior has regularly reinforced its isolation, confirming that Microsoft is the company everyone loves-to-hate.

4   Eric Schmidt, now the head of Novell, when he was chief technology officer at Sun, as reported in *Web Week*, Vol 2 (1996), No 4 (April), p 10.

In this opposition, Netscape first carried the standard against Microsoft, with the "browser wars" setting off the tumult—Netscape's Navigator versus Microsoft's Internet Explorer. The antipathy has renewed and continued, across repeated conflicts, including standards for style sheets and later push technology, to name a couple. Over the time, the browser has metamorphosed into a vastly multi-functional groupware client; the conflict which began with clients spread far and wide, to servers and beyond.

In a finish to setting this scene, Sun has lately started to carry the standard against Microsoft. Sun's Java computing—both the Java programming language and the from-the-ground-up operating system/OS based on new Java chips, along with Sun's championing of a Network Computer/NC—squares off directly against Microsoft's prime preserve in the desktop OS. Microsoft, for its part, has demonstrated that it can find partners, certainly among major hardware vendors, beyond those industry actors who simply take comfort behind a Microsoft shield.

1.1 The two provisional models compared

With this as setting, our interest for this paper is the way in which Netscape and Microsoft came, at least initially, to typify two alternatives to industry organization. In the crispest comparison, Netscape promotes inclusiveness for people and ideas, across the industry; Microsoft by contrast maneuvers at all costs to keep control to itself. Related to this, Netscape promotes "open" standards; Microsoft instead aims for what here will be called "vertical integration." These are the ideal characterizations, unmuddied by the reality of actual behavior.

We will see how the first of the contrasts—inclusiveness vs control—regards industry organization, its conduct and structure finally. The second of the contrasts regards the information "product" of industry behavior—the shared (or not-so-shared) conceptual/logical structure that emerges. To introduce this notion, consider an example of contrasting 'information products:' The cross-platform Java language serves as an intermediary layer between server and any of several client platforms, such as PC, Mac or UNIX. The information product is, in this case, layered. By contrast, ActiveX worked only vertically to connect client and server, that is just within the Microsoft Wintel world, at the outset anyway. (Graphics to depict the contrast are developed from page 116 on.)

Netscape

Netscape actively espoused participation, by individuals across the industry, in the development of innovations. This was particularly in contrast to a Microsoft, characterized as trying to set all the standards by itself. Netscape's public advocacy was in addition to the concrete steps which it took. For instance, Netscape early-on published some of its code, as an invitation to outside input. Now it has made the source code for Navigator available explicitly to encourage input from the whole developer community.

Open standards were certainly a talisman. 'Open' was meant in practice to be the ability to substitute different companies' products for each other. In fact the main symbol for openness became operability across OS platforms, particularly against Microsoft's devotion to Windows by itself.

Microsoft

Microsoft's prowess as competitor—the epitome of the policy ideal—proved almost legendary. Surely, by prevailing standards Microsoft pushed so far that it fell over into being markedly anti-competitive. The story of Microsoft's zeal in pursuit is fascinating. Microsoft seemed to have written the book on cornering a market (for which in this case read 'predation'), then added new wrinkles for good measure. Microsoft seemed massively to deserve its reputation for being devoted entirely to control, against inclusion.

Gates is quoted as saying in December 1995 that he intended to make browsers a "zero-revenue business."[5] By zero-pricing both Microsoft's browser and Microsoft's server, he moved to deny his main competitor, Netscape, revenues in its principal markets. This, when Microsoft had at the time a $2 billion cash hoard, and its upstart competitor depended entirely on its capital financing and the ability to prosecute a few limited markets. And the story certainly did not stop there. Microsoft

5   *Web Week*, Vol 2 (1996), No 15 (October 7), p 19.

made tying deals with sites which provide content. Access to the site would be free, but only to those who used the Microsoft browser, Explorer.

Microsoft also made real an innovation on monopolistic behavior, a theory originally presented in a Silicon Valley white paper.[6] Microsoft levered its high-dominant position in the desktop OS, to overpower competitors in adjacent nascent markets. The company had no more position than did others in the new market, of course. But because of the technical interconnection among markets, Microsoft could use its overwhelming dominance in the mature market to extend its power, above other entrants, into the new market.

Specifically, Microsoft made online services a deal they could not refuse. In return for a place on the dominant Windows desktop, the online services gave Microsoft's Explorer a favored position over Netscape's Navigator. Netscape announced a deal to *be* that favored browser, and one day later was reversed by Microsoft. One by one, each of the online services fell to Microsoft's Explorer—America Online, CompuServe, and so on. With online service interconnected to the desktop, Microsoft dominance in the desktop was irresistible to the online companies, who would control the new use of browsers in their services.

In just the same vein, Microsoft has moved to convert the desktop to a Webtop. The browser interface becomes the desktop, as well. Netscape is doing the same, but its software is a layer on top of the Windows system. Because Microsoft's new Webtop integrates directly into Windows, it will always enjoy some better functionality for Windows users. In this case, interconnection itself, specifically the closer integration, conveys advantage over Netscape, the other entrant to the Webtop. Dominance in the original market, the OS, is not only extended, but reinforced.

Other moves have been subtler. Though Microsoft later concluded that its reputation against public standards bore too great a cost, Microsoft pointedly omitted Netscape from some key, early deliberations over standards-setting, such as regarding push technology. Once again Microsoft proved exclu-

---

6 Though not formally attributed, said to have been authored by two Stanford economists.

sive, rather than inclusive, even though the new standard would purportedly be open. Or again: When Microsoft finally committed ActiveX to a standards body, the Open Group, it closely controlled the process, seeming to arrange a 'friendly' caretaker, even excluding an alternate body, the Open Management Group.

In perhaps the grandest statement of Microsoft in control, Gates convened a "summit." Held at his palatial new home, still under construction, numerous CEO's of major companies gathered from around the world. To underline the exclusiveness, apparently some companies in a given industry sector were favored, when others were not invited. To bring home that the influence extends beyond just industry, to the highest political realm, the Vice-President of the United States was also in attendance.

Microsoft richly earned its reputation as favoring control over inclusion. Vertical integration, the counterpoint to open standards, is the other element in the comparison with Netscape. What is vertical integration (in information product, *not* traditional vertical integration in industry organization—so, hereafter "*idea*-vertical integration"[7])?

Microsoft *idea*-vertically integrates, as an example, by tying to its existing—"legacy"—desktop Windows OS. The move to a Webtop, described above, is a case. The new Webtop interface, because it is more tightly integrated, helps to preserve Microsoft's position in its legacy desktop software and so reinforces it. Another example is preservation of Microsoft's legacy object model, Object Linking and Embedding/OLE, which it developed for Windows. Other industry members moved toward the Common Object Request Broker Architec-

7   The reader naturally associates vertical integration with industry organization, not with the present topic of information product (and industry organization is also a key topic in this paper, which increases the potential for confusion—indeed, later in the paper a similarity emerges to *connect* idea- and organization- integration). But the notion of vertical integration suits the information product phenomenon too aptly to be substituted with something else less descriptive, even if a substitute would not so directly conflict. To help distinguish the two uses of the notion, between information product and industry organization, the balance of this paper uses '*idea*-vertical integration.' More rigorous attention to the particulars of information (and communication) in the economy, as Don Lamberton encourages, will likely lead to other similar distinctions. [See for instance Lamberton's "Information : pieces, batches or flows?" Stirling: Loasby Conference, 1997.]

ture/CORBA and its Internet InterORB Protocol/IIOP. But Microsoft fought fiercely to sustain its old OLE technology by extending it to network play, cloaked there as the Distributed Common Object Model/DCOM.

Before leaving the direct comparison of Microsoft and Netscape, we should note a point that will presage later discussion. While Microsoft has used zero-pricing in classic predatory fashion, Netscape made a point early-on also to give away some of its software, mainly to students (and now has been forced by Microsoft's zero-pricing to make the Netscape browser free, too).

Not revealed by either case, however, is a more basic phenomenon. The server software, Apache, which continues to dominate the Web—its share is on the order of three times that for either Netscape's or Microsoft's servers—is freeware. The motivation behind *this* zero price is, however, essentially opposite to Microsoft's. The freeware tradition (a tradition strong in the university world of Netscape's origins) makes code available to build a better system, and with it a better community. The emphasis is on the community of reference and its better future (not on a positive price for one or the other of the community members).

1.2 Summarizing ... with conflicting straws in the wind

The comparisons and contrasts, so far, are clear. Netscape champions inclusion, which is paired with open standards/cross-platform interoperability. Microsoft epitomizes the opposite with its lust for control and exclusion, which is paired with a penchant for vertical integration.

But Sun, demonstrably on the Netscape side, has pursued exactly the same course as Microsoft—vertical integration—for its Java language. To keep Java "100% pure," Sun has tried tightly to control the standardization process, among others submitting Java to the unaccustomed International Standards Organization/ISO. Vertical integration, and control, apparently have their place on the opposite, 'Netscape' side of the contrast, too.

Beyond that, not just Microsoft but also Netscape has broken the mold of a standard, previously committed, to extend capabilities in a proprietary way. Both, as an early for instance, wrote proprietary tags to extend Hypertext Markup Language/HTML.

How do we understand the conclusions to be drawn? Netscape we characterized as bringing the style (without specifying what that was) which earlier had served the 'Net so well. The contrast between Netscape and Microsoft might, it seems we could hope, illuminate what makes for the remarkable success with innovation. But the comparison, though it will prove useful, encounters the two inconsistencies just above.

We can resolve these contradictions, and also build on the contrasts, if we move beyond the essentially static characterizations in the comparison so far—if for instance we incorporate the dynamics behind both the Netscape and Microsoft proprietary extensions to HTML. The process by which the 'Net originally developed seems to offer such a dynamic model. We now (re)turn to it.

In preparation, what in summary can we conclude so far about the results of the opposition that set Microsoft and the Netscape/Sun/allies coalition against each other?

In fact, Microsoft is now seen as innovative, when previously it was taken more to be a copycat. The competition seems to have been effective in that regard. (Microsoft has also embraced the standards process, for instance with the fourth largest contingent pre-registered for a recent Internet Engineering Task Force/IETF meeting. It has even grown more cross-platform, with for instance one of the largest Mac developer teams outside of Apple. But many doubt the motivations behind both the standards and the cross-platform work. And the cross-platform implementations often do not perform nearly as well as on Windows. Nor is it uncommon to find Netscape lambasted for contravening its own public rhetoric to be open.)

The competition may have worked; the consensus, however, failed. Despite fleeting occasions for agreement (as captured for instance in one of the opening quotations), long-running feuds continue to separate Microsoft particularly from Netscape and Sun, some of the cases being those above.

2 The IETF—a dynamic model

The history of the 'Net now covers several decades. We focus on the recent period of accelerating innovations.

The ongoing flow of innovations in the 'Net is constructed from a simple building block. For each innovation, the 'Net community first generates, then incorporates the new idea. This simple, though dynamic, building block—a cycle between first innovation, then standardization[8]—is repeated for each new step.

In the first half of the cycle, a new idea generates, which may spur other new ideas on the same topic. These new possibilities must be tried out, in a competition with each other—they must be tested for their usefulness.[9] After a period of trial, the mode switches to the second half of the cycle. Now the new possibilities must be winnowed, perhaps melded with each other, to find a 'best' composite.

In the first—innovation—phase of the cycle, the community devolves to its individual elements. Each competes with the other to produce the best innovation. In the second—standardization—phase, the group re-assembles to sort the trial results and reach consensus on a new, perhaps melded, stan-

8   Petros Kavassalis has developed a set of ideas focused on just the same phenomena. A recent paper with Richard Solomon, for instance, discusses an iteration between fragmentation and convergence (which specific phenomena we will see in industry structure), "Mr Schumpeter on the telephone : patterns of technical change in the telecommunications industry before and after the Internet," in *Communications & Strategies*, 1997, No 26 (2nd quarter), p 371. There are earlier papers on the subject from Kavassalis. See also my "Telecommunications policy between innovation and standardization : the evolving network." Sophia-Antipolis, France: Ninth Biennial ITS Conference, 1992.

9   Gunnar Eliasson has particularly emphasized the 'experimental economy.' His policy conclusions differ a bit from those here, but the work is parallel in some other key respects. Among his several contributions on the subject, for a discussion of experimentation that parallels the innovation phase here, see his "Commentary" on "Gateway technologies and the evolutionary dynamics of network industries : lessons from electricity supply history," by David, P A & Bunn, J A, in *Evolving technology and market structure : studies in Schumpeterian economics*, by Heertje, A & Perlman, M (eds). Ann Arbor: University of Michigan Press, 1990, pp 157–163.

dard for the best future system. With its committees and chair structure, the Internet Engineering Task Force/IETF forms a loose hierarchy to reach consensus (however the idea of hierarchy may contravene 'Net ideology).

Thus Netscape's inclusiveness is appropriate, indeed fundamental, to consensus for the standardization phase. But the hierarchy does take control over the outcome. Though Microsoft failed to situate control in appropriate hands, control is necessary, as we saw also with Sun and its Java. And Microsoft's fierce competitiveness is essential to the innovation phase.

Thus is innovation both generated and incorporated. In fact the cycle is a necessity—here we come to the normative. Network technology must interconnect[10], and this drives the result. An innovation by its nature breaks the connection; for interconnection to be re-established, the innovation *must* eventually be resolved into a new, interconnecting standard.

We can test this, with results from the opposition between Microsoft and Netscape, Sun et al. As noted in the summary above, competition produced more innovation from Microsoft; but consensus failed. The test of our normative proposition is whether failed consensus retarded the uptake of innovation [implicitly, but nonetheless from the opening lines of the paper, the objective function in this dynamic model is successful adoption of innovation[11]]—did the failure to agree around successive new standards prevent new uses which might otherwise emerge? Decidedly.

For instance, developers regularly report that they avoid new technology which they would otherwise choose, because Microsoft and Netscape have failed to agree on a standard approach. Instead a developer will use an existing lower common denominator, avoiding investment in more interesting technology because it is of uncertain future.

10 Computing, in contrast to networked computing, is an intermediate case, one where there is some interconnection—externalities—but where strict interconnection is not a necessity. Though not dealt with in this discussion, the case is included elsewhere.

11 This relatively straightforward objective function creates a basis to introduce the model, which is the purpose of this paper. In other discussion, the real complexity of (technical) change in human affairs—certainly, limits on the rate of desirable change—takes due place.

One news report even attributes multi-millions of dollars of loss to the failure of consensus, in this case the choice between the two distributed object models, DCOM and CORBA. Lacking a clear industry choice, the Union Bank of Switzerland, or UBS, was unable to deploy an intranet application related to its role as a clearing-house. Without the application, the bank loses $10 million *a day*—and a delay of even a calendar quarter is about a hundred days, or the vicinity of a billion dollars.[12][13]

With this dynamic cycle there are two points of inflection. *First*, in the shift to the innovation phase, the cloak of hierarchy falls away and the industry actors assert their individual positions; thought turns from consensus standards to new possibilities; consensus shifts to competition.

Thus we see, through this dynamic lens, how both Microsoft and Netscape served the cycle when they extended the HTML standard with proprietary tags.

Second, in the shift *back* to the standardization phase,[14] focus moves from individual ideas and individual betterment to concern for the best technology that will suit the group; the roles and rules for conduct in the loose IETF hierarchy once again become the harness; competition shifts to consensus.

These essential dynamics distinguish this model; they convey its power both to explain and to guide. The two points of inflection are of course captured by the two opening quotes from Tim Berners-Lee, one of the originators of the Web. Likewise, the two parallel quotes from the Microsoft-Netscape saga chronicle the two points of turn—perhaps largely unbeknownst but nonetheless, Netscape and Microsoft vivify the dynamic 'Net model, despite an imbalance with too little consensus between them. (Both pairs of quotes are presented in the reverse order: shift to standardization, *then* to innovation.)

We should also notice that a zero price philosophy profoundly undergirds the proceedings. A torrent of innovation has been necessary to fuel the development of the 'Net and

12 Inter@ctive Week, Vol 4 (1997), No 11 (April 14), p 47.

13 Almost a year later as the stand-off between DCOM and CORBA continues to fester, the effect is sufficiently debilitating across the entire industry that Intel has undertaken to negotiate a 'middleware' middle ground between the warring sides. See *InfoWorld*, Vol 20 (1998), No 9 (March 2), pp 1, 3.

14 Petros Kavassalis has spoken of "creative accumulation," ibid.

Web. Hackers make their code freely available for the purpose. Their interest is a better 'Net. As an example, we have already seen the case of Apache freeware for servers. This underlines the shift at the second inflection point: the community and its larger interests become the object of the consensus decision, instead of individual gain from (positive) prices.

Finally, we turn to the conflict over generic top level domain/gTLD names, to illustrate a last feature of the model. The IETF undertook to expand the number of gTLD's, such as .com, also to change the regime for assigning names. To assemble the necessary consensus, it consulted and brought into the process a large number of actors. This included several parties not ordinarily thought of as participants. Despite this, both the United States Government and the European Commission expressed public dissatisfaction with the process and outcome.

The purpose of this case is to illustrate the expansion of the community. Though the IETF is vastly inclusive, it is finally, of course, only a sub-community within a larger group. It is a (loose) hierarchy nested within a larger (loose) hierarchy—in fact I will use 'nest' rather than 'hierarchy,' to signify the loose/tight flexibility of the bonds. In the gTLD case, the boundary would expand to bring inside those who had previously been outside (or two groups may merge to form a new encompassing entity). Then the group's implicit groundrules—such as for handling disagreement, and for assembling consensus—are no longer shared among all parties.

The routine shifts between individual and group, which are characteristic of the cycle, also amount to an expansion and contraction. But they take place within a given group, and so with an implicitly shared set of behavioral protocols across the cycle. In the expansion of the group itself, however, the groundrules become indeterminate. Groundrules from the original group collide with different groundrules held by those outside the group. A new set of shared groundrules may eventually emerge, for the merged sub-groups, but there is a "law of the jungle" in the interregnum. Dissatisfactions, such as with the new gTLD's and with the process surrounding them, are a symptom.

To summarize the model: At its core is a simple repeated iteration, between innovation and standardization. The behavioral and social implications may seem less simple. Individuals or individual firms, promoting new ideas, repeatedly alternate temporally with loose hierarchies of these same individuals, now harnessed to the work of the larger community with pursuit of individual gain momentarily submerged. In this dynamic characterization of industry, borders repeatedly shift in response to the on-going cycle between fragmentation and (re-)coalescence. Expansion of the community engaged in the cycle unsettles the shared social protocols, which are the glue holding together the process in the first place.

The foregoing is the model I see embedded within the development of the 'Net, now Web. This dynamic model has been pivotal, I suggest, in the extraordinary flow of innovations, successfully implemented. Besides the evidence of success, the model is self-confirming, through its internal normative logic.

Now we can turn to the implications for industry structure and conduct; also to the raison d'être for the cycle, its output, namely, the 'information product.'

2.1 Industry organization: model structure and conduct

What are the implications for industry organization, both model structure and model conduct?

Conduct (individual and group)

Industry participants are expected to interleave two opposite behaviors temporally—competition, then consensus, and repeatedly. First, in the *innovation phase* of the cycle, classic competition is essential to bring out and test the best new ideas. As noted, Microsoft's competitive fervor, at least, is some sort of ideal.

Second, in the *standardization phase*, the opposite behavior is required. A constellation of behaviors make up a consensus. In a shift away from the individual and self-aggrandizement—just for this phase of the cycle, of course—the focus turns to a better 'Net and improving the lot of the group as a whole. This means an openness to new ideas from others—access for them—to enable the best result. So Netscape's advocacy for inclusiveness is fundamental. To sift and meld contesting innovations into the best standard requires that each participant take an allotted part in the standards-making loose hierarchy. An implicit set of group groundrules guides the behavior in the hierarchy.[15] As evident from the standards process, there is a conscious choosing of the best outcome.

With shared protocols across the group, at some level each member also engages in evolving forward the shared visions of the 'good' 'Net, the shared groundrules, and the shared objectives overall.

Structure

Mimicking an accordion, the oscillating musical instrument, the dynamic industry structure alternately fragments to its atoms, for the competition among new ideas; then re-gels into the loose hierarchy—the nest—for consensus around a new standard. This virtual industry organization is, at one point, disparate individual and corporate actors; then at a later point, it becomes a loose group, transcending the individual and corporate borders and linking them inside a larger common, if loose, border—borders are dynamic in the model.

Perhaps the single constant is the sharing of behavioral protocols, the groundrules, across the whole group.

What of the notion of 'openness'? Does everyday usage of the word denote and intend the intricacies of the foregoing dynamics? Is this what industry participants mean when they say 'open'? A recent example offers some evidence. Objections heard during Apple's forced end to Macintosh cloning seem clearly to plead for the importance of a community of protagonists, if the Macintosh platform is to have any hope. More than the ability to substitute one company's machine for another (certainly more than cross-platform operability), the sentiments expressed seem to recognize the primacy of an 'inclusive community.' There was no reference to the detail gyrations used here to analyze the basic cycle, but there seems to

---

15 Sometimes the groundrules are even explicit, such as in FAQ's about acceptable behavior for IETF newcomers.

be deep recognition of the competitive/cooperative tension essential to a vibrant, ongoing enterprise of improvement.

The dynamic structure—graphically

To represent the dynamic model graphically, imagine a three-company industry, say, Microsoft, Netscape and one other. In the innovation phase, the three actors are disparate.

Figure 1

The innovation phase [industry structure]

For the shift to the standardization phase, the three assemble into a loose hierarchy.

Figure 2

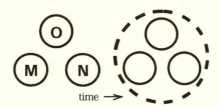

The cycle, innovation *to* standardization

For the *next* cycle of innovation and standardization, the two phases repeat, and so on with each cycle.

Figure 3

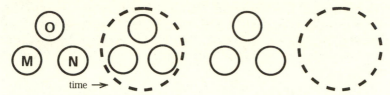

The cycle, repeating

To visualize the expansion of community, the case of gTLD's for instance, we start from the two steps in the basic innovation and standardization cycle, in other words we build from Figure 2. For expansion of community, there is effectively a third step, to bring in those who do not ordinarily participate.

Figure 4

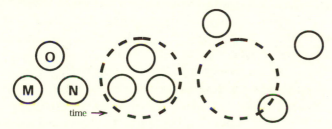

The expansion of community: Three levels

2.2 Information product

A shared view—the information product—is a key result from a group's interaction. Each person has a different experience of the world, and so sees phenomena of concern with an eye that has some privileged access. Information is a confection that arises as the experiences of separate individuals are mingled together. Nor can the mingling be avoided; even the frameworks for thought—the categories into which raw perceptions are fitted—are a legacy of those who have come before. The raw input is individual, but the resultant—information—is conjoint. Done right, the joint result is stronger, taking advantage of each person's different access to the real world.

Of course a 'strong' information end product is the whole point of the dynamic alternations in the model, specifically the model conduct and structure just reviewed—it is the whole reason to foment and support this complex ritual across time.

Open standards versus *idea*-vertical integration were the two extremes in Netscape against Microsoft. These two templates for an information product implicitly argued, one for looser integration among the logical parts, the other for tighter integration. Choosing where to fall between the two determines the number of points at which new variety may be introduced—*idea*-vertical integration offers fewer points, and open layering more points. (See the graphics immediately below.)

In fact neither open standards nor *idea*-vertical integration proved to be a naturally correct choice. This is despite the rhetoric for openness (not to be confused with inclusion).[16] A fundamental thrust of this paper, of course, is to deconstruct the architecture of the information product from the industry behaviors which produce it.

For an example that 'open or vertical' (in information product) is a choice and not normative, we saw how the-usually-castigated integration was in fact important for Sun with Java. Beyond that, both penalties and benefits have accrued to *both* ends of the loose/tight scale in logical structure; for example:

- Tighter integration—*idea*-vertical integration—could serve badly. We have seen already that Microsoft fought to keep

16 There is a pivotal case for the view that 'open or vertical' (again, in logical structure, not in organization) is a choice, and not dictated normatively: that is the case in which vertical integration in logical structure is *not* incompatible with inclusion for industry organization. The original Apple model for 'cloning' its Macintosh was such a case. That Apple model carefully balanced inputs from multiple industry participants with protection for the Mac's hardware/software integration, a key to the Mac's appeal. Though Apple's cloning model has now failed, in fact was not ever fully implemented, it appears clear that the reasons for failure were other than the practicability of the model. This test case will have to be a discussion for another occasion, however.

its old Windows-based component architecture, OLE, though OLE is pretty widely seen not to rival even closely a "modern" alternative, such as OpenDoc. In fact, the Microsoft juggernaut helped to kill OpenDoc. Outdated but vertically protected technology stopped a (much) better new alternative.

- Or, vertical integration could serve well. Sun's Java was a case. The Microsoft Webtop we also saw to be such a case, where closer integration meant better performance. The same holds for ActiveX performance, because it is integrated with Windows. The hardware/software integrated Mac is one of the most obvious cases.

- Open standards may offer benefits. The PC/Wintel open hardware platform, with many more points at which variety may be introduced, has allowed the rapid introduction of some innovations.

- Or, open standards may perform less well. Microsoft struggles to keep a *vertically*-integrated software OS (Windows), in part as a response to the great difficulty presented by so many variations in the *open* hardware PC platform! Slow performance by cross-platform Java is another case.

As these (implicitly 2x2) cells suggest, one of the trade-offs is between the performance which *idea*-vertical integration may bring as against opportunity for more innovation at more entry points with the opposite. In turn, the degree to which the performance of a given technology benefits from *idea*-vertical integration—the "system-ness" of the technology, we might say—becomes a parameter. This just sketches the complexity of the choice.

Where to land on the choices between open and vertical logical structure, including when and how to shift the mix, is one of the most important decisions. It is high on the agenda of the consensus decision-taking in the second phase of the cycle.

Both industry organization and its information product become looser or tighter hierarchies, with variety nested at lower levels. For the industry organization, that is in the concatenated communities and sub-communities into which the group fragments and alternately rejoins. For the information product, that is the looser or tighter logical structures, and the greater or lesser variety enabled. It is this which brings the model, and its analysis, real complexity.

Since industry organization and its information product are both looser/tighter hierarchies, both can be described by the same analytic graphics. The above graphic which portrays the *dynamics* (see Figure 4 on page 117, the fullest, three-stage diagram) effectively illustrates the concatenation of variety at levels in the *organizational* 'nests.' Earlier, or disaggregated, stages display variety which subsequently is subsumed at later, or higher, stages (for a given cycle). (And now we can also notice that only the relevant variety is subsumed into a new standard; other variety continues to persist at the disaggregated layer.)

If we switch to a more typical *static* view, the layering of variety in *an information product* will be more obviously on display. Here I use the convention that a pyramid may represent a [static] hierarchy. To convert from the dynamic stages in the graphic above to a static pyramid, each of the three stages above becomes a layer in a pyramided stack. Each stage is a successively higher aggregation, across time. To convert to the static view, and so omit a time dimension, the first stage above becomes the foundation layer, the second stage/aggregation the second layer, and so on (with the largest aggregation converting, perhaps unintuitively, to the narrowest layer).

Figure 5

Looser/tighter hierarchy: Static view

120

For the information product, looser coupling among the layers—'open layering'—allows more points at which new variety may be introduced. Tighter coupling—*idea*-vertical integration—offers fewer points.

Figure 6a
Open layering

Figure 6b
Idea-vertical integration

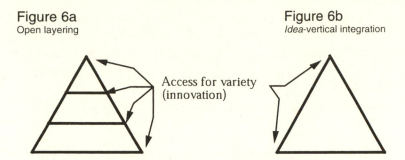

Access for variety
(innovation)

Open vs vertical and access for innovation

In fact, both the dynamic and the static graphics characterize *both* loose/tight hierarchies (notwithstanding that one or the other graphic fits more closely our predilections for organization or for its information product)—this because dynamic or static, both describe the same thing analytically, only from different views. A single analytic device characterizes industry organization and its information product.

To summarize overall: A key function of the industry organizational dynamics is to choose an information product. Analytically, both the organizational dynamics and the information product entail the same interplay between whole and part, as a central feature. When viewed dynamically [for organization], across time the interplay between whole and part juxtaposes variety, the trace left by innovation, against commonalties necessary for a standard (other variety continues to persist at 'lower' levels in the nest). When viewed as a static slice across the time stream [for information product], we can choose the relative number of points at which the variety from innovation may enter, as against performance of the technology system.

Part two
Theory and policy

3 The model and prevailing theory

How does this new model comport with prevailing views?
The bluntest comparison is with neoclassical views. There is
also one observation about evolutionary economics. The notes
below intend just to prepare the ground for a comparison.

3.1 Comparisons with the neoclassical viewpoint

The neoclassical position is founded on the individual, and individual action. This new model treats the individual in a
community. The neoclassical position is wary at best of social
ties, particularly the threat that group power may overwhelm
individual choice. The new model celebrates social ties—for
the 'better' shared information;[17] but underlying that, for the
power of social ties[18] to lift joint performance.[19]

But to say, as I do above, that "the community and its larger
interests become the object of the consensus decision" invites
neoclassical exasperation at defining the 'community interest.'[20] Thoughtful neoclassicists have created the lively litera-

---

17 Though, stalwart neoclassicists also appreciate shared information. I am
indebted to Don Lamberton for bringing to my attention Kenneth Arrow on
the subject ("Some ordinalist-utilitarian notes on Rawls's Theory of justice,"
in *The Journal of Philosophy*, Vol 70 (1973), No 9 (May), pp 245–263). A phrase
from Don's note to me captures it most succinctly: Arrow especially applauds
Rawls's Theory of Justice for arguing the "importance of the 'natural complementarity' amongst people because no one has all information." The Austrian
school also takes the assembly of shared information as a major departure.
Perhaps ironically, the view is commonly considered staunchly conservative,
with laissez faire producing an "autonomous, decentralized, non-
bureaucratic information system." The seminal work is Friedrich A Hayek,
The road to serfdom, Chicago: University of Chicago Press, 1944. (My appreciation to Marcellus Snow for his guidance about the Austrian school.)

18 Hierarchy is of course one element in the Coase/Williamson school of
work.

19 For instance in the case above, re objections to the forced end of Macintosh
cloning.

ture on [not] comparing preferences; but the shared notion of community seeks an analytic approach which will be fashioned anew, expressly for the purpose.

The prospect for group dominance is more than a threat—the news headlines daily remind us of human nature. But humans operate in groups—exclusively in groups. Virtually all our proudest achievements have depended in *some* way on group ties. Certainly, today's complex innovations depend intimately on close human interaction, and always a mix of the push and the pull. Economics is a science of aggregates—it seems appropriate to try and incorporate that most fateful of aggregates, the human group. To deal explicitly with the *power* of the group is essential. That is why the shared ethic of group behavior—here, the mandates around industry conduct and structure—plays a central role in this thinking. The embedded power-sharing is carefully balanced. Other power outcomes are possible, even prevalent; but if we are to grasp the essence, we had better start with the productive form.

An adequate characterization in this model becomes a little complex, to represent experience with some fidelity—but it is no more complex than the daily reality of all economic activity. And the IETF process for developing the 'Net indulges this complexity with stunning results—and seeming effortlessly!

What are the "primitive" assumptions, the bedrock? The objective function is speed and quality of innovations incorporated.[21] Does the model falter, if this is suspended? A more sophisticated treatment, for another occasion, would make more explicit the group evolution of objective function.

Will the model extend to non-networked industries? Though hardly a question for this paper, I believe we can look to another question and its answer: Will the quintessential network industry, telecommunications, become a 'normal' industry? Yes—in that the 'normal' industries will prove to have the characteristics essential to *network* industries when group dynamics are incorporated into the analysis.[22]

---

20 My balance between individual and community is of course not collectivism. Though not for this paper, I have in other places scrupulously worked out nominal group phenomena in terms of individual action.

3.2 Evolutionary economics and the selection environment

This paper is of course implicitly in the tradition of evolutionary economics. Though a bit self-reflective, there is one observation.

Defining the selection environment is an interesting question. The new model makes it even more interesting. Once group choice is recognized, what may previously have been seen *as* a selection environment can shape itself proactively, both the human and tool-based environments.

4 Policy

Network—for which currently read telecommunications—policy is headed massively in the direction of competition. This model is clear about an alternation between competition and consensus (with no diminution of the importance of competition, [though competition in the model focuses among ideas, not commodities]).

In the model, a group "picks winners," to which those who eschew industrial policy would object strenuously. The key point, however, is that the correct layer of 'private government' is identified to do the 'picking'—in the 'Net case, that is the IETF 'layer.' The conceptualization as concatenated hierarchy, or nest, provides new tools for identifying who/what layer appropriately chooses. Rather than a blunt divide between government and private sector, there is a gradation of levels each of which has a distinctive sphere of competence.

Anti-trust and intellectual property rights are two policy areas where the impact of the new model is particularly plain.

21 However, see footnote 11.

22 Further to be noted: It is not uncommon to equate standards with neoclassical scale economies. The notion of scale is often taken in a narrow sense, distilled essentially to a continuing decline in costs. Because the standards phenomenon is multi-faceted, certainly involving organization among others (as described), I have not chosen to invoke neoclassical scale as a descriptor.

4.1 Anti-trust

The root proposition for anti-trust holds that corporate size must not be allowed to become dominant. Otherwise in this view, size will be used to disadvantage other actors (with deleterious effect economically). This proceeds, of course, from neoclassical protection for the individual and freedom of movement. In contrast the model here, which has produced such successful innovation, holds that it is crucial to use the power of the group—not just of some large company, but of the entire group. But the point is to use that power productively.

Lying behind these contrasting models seem to be two divergent conceptions of human nature. One extols self-interest, even avarice; the other sees self-interest set in the social context. In fact, the protocols into which we are socialized may emphasize one outcome or the other—what we get is to some extent what we preach and ask for. Evidence in the cases above makes clear that both outcomes are possible, interestingly even within the same US culture.

How does the model modify traditional anti-trust? Two basic differences are worth inspection, alongside the many details.

First, the concern in the model is not size, but behavior. The model relies on relatively sophisticated social protocols, which allow for fluid transversal of the cycle, between self-interest and shared objectives, repeatedly. How is a "spoiler" handled, the actor who transgresses the protocol?[23] The Amish in the US for instance use 'shunning'—the exclusion of the offender from usual social perquisites—and so do all social groups, in one way or another. (Recent treatment of Saddam Hussein in Iraq is just another example.) That illustrates the role of informal social processes, over the relative formality of judicial systems.

Does size matter? Yes, both in that the power of the whole group is needed for successful outcomes *and* in that the atomized individual actor is also cherished for the creativity of un-

23 For a more detailed treatment of this and other previous topics here, see my "Beyond competition : where are we in the dialog about policy for telecommunications?" in Lamberton, D (ed), *Beyond competition*. Amsterdam: Elsevier, 1995.

fettered impulse. Perhaps most to the point, the joining of ideas, not the joining of people into relatively inflexible 'merged' organizations, is the objective. The creativity of the smaller group, with equal ability temporarily to join others when indicated, is the model of course.

Second, the focal scenario is dynamic, not the static conception of a relatively frozen 'market.' The furor between Microsoft and the US Department of Justice, over whether the browser Internet Explorer is part of Windows 95, amply illustrates. Object-oriented software design only recapitulates the juxtaposition between part and whole, which we have seen underlies useful understanding of organization and of *idea*-vertical integration.[24] Explorer, as an accumulation of objects 'in' Windows, is a part which is to be understood relative to a whole. Only when we take a dynamic view do we see that it may be *both* a separate part and part of the whole, depending on where we are in the basic organizational cycle.

Rather than caught in a conundrum which serves really no useful purpose, trying to parse Explorer re Windows in a static world,[25] we might take a dynamic view, which instead gives a framework to take sensible steps. Then we can bend ourselves to the real, hard work of sorting out choices for the Explorer/Windows information product (among others), between vertical and open.

Practice

What are the practical implications for policy? A quite significant change is indicated, obviously. An 'ideal,' up-and-working new regime is one topic; requirements for transition is another.

A new regime requires (quite) different institutions. Rather than an approach in which compliance is forced from outside, by some policing agency such as the US Department of Justice or other competition authority, the outcomes depend on internalized protocols of conduct. The pivotal institutions are the loose hierarchies, such as the IETF. In fact, a given hierarchy

24 I am grateful to John Markoff for reminding me of the object-oriented design. See for instance his *New York Times* article, March 2, 1998, p D5.

25 Or the equally hollow conundrum: Microsoft is a predating monopolist, but sets [bad] standards that are necessary.

or group must be able to find common ground with other such groups; that means that even looser aggregations, at 'higher' levels, finally extend up to what we ordinarily think of as government (so the 'expansion of community,' earlier, is actually necessary for coherence across a society—a topic touched again below). Early socialization is the real source of the behavioral outcomes which are the focus of a dynamic approach.

Are there difficulties deciding whether a given behavior is a 'good' consensus or an abuse of the group's power? Of course. (Schisms internationally over how to treat Saddam Hussein are also a useful illustration of such problems in more informal systems.) Do our present anti-trust regimes also fail to stop predation? The answer seems decidedly to be yes. The question is which process can work effectively.

From the cases above, it is clear that the new model can work remarkably well. All social groups come equipped with internal policing mechanisms, in some form. Gunnar Eliasson has suggested an encapsulation: that in this policy we do not allow "predation of the family." That is the succinct summary, I think (with thanks to Gunnar). Then we ask about our ability to mobilize those devices, when the participants may start from (very) different cultures, in a globalizing world.

Transition is another large topic. Ultimately, the emphasis has to be on early socialization. Immediately, there would be acute problems with the 'spoilers' who already have huge positions and have no intention of abandoning their style. 'Shunning' in this case could take very large proportions, such as not buying from internal company units which were not allowed the freedoms endemic to the innovation phase of the cycle,[26] even removing offending magnates.

The implications are too blasphemous, generally, to be considered—except that we are addicted to the success of just such a policy model for the dynamics of innovation. Are the policy dictates too fanciful to be taken seriously?

---

26 An extreme case would be an (unacceptably unfreed) internal unit which sells a popular OS. Then the 'shun' would entail shifting to purchase an alternate OS, rather than buying from that unit—with all the profound economic ramifications.

Constantly shifting organizational borders are hard to square with notions about firm identity, for instance. Consider the 'social architecture' which underlies the experience each of us has every day (and also underlies the analysis of the model, above). We are each members of several different 'groups'—family, work, play, perhaps religion and so forth. For any group we have membership in a widening set of concentric circles, with the bonds looser as the circle widens—at work, for instance, the most intent links are typically with the work group, but there may also be affiliation with a division, the company, even the industry. (The axes through the centers of *each set* of concentric circles—family, work and so forth—may overlap to some extent, but they will also be significantly orthogonal.)

Many times during the day, for any of the several groups, each person first exercises judgment based on membership in a circle of given scope (the work group, say), then may immediately shift to consider a question for a wider or narrower circle (the industry, for instance). Daily experience reproduces constantly shifting borders, our preconceptions notwithstanding.

Actually to sanction the power of the group, then to manage that informally rather than through strict rule-based procedures, seems to ignore, even threatens to trample cherished icons in our (Western) ideology. In the Asian financial crisis the regime in Indonesia has been held up as illustrating the excesses of 'crony capitalism,' when the Indonesian constitution enshrines the family as a model for economic policy-making.[27] With the net wealth of Suharto's ruling family thought to be in the same league as Bill Gates' ($30 billion and beyond), concern about informal mechanisms and about trusting a group's use of power does have to be taken seriously.

The discussion here can only frame a dialog on these two fundamentals, to be taken up later. The arguments favoring the novel model—dramatic productivity enhancements—are clear; it is the concomitants which may give pause. Let's be

27 The 1945 Indonesian Constitution holds that, "The economy shall be organized as a common endeavor based upon the principle of the family system."

plain about the main elements; then we can ask how different they are from actual practice today:

> Some coherence is maintained between 'higher' and 'lower' layers, ultimately throughout a society. Equally, there is opportunity for entry by new—dissenting—ideas. This is the essential, careful tension—coherence and, at the same time, entry for the novel idea—carried forward by agreed social protocols. The protocols are maintained by active 'jawboning,' including shunning for spoilers (those who would spoil the *process*; 'spoiling' a soon-to-be-outmoded idea is indicated of course). Care is taken to distinguish the inclusion of voices with new ideas from the choices to be made about the degree of integration for a given system—including individuals and choosing technology are not to be confused with each other.

Then a Microsoft is expected—not to wrest the control of standards to itself—but to join with the community, bringing its contribution alongside others and taking its part in the choices. For an example (again), the IETF has been remarkably good at keeping the use of power exercised by the group trustworthy. The difficulties arise at the 'higher' layers, where more tenuous ties (with implicitly greater differences at the [submerged] 'lower' layers) make consensus a greater challenge. Despite the intrusion of some hierarchy, this regime seems hard to distinguish from cherished notions of democracy. How different, in the end, is the maintenance of (these procedural) 'informal social protocols' from the evolution of law in formal judicial systems? Which is the more robust? (Steps for an Indonesia which has got off-track will open, hopefully, to the dialog which should be framed here for later.)

4.2 Intellectual property rights

There have recently in the US been two interesting lawsuits about Web content. Both concerned information—Web pages—that one service had "linked" from another service. In one suit, a group of newspapers objected to their site content being linked by another news service. In the other, Ticketmaster sued Microsoft for linking in a fashion that bypassed Ticketmaster's home page.

We have already seen how the hackers who largely created the 'Net and Web operate with freeware and typically disregard their intellectual property rents. The Web's fundamental, distinguishing quality—its hypertext links, which tie one set of information to another—is orthogonal to the usual tenets of intellectual property rights/IPR.[28] Elements of information, rather than being strictly compartmentalized as to one source or another, are linked, much in the way that individual ideas also connect in human cognition.

That is the parallel with individual thought; if we analogize with the social production of information: The architecture of hyperlinking recapitulates the creation of the information product, where each person's separate ideas may also contribute to a larger, joint whole. In hypertext linking, the loose dependence between whole and part, each upon the other, is perhaps nowhere clearer. The two lawsuits only begin to bring to the surface the inherent conflict between IPR and real world complexities of information which the Web can finally spin.

How does the model impinge on the regime of intellectual property rights? In basic terms, IPR is inflexible relative to the dynamics endemic to the model. Also, the control in IPR is situated with the individual, rather than socially. Finally, the social context essential to innovation is underplayed or missing entirely. IPR does protect the individual's pivotal role in creativity.[29] Can we operate without IPR? John Perry Barlow[30] argues that authors' incomes will actually rise, absent rent-accumulating intermediaries in the distribution chain.

28 For a classic treatment of IPR, see Kenneth Arrow, "Economic welfare and the allocation of resources for inventions," in Nelson, R (ed), *The rate and direction of inventive activity: economic and social factors*. Princeton: Princeton University Press, 1962, pp 602–627.

29 A full treatment of the question is in my "Intellectual property rights : an evolutionary reappraisal," in Lamberton, D (ed), *Communication & trade : essays in honor of Meheroo Jussawalla*. Creskill NJ: Hampton Press, forthcoming.

30 See for instance http://www.eff.org/~barlow.

But more profound are the implications for social and economic organization which arise, once the shortcomings of IPR are confronted. Rather than reward an individual with overflowing rents, for a big 'hit,' benefits would be spread among the entire social group. By raising the basic questions about property itself,[31] the implications for economic organization, for 'making a living,' become fundamental. To pursue a dialog about a future intellectual property rights regime, I believe the focus needs to be on actual practice among those who would espouse the new model: namely, there is *both* attribution (to individual authors) for 'good' ideas *and* a sense of shared ownership of the resultant information product.

> For both theory and policy, a single thread underlies the new model. That is a back-and-forth, a tension, an alternation between order and its opposite, whether we want to call that opposite by the name disorder, chaos, non-structure or use another label. We find this tension throughout. In industry structure: hierarchical form and inchoate atomization alternate to provide both for the stable agreements which are necessary and for the flights of creative fancy which are equally necessary. In industry conduct: fidelity to agreed norms alternates with self-propelled choices for innovative directions. In the underlying, basic cycle—and in its information 'product': the order of standards alternates with a free-form for innovation—the ideas themselves are alternately congealed with the consensus and made fluid for independent, creative thinking.

We might speculate that some order is essential to gain the advantages of its opposite: that innovation flowers when those who would create also have some stable footing from which to launch. That parallels a 'market place' set within a more ordered context or 'level playing field.' However we do speculate, which later we then need test, the implications across both theory and policy are unmistakable.[32]

---

31 Wherein important classes of real property are, alongside intangibles such as information, also 'both-shared-and-individual.'

One of the most remarkable runs in the annals of innovation has apparently been the product of a novel model for industry organization. With dynamic borders and alternating behaviors, the model stands at some variance from the prevailing views. But it builds, or tries to anyway, faithfully upon the underlying human experience. At stake in our choice of such models are the productivity and standards of living for our societies.

32 A conversation with Bertil Thorngren, during a respite between ITS deliberations and the Calgary conference, brought out how pervasive is the alternation between order and its opposite, particularly as he traced through his prior analysis of the phenomenon in the practicalities of managing an organization.

Chapter V

The case of Telecommunications in Europe

Regulatory Body, Rent-seeking and Market Activities

This paper is a revised version of one presented at the Sixth Conference of the International J A Schumpeter Society (Stockholm, June 2–5, 1996). We thank Gunnar Eliasson and participants for comments and Daniel Catherwood for editing.

Jean-Philippe Bonardi & Bertrand Quélin

Abstract

The purpose of this article is to explain to what extent the regulatory body, created during deregulation, can incite the former monopoly in telecommunications to discard rent-seeking assets and to develop market assets. Two main features of the regulatory body are enhanced. On this basis, we study three cases: France, Germany and Britain. We show that the regulatory body can only be effective if it has freedom of action, and if its role is above all to favour the entry of new competitors.

Introduction

The economic theory of regulation argues that the decisions made by firms, in a highly regulated environment, are mainly rent-seeking ones (Stigler, 1971; Peltzman, 1976; Noll, 1989). Indeed, the institutional structure indicates better pay-off for rent-seeking activities than for economic activities. This is particularly the case for regulatory monopolies which are encouraged by politicians to employ too many people, to produce goods desired by politicians rather than by consumers, or to locate their production in politically desirable rather than economically attractive regions (Schleifer & Vishny, 1994). Public Telecommunications Operators (PTO) in Europe have belonged to this category for a long time. Consequently, many scholars predicted that deregulation of telecommunications markets would help stop these rent-seeking activities that generated a sub-optimal result for society (Krueger, 1974; Winston, 1993).

However, more than ten years after its beginning in Europe, deregulation has not yet been brought to completion and rent-seeking activities still exist. Deregulation appears to be a slow and complex process that can be influenced by rent-seeking and market strategies of many actors. Especially, former monopolies can use their know-how of the political market's mechanism to influence regulatory decisions and to try to freeze the deregulation process. An important question for the deregulation of telecommunications, and in reaching a more optimal situation, is thus to know how to reduce this kind of rent-seeking activity and, at the same time, spur the development of market activities within PTOs in Europe.

Many works about the deregulation of telecommunications stress the importance of the creation of a regulatory body to set up an adequate framework (Gillick, 1992; Levy & Spiller, 1994; Tyler & Bednarczyk, 1993). The creation of a regulatory body can be considered as one stage of the deregulation process, among other important debates such as privatisation, dismantling, opening of the various markets, price controls, interconnection, etc (Bonardi & Quélin, 1998). The existence of a regulatory body is an important stage in this process, since it may be a changing factor in the existing institutional framework of the sector. However, not all regulatory bodies have the expected positive effect on the strategic behaviour of the PTO. It is thus necessary to determine which features in the role of the regulatory body really reduce rent-seeking activities and spur market activities.

In this article, we argue that the creation of a regulatory body can trigger a reducing of rent-seeking behaviours and fuel market activities of PTOs, but only if this regulatory body has the power to change the regulatory governance of the telecommunications sector. We show that this power must be based on two attributes: a freedom of action, i e independence from political authorities, and a clear incentive to favour the entry of competitors into the sector.

The article falls into two parts. First, we propose a theoretical discussion about the impact of the creation of a regulatory body on the strategies of former monopolies during the deregulation process. Secondly, we show the relevance of our insights through the comparative study of three cases (France, Germany and Britain), a few years before the opening up of the European market.

Part one
Strategies of the former monopoly and deregulation process

1 Deregulation and strategies of the former monopoly

1.1 What is deregulation?

Deregulation is a process (Weingast, 1981; Dixit, 1996), far more complex than many people expected. It creates surprises (Crandall, 1988; Kahn, 1988), and no one really knows how it is going to end up (Vietor, 1994). In this process, actors can adopt rent-seeking and market strategies, either if they want to put a brake on the deregulation process or if they want to accelerate this process (Bonardi & Quélin, 1998). If rent-seeking activities prevail over economic activities, the deregulation process will lead to a sub-optimal solution. Conversely, if market activities prevail over rent-seeking activities, the deregulation process is likely to create a more optimal situation. It is particularly the case for strategic behaviours of the former monopoly, because this organisation has a real influence on the political market.

Here, we view the firm as a crucible of resources and competencies (Verdin & Williamson, 1994), i e, a collection of tangible and intangible assets that are developed and selected along the history of the firm. It is the only way to understand strategic choices during a process in real time (Langlois, 1992). Former PTOs have two kinds of resources and competencies: political and economic ones. Because of years of regulation, the former monopoly has huge political competencies and resources, which render rent-seeking activities effective.

1.2 Political resources and competencies: keys to the political market

On the political market, the former monopoly has many things to trade with the government: it is a huge employer, it generally invests in many lame ducks, its privatisation is an extremely important issue for politicians, etc. All this means that the former monopoly has a great stock of political resources, contributing to social peace for a government aiming at being relocated. Besides, years of regulation have created significant know-how in dealing with public authorities. The former monopoly knows how to use its institutional environment to get favourable regulation or how it can react to an unfavourable regulation. It thus has political competencies. Combined political competencies and resources allow the former monopoly to be particularly efficient on the political market. It can put a brake on the deregulation process and try to keep high rents, even after the beginning of deregulation.

Figure 1: The political market in an era of deregulation

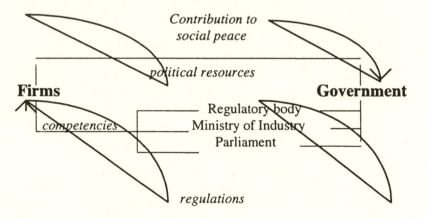

1.3 Political resources of a deregulated PTO

PTOs have various kinds of political competencies and resources. Table 2 summarises these political assets. We distinguish four kinds of political resources. The first kind corresponds to the influence of the firm on macro-economic variables, which depends highly on the size of the firm, the number of its employees, its contribution to national investments, etc. The second kind is the influence of the firm on budget deficit. This resource is particularly high when a company is to be privatised. Indeed, privatisation demands the high concern of the Treasury that must assure its success, and that must attract potential private investors. Thus, the company may be given favourable regulation to guarantee future benefits.

Whereas the two first resources are more macro-economic, and so have an "absolute value", the two others are more relative. They depend on the competition of other firms on the political market. First, there is the role of the firm in public interest missions, such as providing telecommunications services to everybody in the country. If the firm is considered as the only one that has to face this goal, the political resource is high and allows the firm to keep its monopoly. On the contrary, if there are other firms that can provide better services and at lower costs, and if these firms have support on the political market, it reduces the rent-seeking resources of the incumbent firm. In the same way, we consider the international prestige of the firm. If this firm is considered as the "national champion" of the country, it can obtain favourable subsidies or protections. This level of this resource depends on the number of firms that can be national champions, which are representing the country in international markets.

1.4 Political competencies of a PTO

Political competencies allow the firm to discover rent-seeking opportunities. They can be considered either as a way to exploit rent-seeking resources, or as an ability to analyse and forecast institutional evolution. We distinguish three kinds of competencies. The first is direct access to public decision. This allows the firm to reduce transaction cost in rent-seeking activities. It is related to the participation in pressure groups or lobbying activities directed to members of Parliament. The second rent-seeking competence is the length of the relation between a firm and a ministry or a regulatory body. Political know-how can just be acquired with time. There is a strong experience effect (Dean & Brown, 1995). The third rent-seeking competence is related to asymmetries in information between a firm and its regulating administration. This allows the firm to hide a part of its situation in order to obtain more favourable regulation in the political negotiation.

Table 1: Political competencies of the deregulated firm

Resources	Competencies
• Influence on macro-economic variables	• Direct access to public decision
• Influence on budget deficit	• Length of the relation
• Role in public interest missions	• Information asymmetries
• International prestige	

The former monopoly can use its high political resources and competencies to influence the making of regulation, thus assuring the success of rent-seeking activities. The question that must be raised now is the following: to what extents can the creation of a regulatory body reduce the political resources and competencies of the firm?

2 The impact of the regulatory body on the strategic choice between rent-seeking activities and economic activities

In this part, we show that the role of the regulatory body is very important during the deregulation process. But above the decisions that this body may make, the greatest aspect is its capacity to create change in the regulatory governance of the sector. Only this capacity can reduce rent-seeking activities, and drive the process to an optimal situation.

2.1 The regulatory body as an actor changing the regulatory governance

To analyse deregulation, Levy & Spiller (1994) distinguish two aspects: the regulatory incentives and the regulatory governance. Regulatory governance is defined as the mechanisms that societies use to constrain regulatory discretion and to resolve conflicts that arise in relation to these constraints. Conversely, regulatory incentives comprise the rules governing utility pricing, cross-subsidies, entry, interconnection, etc. The authors put emphasis on the regulatory governance, since the study of regulatory incentives has already been the central preoccupation of many theoretical works. In our present work, we operate using a similar distinction, since we believe that regulatory incentives are the result of actions on the political market. The regulatory governance is the system of rules that constrain rent-seeking activities on the political market. But, to address questions related to the deregulation process, we suggest taking time into account. Thus we adopt a dynamic view of the regulatory governance, that changes during the deregulation process.

Two regulatory governances can be defined: the regulatory governance before the creation of the regulatory body, and the regulatory governance after the creation of the regulatory body. If the regulatory governances are different enough, i e if there have been many changes in the regulatory governance, the functioning of the political market will be different after the creation of the regulatory body. If this is the case, the PTO will not be able to apply its existing political competencies and resources, and will turn towards the development of market resources and competencies. If this is not the case, the rent-seeking activities of the former monopoly will remain effective enough to assure the persistence of the monopoly position. This is the current situation of the trucking deregulation in the United States (Teske et al, 1994).

The new regulatory body, which has been created in all countries during deregulation, is thus the central actor in our approach since it constitutes the most important source of change in the regulatory governance, i e in the rules of the game on the political market. Here, we propose two features to assess the regulatory body's capacity to modify the regulatory governance: its freedom of action and its ability to favour the entry of competitors.

2.2 The two main features of the regulatory body

The first direction corresponds to the *freedom of action* of the regulatory body. If it does not have this freedom of action, changes that may be expected from its creation are very weak. Freedom of action provides a capacity to limit the rent-seeking influences on the political market, as well as a strong reactivity. It can be addressed through the following four questions.

- Is regulation under the responsibility of only one regulatory body?

If there are different regulatory bodies, [1]there will undoubtedly be disagreements about the right way of regulating the market. It also creates political competition between the different agencies, which will give rise to political opportunities for the incumbent firm. For instance, competition may occur between regulators at the European and the domestic level.

- What is its autonomy with regard to the political powers?

If it is not autonomous from political powers, the decision still comes from the traditional functioning of the political market, and the PTO can bet on its existing political resources and competencies. Then, the incumbent firm can pass over the authority of the regulatory body.

- What is its autonomy with regard to other government entities?

Above all, the question is about its legitimacy to be able to set up a new regulatory framework. If this autonomy is not strong enough, its ability to build up a new competitive framework will be weak.

---

1   Like in the UK, where both the Department of Trade and Industry (DTI) and the Office of Telecommunications (Oftel) have an authority to regulate the telecommunications sector during the 1980s.

- What are the potential appeals against the regulatory body's decisions?

This possibility of appeal allows us to assess institutional limitations to the decision freedom of the regulatory body out of administrative limitations, especially the ability for each actor to go to the Court of Justice.

The second direction corresponds to the *ability of the regulatory body to favour the entry of competitors*. We here refer to the view of competition in terms of a process that argues that competition mainly comes from the potential entry of competitors (Hayek, 1949; Eliasson, 1991). It depends on four points:

- Is the mission of favouring entry precisely expressed?

If it is not the case, it will be very difficult for the regulatory body to change anything. We join here the opinion of Levy & Spiller (1994) when they explain that the regulatory regime must be inflexible to guarantee the credibility of the regulation. Furthermore, if the mission of the regulatory is not clear enough, it will create political opportunities for the incumbent to pass over its authority.

- Are there points of the mission of the regulatory body which are incompatible with that of favouring the entry?

Opposing objectives, such as universal service and competition, can both be part of the task of the regulator, thus limiting its ability to concentrate upon an entry. Actually, the point is the overall framework to be built on its consistency and coherence.

- Which jurisdictions does it regulate?

If its powers are limited to a small part of the sector, political changes won't be important and the political resources and competencies of the incumbent firm won't really be questioned.

- Is it supported in the mission of favouring an entry by national or international institutions?

We will consider here the role of the European Commission, or of institutions as Commissions protecting competition in markets. Indeed, the support of such institutions that are supposed to be independent from political interests may be important to favour an entry.

3 Theoretical propositions

Note here that we do not propose any theory regarding the beginning of the process. As indicates Keeler (1984), we may find that it becomes too costly for the government to continue to satisfy only private interests. So, it has to take into account the general interest and decide to promote deregulation. In this view, deregulation begins with rent-seeking actions of consumer groups and large users in the political market. Here, we focus on the role of the regulatory body.

If the regulatory body has enough freedom of action, it can trigger huge institutional changes during the deregulation process. Especially, it can question established rent-seeking competencies of the former monopoly. The regulatory body has a large scope of liabilities: rules of the game, market structures, price controls, entry of competitors, etc. It has the freedom to change these regulatory incentives, without suffering from the political influence of the former monopoly. Regulation is not produced by the same political rules as before, and the rent-seeking strategies of the firm designed to brake the deregulation process are not as effective as they were. Besides, the regulatory body can use its freedom of action to try to reduce the information asymmetries, for instance by modifying price controls to get a better idea of the real costs of the former monopoly. Consequently, the PTO can not rely on its existing political competencies anymore to discover rent-seeking opportunities.

Proposition 1: Rent-seeking competencies of the incumbent firm decrease when the regulatory body has freedom of action.

Besides, the creation of such a regulatory body reduces the lobbying power constituted by the political resources of the firm. In effect, "abilities to favour the entry of competitors" allow the regulatory body to spur the development of competitive technologies (cable telephony, Internet telephony, satellites, etc) or techniques (call-back, Intranet, etc) that question the importance of the former monopoly for the supply of basic telecommunications services. Consumers, who are also voters, realise that the PTO creates inefficiencies and slows down the development of new technologies and techniques. With this evolution in mind, the PTO loses many political resources, and has less influence to defend a status quo position in deregulation debates.

Proposition 2: The rent-seeking resources of the incumbent firm decrease when the regulatory body has strong abilities to favour the entry of competitors.

Conversely, the entry of competitors creates economic opportunities for the incumbent firm, since entrepreneurs penetrate the market (with new products or services, lower costs for basic services, etc). Therefore, the PTO can develop market competencies and resources through imitation of competitors. These new economic assets will be complementary to older assets of the former monopoly, like a well-known brand (Cave & Williamson, 1997), this complementarity creating other market opportunities. It means that the incumbent firm accumulates economic assets more and more rapidly. This process of accumulation transforms the firm into a competitive player.

Proposition 3: The entry of competitors spurs the creation of market competencies and resources within the former monopoly. It drives it to discover long-term sources of profits on economic markets.

As explained by Mises (1949), it is competition that allows entrepreneurs to use economic calculation. This economic calculation drives entrepreneurs and firms to distinguish short-run profits from long-term returns brought about by time preference and risk. In the deregulation process, if the regulatory body favours the entry of competitors, long-term returns are based on the development of market competencies and resources. Indeed, since political competencies and resources of firms are decreasing, rent-seeking activities can just generate short-term profits. Conversely, since economic resources and competencies are increasing, market activities can generate long-term profits.

Proposition 4: The former monopoly will prefer long-term profits generated by market opportunities to short-term ones expected from rent seeking opportunities.

This evolution leads to the cumulative development of economic competencies and resources, rather than development of political competencies and resources. Thus, the firm reduces its rent-seeking effort to brake the deregulation process. In many cases, it may even decide to accelerate this process. Indeed, the great power provided to the regulatory body gives it the power to limit the strategic action of the incumbent firm to protect competition. For instance, the former monopoly will not have the right to diversify into some promising sectors related to telecommunications (cable television or multimedia services for instance). The deregulated firm will then lobby against this "over-regulation" of its activities (Majone, 1990), and so will try to accelerate the deregulation process. It will develop political competencies to do so. The main difference between these new political competencies and the former ones is that the new ones are complementary to economic resources while the older ones are complementary to political resources. Consequently, the development of new political competencies does not slow down the accumulation of economic competencies, but even accelerate it.

Proposition 5: The incumbent firm creates new political competencies to lobby against "over-regulation" by the regulatory body. These new rent-seeking activities are complementary to economic activities.

Therefore these theoretical propositions about the deregulation process stress the ambivalent role of the regulatory body: it is an essential factor in changing institutional incentives, but can also bring about over-regulation of the market, and thus rent-seeking activities by the former monopoly to accelerate the deregulation process. In the following part, we show the relevance of our five propositions through the comparative case studies of telecommunications in France, Germany and Britain from 1985 to 1995.

Part two
The cases of telecommunications in Britain, France and Germany

Our empirical analysis compares our theoretical propositions with the deregulation processes of the telecommunications in France, Germany and the United Kingdom. We here consider that the deregulation process had started everywhere in Europe at the beginning of the 1980s. This proposition is obvious in the British case, but less in the two others. Nonetheless, two factors indicate that deregulation went across frontiers, and also started in Germany and France either in facts or in minds. The first is the external threat of the US, that took in 1982 the decision to break up AT&T. All European countries saw this decision as the sign of a more intense phase of competition in domestic and global telecommunication markets. The second factor is the opportunity offered by new technologies such as optical fibres, new cables or satellite links, which are eroding the industrial boundaries between telecommunications, data processing and audio-visual media (Cawson et al, 1990). This technological evolution was to trigger the deregulation process in all western countries.

We chose these three countries because they are quite similar as far as general criteria of economic analysis of institutions are concerned (Ghertman & Quélin, 1993). There are of course differences in constitutional frameworks (role of the central leadership in government, role of parliament) or in legal systems. But, considering North's criteria (1990) like social conflicts, social norms or administrative capabilities, these countries are not as different from each other as Argentina, Chile, Jamaica and the Philippines, all countries studied by Levy and Spiller (1994). This relative proximity of the three countries for their overall institutional environment allows us to concentrate upon differences in the role of the regulatory body, and to enhance their ability to transform the existing regulatory governance of the telecommunications sector.

147

Table 2: Regulatory bodies at their origins

	Regulatory body	How regulatory body was established or received its mandate	Type of entity within the government structure
France	DRG (Direction de la Réglementation Générale)	Established in May 1989 Current legislative framework is Code des Postes et Télécommunications (Dec 1990)	Separate regulatory division within Ministry of Post and Telecommunications
Germany	No distinct telecommunications agency: the functions are performed by regulatory staff in the Ministry of Posts and Telecommunications	Postal Constitution Act (July 1989)	Separate regulatory division within Ministry of Post and Telecommunications
UK	Oftel (Office of Telecommunications)	Telecommunication Act of 1984	Semi-autonomous agency (related to the DTI)

Table 3: Processes by which the regulatory agency places issues on its agenda

	By statute	By initiative o government	Responses to petition / private initiative	Own discretion	Through mandated periodic review
France	No	Yes	Not usually	Yes	No
Germany	No	Yes	Not usually	Yes	No
UK	No	No	Not usually	Yes	Yes

Source: Tyler & Bednarczyck, 1993

149

4 Regulatory body and changes in institutional incentives in the three countries

To compare the three deregulatory frameworks, we focus on the two directions developed above for the role of the regulatory body: its freedom of action and its ability to favour entry.

4.1 Assessment of the freedom of action in the three countries

We keep our analytical framework based on successive questions about the regulatory body.

- Is the regulation under the responsibility of only one regulatory body?

The answer is positive for the three countries, as displayed in table 3. But we can already notice strong differences concerning origins and forms of the regulatory bodies. The United Kingdom is more than five years ahead on France and Germany. Besides, they go further in defining the regulatory body's status, since the Oftel is what Tyler & Bednarczyk (1993) call a "semi-autonomous agency," i e a non-ministerial government entity, independent but related to the Department of Trade and Industry (DTI). In France the DRG, created at the end of the 1980s, is a distinct body but stays within the government ministry. The difference from the German one is that the latter is not clearly distinguished from the Public Telecommunications Operator (PTO), which is still a public administration.

Table 2: Regulatory bodies at their origins (Page 148)

- What is its autonomy towards the political powers?

Data in table 3 clearly stress the differences concerning the autonomy of each regulatory entity towards the political powers. Indeed, even if the Oftel is not totally independent since it is still related to the DTI, it has more autonomy than the German and the French ones, which continue to belong to the Ministry of Post and Telecommunications. Administrative

150

Table 4: Influence of government entities in shaping telecommunications regulation in the 1990s

	Legislature	Courts	Antitrust agency	Parent ministry	Other ministries	Other regulatory bodies	European Commission
France	lesser role	no role	no role	Major influence	Major influence	lesser role	Major influence
Germany	Major influence	no role	lesser role	Major influence	no role	lesser role	Major influence
UK	Major influence	no role	lesser role	lesser role	no role	lesser role	Major influence

■ : Major influence   ◧ : lesser role   □ : no role

Sources: Adapted from ITU (1993), OECD (1997) and Quélin (1996).

151

steps have been taken in France to reinforce the independence of the DRG, which will be replaced by the "Agence de Réglementation des Télécommunications (ART)" in 1997, but these efforts can only bring few results as long as the regulatory body won't be clearly distinguished from the Ministry and its political objectives.

Table 4 confirms this analysis. Trying to assess changes provoked by the setting up of a regulatory entity, it is interesting to know how this entity places issues on its agenda from 1991 to 1995. This gives indications about autonomy of choice as far as deregulation is concerned. We see here that each entity has discrete powers, but also that only Oftel doesn't depend on government initiatives. Besides, we can notice the existence of mandated periodic review in Britain. This formal practice can be a source of autonomy for the regulatory body, which does not have to negotiate dates of changes anymore. That may be a way to institutionalise deregulation changes, and to overcome political obstacles or agenda.

Table 3: Processes by which the regulatory agency places issues on its agenda (Page 149)

• What is its autonomy towards other government entities?

In the three countries, the influence of other ministries and bureaucracies is quite weak. That is a positive point for institutional changes.

Table 4: Influence of government entities in shaping telecommunications regulation in the 1990s (Page 151)

• What is the appeal against the regulatory body's decisions?

This possibility of appeal allows us to assess institutional limitations to the decision freedom of the regulatory body out of administrative limitations. It appears that limitations in the three countries are weak. This is especially the case in the UK since appeal to courts requires a lot of time and financial resources. Then, the conflicts between the former monopoly and the regulator generally take the form of personal conflicts in newspapers or TV between the managers of the two organisations (Dumez and Jeunemaître, 1991). Thus, the PTO has no real appeal solutions against decisions of Oftel.[2] This point may be a positive one for institutional changes, but also favours over-regulation.

Table 5: Regulatory appeals process (1984-1995)

	Mechanisms for appealing regulatory decision
France	Appeal possible to all DRG decisions by same process as all administrative decisions of the government
Germany	Within the limits set by law on Administrative Proceedings, objections may be filed in regard to any administrative act. Review is then undertaken in a new administrative proceeding.
UK	Appeal to courts is possible, but grounds for appeal acceptable to the courts are very limited

Source: ITU, 1993

4.2 Assessment of the ability of the regulatory body to favour the entry of competitors

• Is the mission of favouring an entry precisely expressed?

As indicated in table 6, favouring an entry appears explicitly in the regulatory body's mission of the three countries. But there is an apparent objective in French and German texts to move cautiously and to preserve the interests of the PTO. This cautious attitude limits the ability to provoke important changes in the competitive regulation, and sustains the rent-seeking resources and competencies of the PTO.

The position of Oftel is different since it is not a Ministry department. This more independent position enhances the importance for Oftel to reach such goals as introducing competition and boost innovations.

---

2 This point is a feature of European deregulation. For instance, it is not true of the FCC in the US, whose decisions can be more easily questioned in courts.

153

Table 6: Missions of the regulatory entities

	Key elements of the mission	Points concerning the origin of the approach
France	• Incentive for efficient operation by fixed network service monopoly (France Telecom) • Controlled increase of competition in other fields (e g cellular)	• Cautiously moving towards competition in cellular, VSAT and Data services — balance with public service obligations and financial perequations. • Compliance with pro-competitive EC directives • Possible trend to free state-owned dominant PTO from political control in new business expansion, e g acquisitions in other countries, joint ventures.
Germany	• Stimulate efficient operation by fixed-service monopoly (DBP Telekom) • Controlled increase of competition in other fields (e g cellular) • Protect residential users	• Tradition of state-owned monopoly, but evolution towards privatisation • Increasing recognition by government and economic adviser of benefits of competition •Transitional need to meet high cost of catch-up in eastern Germany • Compliance with pro-competitive EC directives
UK	• Nurture growth of competitors • Protect low-income residential users	• Mandate in 1984 Telecommunications Act to introduce / encourage competition and safeguard user interests • Enlargement of competition.

Source: Adapted from ITU (1993) and Quélin (1996).

Are there points of the mission of the regulatory body which are incompatible with those of favouring entry?

In the three countries, regulatory mission can seem contradictory. On the one hand, it has to assure universal service goals, which suppose for instance the sustaining of crossed

Table 7: Major roles of the regulatory bodies

	Universal service goals	Affirmative mission to change industry structure	Move rapidly towards a " no discrimination policy "	Supervising the dominant PTO	Stimulating innovation	Achieving technical preconditions for effective operations
France	■	◨	◨	■	◨	■
Germany	■	◨	◨	■	◨	■
UK	■	■	◱	■	■	◨

■ : Mission listed as a major role   ◨ : lesser role   □ : no role

Source: ITU, 1993

155

subsidies. On the other hand, the regulatory body must favour entry, supervise the PTO and stimulate innovation. This internal contradiction reduces the impact of the regulatory body on institutional changes.

But the situation is not exactly the same in the three countries. Indeed, it is only in the UK that the regulator has the affirmative mission of changing industry structures and to promote innovations. In Germany and France, the role of the regulatory body concerns much more the supervising of the PTO than institutional changes. This maintains high rent-seeking competencies and resources for the PTO to bet on status quo.

Table 7: Major roles of the regulatory bodies (Page 155)

- Which jurisdictions does it regulate?

There are no important differences concerning the extent of regulated jurisdictions in the three countries. In Germany and France, splitting the regulation between telecommunications and broadcasting organises a competition, which is actually not well adapted to the future. One can forecast conflicts between different regulatory bodies, which can help incumbent firms to maintain rent-seeking activities.

Table 8: Jurisdictions of the principal telecommunications regulatory bodies (Page 157)

- Does national or international institutions support it in the mission of favouring an entry?

As it appears in table 5, the European Commission plays an important role in supporting regulatory bodies' ability to favour an entry in the three countries. Although the European Commission had been concerned about Europe's position in the videotext sector back in 1970s, it was not until 1983 that a serious strategy for telecommunications began to emerge. The Action Program for telecommunications in 1984 was the first concrete manifestation of this strategy. The second would be a Green Paper published in 1987. Compared to past proposals, this Green Paper was a radical document, designed to "*initiate a common thinking process regarding the fundamental adjustment*

Table 8: Jurisdictions of the principal telecommunications regulatory bodies

	Communication services included in telecommunications regulator's jurisdiction					Other aspects of telecommunications regulation	
	Fixed public network	Private corporate fixed networks	Public Mobile networks	Cable TV	Broadcasting	CPE type approval	Radio spectrum regulator
France	■	◱	■	□	■	□	▨
Germany	■	■	■	▨	□	□	▨
UK	■	■	■	◱	□	■	□

■ : Major role of telecommunications regulator   □ : Regulator partially responsible

◱ : Regulator has limited role   □ : Regulator has no role

Source: ITU, 1993

157

of the institutional and regulatory conditions which the telecommu-
nications sector now faces."[3]

However, the support of the European Commission to fa-
vouring an entry was not always very intense because of internal divisions over the implementation of the Green Paper.
The General Directorate in charge of Competition Policy (DG
IV) develops the idea that the telecommunication market is
covered by the pro-competitive powers of the Treaty of Rome.
Its influence is very positive to supporting a competitive entry. On the contrary, concerned about the interests of the
Community's equipment and services industry, the General
Directorate in charge of Information Technology (DG XIII)
feels that it is important to accept the telecom administration
monopoly, particularly in voice telephony. Somehow, one can
say that the European Commission has a positive influence in
modifying institutional incentives, particularly through di-
rectives fixing the opening of the national market in 1998. This
reduces the rent-seeking opportunities on the middle term,
and incites PTOs to develop market competencies.

In the same way, one can say that the presence of the Monopolies and Merger Commission (MMC) in the UK enhanced the effectiveness of the changes in telecommunications regulation. Indeed, its power to fight against anti-
competitive behaviours can be combined with the Oftel's
right to refer to the MMC matters. It reinforces Oftel's ability
to implement its regulatory initiatives since BT has just the
choice to accept changes or to refer to the MMC.

Conclusion of the institutional analysis

From this analysis of the role of the regulatory body in the
three countries, we can conclude that the British regulatory
body (Oftel) has the most important chances to trigger institutional changes. Oftel is not totally autonomous from the DTI
and the whole government, but its future depends hugely on
its ability to lead the market to competition. In the two other
countries, conversely, the regulatory bodies can not be considered as changing actors within the deregulation process.

3 Commission of the European Communities, *Towards a dynamic European
economy*, Green paper on the development of the common market for telecommunications services and equipment, DG XIII, 195 pp.

Their freedom of action seems to be so limited that firms' rent-seeking competencies will not be questioned except under a pressure of new entrants. Besides, their mission is more based on protecting universal service and supervising the PTO than favouring the entry of competitors. Consequently, the competitive environment will not be dynamic enough to stimulate a rapid creation of economic competencies and resources.

5 Evolution of resources and competencies in the three countries

5.1 Time periods for case studies

For studying the deregulation process, our time unit of analysis will be changes in the regulation. Thus, in the three countries, we noted some moments of important regulatory changes: opening of markets to competition, privatisation, and dismantling are examples of such major changes. The historical order in which they came to the political agenda are not considered as a fundamental point before the Commission of European Community decided to organise the opening of the telecommunications market by January 1998. In this article, we are concerned with the events and main changes that happened before this term.

The BT case falls out into three periods, as displayed in table 10. In UK, the deregulation process has already gone far. At the end of the first period, British Telecom, the PTO, has been privatised (1984), and the basic telecommunication market opened in order to organise a duopoly. This was result of the Telecommunications Act of 1981. After the second period, Oftel opens all service markets to competition, even if it is with control of the entry.

Table 9: Time periods in BT's deregulation case

	Local network	Intercities network	International	Data transmission	Mobile phones	Equipment
First period (1969-1981)	M	M	M	M	M	M
Second period (1981-1992)	M(*)	D	D	M	M	M
Third period (1992-1995)	C	C	D	C	C	C

(*) Except in the City where Mercury developed a local network
M = monopoly   D = duopoly   C = competition

In the French case, the process made very slow progress. We distinguish two periods. In the first one, the whole telecommunication industry is market monopoly. In the second period, services and mobile phones are opened to duopoly or oligopoly competition, but not classical vocal services. Thus, law changed the PTO's legal form from a public administration to an institution under public law[4] effective by 1991. Another period should be added from 1997, because a new regulatory body has been created and a third competitor has been introduced in mobile phones. Finally, the PTO will be partially privatised in 1997.

The situation in Germany is equivalent to the French one as far as formal evolution of the deregulatory process is concerned. We chose 1989 to distinguish the two periods of the deregulation process in Germany since it is the date of a fundamental reform law that separated telecommunications, postal services and banking. Deutsche Telekom began a government-owned company. Moreover, these reforms opened up the German market to limited competition by permitting private companies to compete with Deutsche Telekom in some markets (mobile phones, enhanced services, and recently personal communication networks). But Deutsche

4 In French: "Etablissement public à caractère industriel et commercial (EPIC)."

Table 10: Time periods in France Telecom's deregulation case

	Local network	Inter-cities network	Interna-tional	Data transmis-sion	Mobile phones	Equipment
First period (up to 1991)	M	M	M	M	M	C
Second period (1991–1996)	M	M	M	D	D	C

M = monopoly   D = duopoly   C = competition

Telekom maintained its monopoly on the provision of basic real-time voice services and on the public networks for other telecommunication services. But the second period in Germany is almost finished since privatisation is being seriously prepared, and since there is clear engagement to open the market to competition.

Table 11: Time periods in the Deutsche Telekom's case

	Local network	Inter-cities network	Interna-tional	Data transmis-sion	Mobile phones	Equipment
First period (up to 1989)	M	M	M	M	M	C
Second period (1989–1995)	M	M	M	D	D	C

M = monopoly   D = duopoly   C = competition

About the three situations, one could say that the French deregulation process lags behind the two others up to 1996. German evolution has been very slow for many years, but seems to be ready for dramatic changes, especially because of the partial privatisation of DT. The British deregulation process has almost led to total competition, even if it now seems over-regulated. The first conclusion we can draw is that these evolutions seem to be consistent with our theoretical proposition 1. In the two countries where the deregulation process is or has been blocked, the regulatory body has neither freedom of action nor great ability to favour competition. Conversely, in Britain where Oftel has partially these two institutional features, the process evolved towards large opening of telecommunication markets. We now confirm the relevance of our other theoretical propositions studying changes of inner resources and competencies of the three PTOs.

6 Compared evolution of resources and competencies in the three countries

As expressed in part one, Section 1.2, we consider the firm (and PTOs) as a crucible of resources and competencies, either political or economic. Their level of resources and competencies of both kinds determine the strategies of the PTOs. We thus compare the impact of the features of the regulatory body on the evolution of these assets, and try to confirm empirically our theoretical propositions defined above in part one, Section 3.

6.1 France

As the French case displays weak institutional evolutions, it also shows little variation of political competencies and resources over the two periods. The resources of the PTO remain high, and privatisation has still many opponents. Thus, the role of France Telecom in public mission is still high. France Telecom does not face a wide political competition (figure 2). Furthermore, its rent-seeking competencies do not shrink since its relations with the ministries remain strong

Figure 2: Evolution of France Telecom's resources

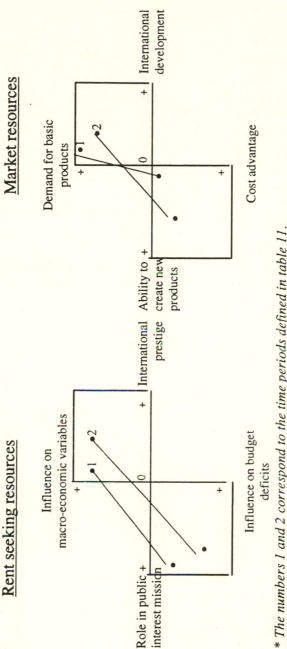

Rent seeking resources

Influence on macro-economic variables

International prestige

Role in public interest mission

Influence on budget deficits

Market resources

Demand for basic products

International development

Ability to create new products

Cost advantage

* The numbers 1 and 2 correspond to the time periods defined in table 11.
** In this representation, the length of the line linking the different types of resources indicates the approximate amount of these resources, either rent seeking or market ones, for the firm. The closer to the centre (0), the lower the value of the resource.

and date back to a very long time (figure 3). The deregulation process is thus very slow.

Figure 2: Evolution of France Telecom's resources (Page 163)

But the status quo is not real as far as market resources and competencies are concerned. France Telecom proposes a high quality of services, better than those of Deutsche Telekom or BT, particularly thanks to a very modern digital network (Table 12). Management structures and competencies have been well adapted to new demands and new markets (Chamoux, 1993). Moreover, strategic alliances in 1995 such as that with Deutsche Telekom and Sprint, a US operator, show the willingness to develop market competencies to be able to discover international opportunities. France Telecom has structures in countries like Portugal, Argentina or Mexico, and in the eastern countries (Table 12). But it does not experience true internal competition, for instance over prices in vocal telecommunications, which creates problems for improving the efficiency of the company.

Figure 3: Evolution of France Telecom's competencies

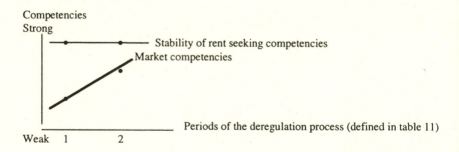

This development of market competencies and resources cannot be analysed as a result of institutional changes triggered by the regulatory body. Changes rather come from international pressures, such as those of the European Commission. Because of this agreement to open up the telecommunications markets in 1998, long-term market opportunities appear. But that does not correspond to a real decrease of the rent-seeking perspectives. Thus, the problem for France Telecom is that its strategic action is often reduced to an imitating behaviour of international actors, such as BT or AT&T. But the lack of experience in competitive markets does not allow it to acquire innovating entrepreneurial capacities.

The relative lack of change in the French regulatory governance should eventually disappear since a new regulator has been created in 1997. It seems to have enough "freedom of action" and "ability to favour the entry of competitors" so as to modify the pay-off expected from the rent-seeking activities. Six carriers have already been given the right to provide telecommunications services (either local or inter-cities) in 1998. In addition to the creation of a new regulatory body, some important evolutions of the deregulation process have already occurred in France since 1996 (partial privatisation, opening of the cellular phones market to a third carrier). These evolutions have also reduced France Telecom's political resources.

Table 12: Some figures about France Telecom

	1985	1990	1995
Number of employees	170 000	156 600	167 660
Share of the state in the capital (%)	100	100	100
% of digital main lines	45	75	93
International diversification[5]	0	3	9
Number of access lines (*1000)	23 900	28 100	32 400
Number of subscribers of cellular phones (*1000)	5	280	1302
Productivity rate (line per employee)	141	179	193

Source: Company annual reports

5   Number of countries in which the PTO has a subsidiary a joint venture, or an alliance.

6.2 Germany

Concerning rent-seeking opportunities, the German situation is quite close to the French one in the two periods. With 11.7 billion dollars in revenues and 203 000 employees in 1982,[6] for instance, its influence on macro-economic variables (figure 4) is important in the first period. It is the same in the second period, its working force growing over 230 000 employees because of the unification with East Germany and the take-over of the phone system (Table 13).

In the first period, its role in social welfare and public interest mission was strong since Deutsche Telekom was a monopoly, and accepted by everybody as such. But this resource declined in the second period because of the political competition of large corporate users, which pressured the government to obtain better services at lower prices so as not to be handicapped in international competition. This decline of the rent-seeking resources of the PTO is illustrated by the fact that the idea of privatisation is today well accepted in Germany. Indeed, privatising the PTO required a constitutional amendment and therefore a two-thirds' majority in the German Parliament. This seemed impossible, but the political opposition (the Social Democratic Party) expressed its willingness to discuss such an amendment.

However, because of the proximity of privatisation, which is important for budget deficits, Deutsche Telekom has kept huge political resources to negotiate a smooth opening up of its traditional markets to competition. Also, because of the moderate changes in the institutional environment, Deutsche Telekom sustains strong rent-seeking competencies (figure 5). All this means that the regulatory governance of the telecommunications in Germany still provide some great pay-off for rent-seeking activities.

The market opportunities in the German process do not seem to be as numerous as in the French or the British cases. Its tariffs are still very high and its productivity does not create a real cost advantage (Table 13). Deutsche Telekom is still a bureaucracy, and for a long time its activities were turned more towards rent-seeking activities than towards discover-

6 Sources: Financial Times, 27 september 1983 and OECD (1983).

ing market opportunities. Nonetheless, Deutsche Telekom keeps high market resources in demand for basic resources because of the need to extend the network to eastern Germany. Besides, the PTO imitated the strategic behaviours of its future competitors, for instance through a major reorganisation which was very similar to the structure adopted by British Telecom (Bohlin, 1995). This is the sign that the strategic choices of Deutsche Telekom are more and more being turned towards market activities. Strategic alliances (with IBM, AT&T, France Telecom...) to develop competencies in new product creation and international markets knowledge are also a significant sign. The market competencies also increased thanks to new management, such as a Chairman recruited from Sony Inc.

Figure 4: Evolution of Deutsche Telekom's resources (Page 168)

The development of Deutsche Telekom's competencies and resources was, at the beginning, more turned towards rent-seeking than towards the market. This is consistent with our theoretical propositions, since the changes in the regulatory governance were not significant. For a few years, the situation has continued to evolve. Deutsche Telekom is developing market competencies and resources, which create market opportunities. Another indication of this point is the fact that significant changes in competition occurred in 1993, when government allowed many companies to use their corporate networks to provide voice and enhanced services. Deutsche Telekom's rent-seeking behaviours ultimately did not block these initiatives.

Figure 4: Evolution of Deutsche Telekom's resources

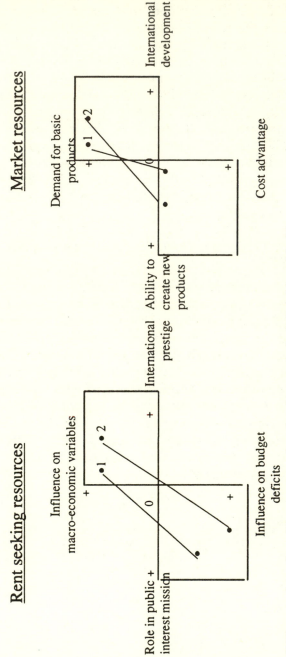

Rent seeking resources

Market resources

* *The numbers 1 and 2 correspond to the time periods defined in table 12.*
** *In this representation, the length of the line linking the different types of resources indicates the approximate amount of these resources, either rent seeking or market ones, for the firm. The closer to the centre (0), the lower the value of the resource.*

Figure 5: Evolution of Deutsche Telekom's competencies

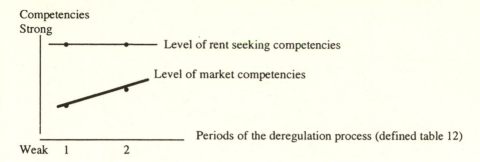

Even if partial privatisation has occurred in 1996, recent evolution of the regulatory governance does not seem to be as rapid as it is in France. Indeed, a new regulatory body independent from the political authorities has not been created. This may engender a slowing down of the deregulation process compared to France, since rewards for the PTO's rent-seeking activities remain high. The best example of this rent-seeking capacity is the conflicts (January 1998) between the PTO and its future competitor, Deutsche Telekom, declaring that customers who want to switch to another carrier will have to pay a substantial tax. This can only reduce the development of real competition, particularly for individual customers.

Table 13: Some figures about Deutsche Telekom

	1985	1990	1995
Number of employees	250 000	212 200	220 000
Share of the state in the capital (%)	100	100	100
% of digital main lines	0	0	55
International diversification[7]	0	0	8
Number of access lines (*1000)	26 700	31 887	40 400
Number of subscribers at cellular phones (*1000)	12	430	3 750
Productivity rate (lines per employee)	107	150	184

Source: Company annual reports

6.3 British Telecom

British deregulation evolved much more quickly than deregulation in other countries. This evolution was partly provoked by the creation of the Oftel, indicated before. This creation and the growing role taken by the regulatory body within the deregulation process really modified the pay-off expected from rent-seeking actions, and obliged British Telecom to turn widely towards market activities.

In the first period, British Telecom is still a public monopoly which has high rent-seeking competencies, based on its particular and long-term relations with the DTI (Department of Trade and Industry). However, its rent-seeking resources strongly diminished in the 1970s because of strikes that caused severe disruption in the financial services in London, and because of the weak quality of services (the number of complaints doubled from 1978 to 1979) while the prices of services had been increasing since 1975. Comparisons with the tariffs of the telecommunication services in the rest of

---

7 Number of countries in which the PTO has a subsidiary, a joint venture, or an alliance.

Europe also reduced the political resources of the PTO linked to its role in public interest mission. In addition, corporate political pressures, especially from the powerful City, created competition in the political market and provoked privatisation and opening up of telecommunication markets to competition. In this first period, political resources only kept a high level because of the support of the Treasury that did not want to jeopardise the success of the first "giant" privatisation.[8] This allowed BT to negotiate limited competition for the second period. Since its market competencies were very weak, BT feared competition of new entrepreneurs about tariffs and new products. Besides, BT's rent-seeking competencies and resources allowed it to avoid the breaking up of the company, as was the case in the US.

Figure 6: Evolution of BT's political resources (Page 172)

In the second period, our propositions about the role of the regulatory body are confirmed. As we showed above, the Oftel has even partially "freedom of action" and "ability to favour the entry of competitors". Therefore, its creation really introduced changes in the regulatory governance of telecommunications in the United States. It took some years for the Oftel to impose its authority, but it finally succeeded. Three points were particularly significant here. First, the Oftel changed the price-cap several times to reduce information asymmetry and get a better idea of BT's real costs (Vallée, 1994). Secondly, it succeeded in forcing BT to accept Mercury's interconnection to its national network in 1987. Thirdly, it spurred the development of new technologies such as cable telephony and cellular phones, promising rights to enter the market to many new carriers in those fields. Through these three points, the Oftel used its "freedom of action" and its "ability to favour competition". Thus, the setting up of the Oftel introduced institutional evolutions that reduced BT's rent-seeking competencies, while its market competencies were strongly increasing thanks to reorganisations and internal efforts.

---

8 It amounted to 3.9 Billion £, the State selling 50.2% of the shares.

Figure 6: Evolution of BT's political resources

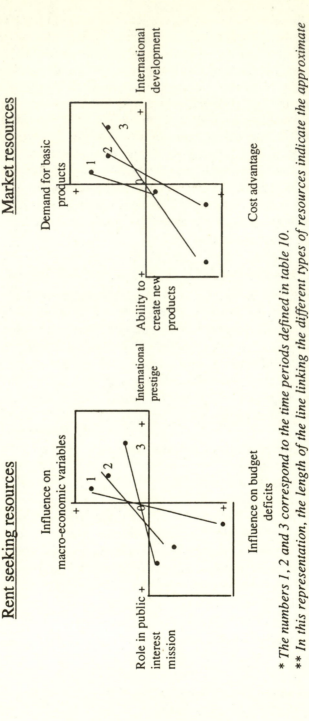

* The numbers 1, 2 and 3 correspond to the time periods defined in table 10.

** In this representation, the length of the line linking the different types of resources indicate the approximate amount of these resources, either rent seeking or market ones, for the firm. The closer to the centre, the lower the value of the resource.

172

All this provoked great efforts from the former PTO to develop its market resources and competencies. Nobody thought that such productivity gains were possible (Table 14). This allowed BT to reduce its tariffs to reply to the competition of Mercury.[9] Indeed, the price-cap chosen by the Oftel incited productivity improvements.[10] BT also improved the quality of its services and improved the digital level of its network. It was now not so far from France Telecom on these criteria, even if it lagged behind ten years earlier. Besides, BT launched into the development of international competencies and resources, even if it did not always lead to success[11] (Table 14). We here find the risky dimension of exploiting entrepreneurial opportunities. BT has become the first European global player (Fransman, 1994).

But the most important point is that the pay-offs for rent-seeking activities are not as high as they were before, since the growing role of the Oftel assures that markets will be opened to market competition in the short run. Therefore, only market activities can bring long-term profits, especially since BT is one of the first European carriers to have real market competencies in a competitive environment. That is why BT renounced its influence on macro-economic variables, for instance by reducing the number of its employees in 1991 with the Sovereign Plan (Table 14).

Thus, in the third period, BT does not strongly resist to Oftel's attempt to question the duopoly. Again, the role of the Oftel has been predominant in this evolution of the deregulation process. Today, more than one hundred firms compete with BT in every part of the telecommunications market. Moreover, BT now appears in Europe as the defender of liberalisation and uses its political competencies and resources at

9   Even if this competition has never been very tough (people are calling it "the cosy duopoly") BT really improved its capacity to lower prices in this period. This became important in the third period, where BT had to face many new competitors on every part of its traditional market.

10 In this way, the price-cap is different from the "rate of return" regulation adopted in the US to control the tariffs of AT&T.

11 MITEL's take over by BT (1985), for instance, was a failure. Conversely, its strategic alliance with MCI (1993) seemed to be promising since it allowed BT to provide global services and penetrate the US market. Nonetheless, the recent acquisition of MCI by Worldcom questioned this global strategy. BT must now find a new partner in the United States.

the European Commission to speed up the deregulation process in other countries. The political resources brought by its international prestige are quite valuable in this view.

Figure 7: Evolution of BT's competencies

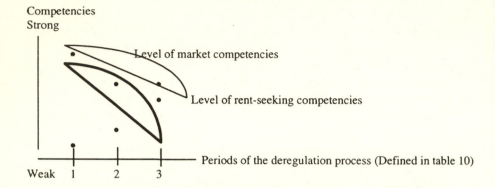

The greatest difficulty for BT now comes from what we called "over-regulation" in our fifth proposition. The Oftel has no obligation to clearly justify its decisions, and the appeals of its decisions are uneasy and costly for BT (Dumez and Jeunemaître, 1991). Thus, some markets are closed for BT, such as that related to television, and the Oftel imposes harsh reviews of the price-cap. Some strategic opportunities, generated by its market competencies and resources, are therefore impossible to exploit for BT, unless its lobbying efforts succeed in accelerating the total opening of the market.

Table 14: Some figures about British Telecom

	1985	1990	1995
Number of employees	235 200	245 665	137 500
Share of the state in the capital (%)	50,2	50,2	22
Number of access lines (*1000)	20 552	24 913	27 072
% of the digital main lines	7	48	88
International diversification[12]	1	3	12
Number of subscribers for mobile phones (*1000)	0	114	5 670
Productivity rate (line per employee)	102	101	198

Source: Company annual reports

7 Conclusion

The deregulation process in telecommunications stimulates market activities in former monopolies, but does not necessarily eradicate rent-seeking activities. The three European carriers considered here (FT, DT and BT) continue to brake the evolutions of regulation. We have tried to show that reducing these rent-seeking activities depends on the institutional changes in the regulatory governance provoked by the creation of a regulatory body that has two features : freedom of action and ability to favour the entry of competitors. None of the regulatory bodies considered here has these characteristics in full, but the British Oftel is the closest form of the three. Today, the British market is almost totally competitive, while there is still a long way to go for the others. Presently, BT appears as one of the world potential leaders for the beginning of the next century, thanks to the development of market competitive competencies and resources. This indicates that BT has renounced some of its rent-seeking resources and competencies

12 Number of countries in which the PTO has a subsidiary, a joint venture, or an alliance.

to concentrate upon market ones. It is the only way to become a competitive player in markets that are becoming very dynamic and global.

In the two other countries, France and Germany, the regulatory body up to 1995 has low freedom of action and low ability to favour the entry of competitors. Therefore, the trade mechanisms within the political market have not really changed, and the PTO keeps a high capacity to influence the adoption of regulation, and particularly to lobby for a status quo position. For a great part, their strategic purpose remains a rent-seeking one. They do not develop economic competencies and resources as quickly as BT does.

All this displays the importance of changes in the institutional environment that create deep evolution in the strategies of firms. It incites the firm to develop one kind of assets or the other, or even both at the same time. If we accept the idea that rent-seeking entails a sub-optimal solution, changes in the institutional environment can put the process on the way to a better solution, stimulating market activities. What is important here, is that the most important effects to give birth to new strategic behaviours are not primarily changes in regulatory incentives (price controls, bureaucratic controls, etc), but changes in the regulatory governance, i e, the mechanisms governing the relations between the former monopoly and the PTO. If these changes do not occur, regulatory incentives can not have a deep effect on the level of rent-seeking existing on the sector.

But the role of the regulatory body is ambivalent, and also creates over-regulation in Britain. That's the price paid to the freedom of action of the Oftel. This generates rent-seeking behaviours by BT to curb this over-regulation that sometimes constitutes an obstacle to the strategic opportunities that the carrier would like to jump at. The deregulation process recreates rent-seeking activities after having reduced them. However, these new rent-seeking activities are not as wasteful as the former ones, since they aim at accelerating the deregulation process, and not at slowing it down.

A good question now concerns the future of the regulatory bodies after 1998. If we have showed their importance for deregulation on a domestic level, it is not obvious that it will be the same when opening will be effective. Three points must be stressed. First, after the achievement of liberalisation in Europe, markets will become more and more global and a domestic regulatory body will not remain the decisive authority for competitive players. Secondly, one can expect more and more administrative competition between the regulatory body and competition such authorities (such as the Conseil de la Concurrence in France, the Merger and Monopoly Commission in Britain, or the DG IV in Brussels). Thirdly, one can also think that there are risks of capture of this regulatory body by global players. If decisive questions are treated in Brussels, one interesting issue for domestic regulatory bodies could be to defend national interests in front of a supranational authority (such as the European Commission). From an active authority to reduce rent-seeking activities within countries, the regulatory body would then become an active authority to promote rent-seeking activities on an international scale.

Bibliography

Bohlin, E (1995), "A changed strategy in search of a changed organization, trends and cases of telecommunications carriers in Europe, Japan and the United States," in *Communications & Strategies*, No 18, 2nd quarter, pp 11–37.

Bonardi, J P & Quélin, B (1998), "From rent seeking activities to economic activities : the strategic transformation of the deregulated firm." Working paper, HEC School of Management.

Cave, M & Williamson, P (1997), "Entry, competition and regulation in the UK telecommunications," in *Oxford review of Economic Policy*, Vol 12, No 4, pp 100–121.

Cawson, A et al (1990), *Hostile brothers : competition and closure in the European electronics industry*. Oxford: Clarendon Press.

Chamoux, J P (1993), *Télécoms : la fin des privilèges*. Paris: PUF.

Crandall, R W (1988), "Surprises from telephone deregulation and the divestiture," in *American Economic Review*, May, pp 323–327.

Dean, T J & Brown, R L (1995), "Pollution regulation as a barrier to new firms entry : initial evidence and implications for future research," in *Academy of Management Journal*, Vol 38, No 1, pp 288–303.

Dholakia, R R & Dholakia, N (1994), "Deregulating markets and fast-changing technology," in *Telecommunications Policy*, Vol 18, No 1, pp 21–31.

Dixit, A (1996), *The making of economic policy : a transaction-cost perspective.* Cambridge, MA: The MIT Press.

Dowling, M J, Boulton, W R & Elliott, S W (1994), "Strategies for change in the service sector : the global telecommunications industry," in *California Management Review*, Spring, pp 57–88.

Dumez, H & Jeunemaitre, A (1994), "La régulation des monopoles au Royaume-Uni est-elle un modèle de référence?" in *Chronique de la SEDEIS*, May.

Eliasson, G (1991), "Deregulation, innovative entry and structural diversity as a source of stable and rapid economic growth," in *Journal of Evolutionary Economics*, Vol 1, pp 49–63.

Fransman, M (1994), "AT&T, BT, and NTT : vision, strategy, corporate competence, path-dependence, and the role of R&D, " in Pogorel, G (ed), *Global telecommunications strategies and technological changes.* Amsterdam: North-Holland.

Ghertman, M & Quélin, B (1995), "Transaction costs and European regulation : a research agenda," in *Telecommunications Policy*, Vol 19, No 6 (August), pp 487–500.

Gillick, D (1992), "Telecommunications policies and regulatory structures," in *Telecommunications Policy*, December.

Hayek, F A (1949), "The meaning of competition," in Hayek, F A, *Individualism and economic order.* London: Routeledge and Kegan Paul.

ITU (1993), "The changing role of government in an era of deregulation," in *The International Telecommunication Union : an overview.* Geneva: ITU.

178

Kahn, A E (1988), "Surprises on airline deregulation," in *American Economic Review*, Vol 78, pp 316–322.

Keeler, T E (1984), "Theories of regulation and the deregulation movement," in *Public Choice*, Vol 44, No 1, pp 103–146.

Krueger, A (1974), "The political economy of rent-seeking," in *American Economic Review*, Vol 64.

Langlois, R N (1992), "Transaction-cost economics in real time," in *Industrial and Corporate Change*, Vol 1, No 1, pp 99–127.

Levy, B & Spiller, P (1994), "The institutional foundations of regulatory commitments : a comparative analysis of telecommunications regulation," in *Journal of Law, Economics and Organisation*, Vol 10, No 2, pp 201–246.

Majone, G (1990), *Deregulation or re-regulation?* New York: Saint Martin's Press.

Noll, R G (1989), "Economic perspectives on the politics of regulation," in Schmalensee, R & Willig, R D, *Handbook of industrial organization*. Vol 2. Amsterdam : North-Holland.

OECD (1997), *Communications outlook 1997*, Vol 2, Regulatory Annex. Paris: OECD.

Peltzman, S (1976), "Toward a more general theory of regulatory regulation," in *Journal of Law and Economics*, Vol 19, No 2 (August), pp 211–248.

Quélin, B (1996), "L'avenir de la réglementation du secteur des télécommunications," in *Revue d'Economie Industrielle*, No 76, 2nd quarter.

Schleifer, A & Vishny, R W (1994), "Politicians and firms," in *The Quarterly Journal of Economics*, November, pp 995–1025.

Spiller, P & Vogelsang, I (1996), "The institutional foundations of regulatory commitment in the UK," in Levy, B & Spiller, P, *Regulations, institutions and commitment*. Cambridge: Cambridge University Press, 1996.

Stigler, G J (1971), "The theory of economic regulation," in *Bell Journal of Economics*, No 3.

Teske, P (1991), "Rent-seeking in the deregulatory environment : state telecommunications," in *Public Choice*, Vol 68, No 1, pp 235–243.

Teske, P, Best, S & Mintrom, M (1994), "The economic theory of regulation and trucking deregulation : shifting to the state level," in *Public Choice*, Vol 79, No 3, pp 247–256.

Tyler, M & Bednarczyk, S (1993), "Regulatory institutions and processes in telecommunications," in *Telecommunications Policy*, December.

Vallée, A (1994), "Le régulateur face à l'asymétrie de l'information," in *Communications & Strategies*, No 14, 2nd quarter, pp 17–24.

Verdin, P J & Williamson, P J (1994), "Core competencies, competitive advantage and market analysis : forging the links," in Hamel, G & Heene, A (eds), *Competence based competition.* (The Strategic Management Series.) Chichester: Wiley.

Vietor, R H K (1994), *Contrived competition : regulation and deregulation in America.* Cambridge, MA & London: Belknap Press of Harvard University Press.

Winston, C (1993), "Economic deregulation : days of reckoning for microeconomists," in *Journal of Economic Literature*, Vol 31 (September), pp 1263–1289.

Chapter VI

Russia's Agrarian Dilemma

The Legacy of an Economy Without Innovation, Entrepreneurs or Market Competition

Andrew N Reed

Abstract

A great deal of the reform effort in Russia's agricultural sector during the post-Perestroika period has addressed the institutional framework within which agricultural enterprises operated during the Soviet period. The main target has been state-owned and managed collective farms which were the main lightening rod for western criticism of Soviet agriculture. The argument implicit in much of the well-intentioned but largely ineffective foreign sponsored remedial assistance offered to date is that the necessary economic infrastructure seems to be in place, so the fault must lie with the public sector institutions. The case presented here is that the superficial similarity is misleading: it is the lack of incentives, entrepreneurs and innovations which constitute the most debilitating legacy of the Soviet period.

Economics in the Schumpeterian tradition was anathema during the Soviet period. Despite the economy's meteoric **growth** during the post-war period and significant technological and social sphere accomplishments, the economic **development** of Soviet society was severely constrained. The resulting inefficiencies precipitated its collapse.

Using Russian agriculture as an example, the paper argues that an evolutionary perspective explains both the current predicament and the policy dilemmas inherent in efforts to transform the economies of Eastern Europe.

The **superficial** similarity of Russia's agricultural enterprises to many of those in the West stems largely from a concerted effort on the part of the Soviet leadership to emulate the modern, industrial mode of production which they believed lay behind the superior productivity of western agriculture. Another, complementary, objective of agriculture was massive consumption of the output of an industrial complex installed to match and surpass that of the cold war competition. The technology of post-Soviet agriculture was created to meet discrete, centrally determined, quantitative criteria, without the feedback mechanism between users and suppliers required for qualitative assessment of alternatives. Economic development is however the aggregate, cumulative consequence of numerous, qualitative, entrepreneurial decisions made to successively enhance economic efficiency. It should therefore come as no surprise to Schumpeterians that Russian agriculture at the end of the Soviet period was "underdeveloped," nor that it collapsed in the first few years of the new era.

The extreme case provided by Russian agriculture not only provides insight into the situation prevailing in the so-called "economies in transition" but also helps illuminate broader economic questions such as the importance of appropriate "success indicators," the distinction between "growth" and "development," the importance of motivation in the mobilisation of human capital, economic development's dependence on a stable policy environment and the critical role of economic feedback mechanisms in the selection of efficiency enhancing innovations.

Although enlightened economic theory may go a long way toward identifying desirable objectives, the question "how does one get there from here?" remains a substantial impediment to the more widespread implementation of development-oriented policies in any context. In "developed" market economies it is acknowledged that public sector infrastructure must evolve in response to changes in its environment, but wealth creation in the non-government sector permits the luxury of redefining the role of government and public infrastructure at a leisurely pace. In eastern Europe, where the economic pressure for institutional change is acute, the role of market economy missionaries has been awkwardly assumed by foreign organisations which are themselves immune from market forces. Although they acknowledge that the economy should not be planned, the belief persists that the intervention they are in business of providing is healthy. As such they tend to ally themselves with the central planners and sustain the status quo rather than facilitate creative destruction. This tendency undermines reform and handicaps the spontaneous development of the robust and competitive agricultural sector Russia now so desperately needs.

183

1 Introduction

Inefficiencies in agriculture played a significant role in precipitating the collapse of Soviet socialism. Mikhail Gorbachev established his credibility as a reformer while Minister of Agriculture and yet agriculture was the sector least prepared for post-Perestroika changes: for historical and philosophical reasons the rural economy has become a political hot potato, sociological and psychological considerations loom large in any policy prescriptions, and the average Russian does not even consider agriculture a sphere of *bona fide* economic activity. Yet failure to address the fundamental **economic** problems of Russian agriculture could prove to be the Achilles heel of "reform"-minded politicians. As a consequence the sector is perhaps the most demanding proving ground, bar none, for any body of theory which claims to broaden understanding of economic activity.

The transformation of east European society in the post-Perestroika era poses unprecedented challenges for economists. This paper aims to address two questions: First, can an evolutionary approach to economics—which counts Schumpeter among its founding fathers[1]—shed light on the current problems and the policy options being contemplated as remedies? Secondly, to what extent may the post-Soviet experience in eastern Europe enrich economic theory in the Schumpeterian tradition?

The two questions are addressed separately: **The first part** deals with the practical problems faced by agrarian reform in modern Russia. First a synopsis of the current situation is provided; attention then shifts to how and why Soviet agriculture evolved in the way it did; finally, the dilemmas facing policymakers are summarised.

The essence of the argument in this first section is that in the absence of market competition and entrepreneurs, the process of technical change during the Soviet period generated an ag-

---

1 As a non-academic, I am acutely aware that there is a great deal I do not appreciate about the lineage of evolutionary economics. What I do know about the influence of Schumpeter derives from primarily from Hinterberger (1993), Rosenberg (1991) and Nelson & Winter (1982). My own attempt at developing an "evolutionary analogue" framework based on personal experience in various economic entities is to be found in Reed (1993a).

ricultural sector which was superficially similar, but fundamentally different, to that in the west. Policy prescriptions which do not take technical change into account will fail now as they failed in the past, irrespective of whether they are formulated by Russian or foreign "specialists."

In **the second part**, the theoretical implications of the current situation are discussed and some tentative conclusions drawn. Sectoral restructuring and redefining the role of government are not exclusively east European problems. Market economies characterised by inter-enterprise competition, considerable down-side risk, and *laissez faire* economic policy are sometimes believed to be immune to economic problems on the scale revealed in the USSR by a concerted and well-funded research effort in the West during the Cold War. Closer examination suggests that this "holier-than-thou" attitude is misplaced.

The agricultural crisis in modern Russia vividly illustrates a number of economic issues with widespread applicability. The distinction between growth and development is a case in point. The Soviet Union attained impressive levels of growth, yet this growth ultimately proved unsustainable. Secondly, the "capitalist" habit of mind which fascinated Schumpeter was evident in **Soviet** agriculture, working around the "system." As was the case in the Soviet period, the primary problem agricultural enterprises now face in Russia is the motivation of the work force. Western businesses under competitive pressure have come to the same realisation and they, too, are attempting to harness the potential inherent in human behaviour to achieve corporate objectives. Thirdly, it is not public policy *per se* which is an impediment to economic activity, but the discontinuities in public policy and the frequency with which policy changes are introduced which are the more serious problem. Fourthly, the Soviet experience in agriculture vividly illustrates the importance of feedback mechanisms in evolutionary economics by providing a large-scale case study of what happens when these mechanisms are impaired or inoperable.

The case of Soviet agriculture is used here to illustrate how technical change governs the co-evolution of economic and institutional infrastructure. During the Soviet period, the state was motivated to invest in agriculture by the political risk inherent in a hungry population. The institutional infrastructure which constrained innovation and ignored market signals promoted resource-consuming and unstable growth, but not efficiency-enhancing development.

Market economy theory suggests that the reverse should also be true: institutional infrastructure which facilitates innovation in response to market feedback should foster robust and efficiency-enhancing development. Yet institutions often constrain pursuit of economic efficiency: as Eliasson (1997) points out, mixed economies too often impede innovation in the public sector and the efficiencies theoretically obtainable from privatisation are often foregone in the face of opposition articulated or threatened via the democratic process.

2 The practical problems

The superficial similarity of Russia's agricultural enterprises to those in the West leads foreign specialists to focus their attention on the institutional framework within which agriculture operated during the Soviet period. These institutions evolved in unique circumstances and, from a western perspective, the results are bizarre. The most bizarre of all, collective farming of land owned by the state on a massive scale, has attracted well-intentioned but largely ineffective remedial assistance. The prevailing argument implicit in much of the foreign sponsored technical assistance efforts is essentially that the necessary physical infrastructure seems to be in place, so the bottleneck must lie in the institutional infrastructure with which donors are unfamiliar.

Technical assistance efforts which fall into this trap do so for a variety of reasons. Chief among these are an inadequate appreciation of the evolutionary path taken by Russian agriculture prior to Perestroika and failure to understand the pivotal role of technical change in economic evolution. There is considerable reluctance to ask the question: "What **should** the infrastructure of Russian agriculture look like given the unique circumstances in which it has evolved?"

2.1 Background and current situation

Marx, as Rosenberg has pointed out (1991, p 8), was acutely aware that socialism was ill-equipped to deliver improvements in economic **efficiency**: he recognised that socialism would only therefore be a (popular) option once society as a whole was satiated with the high standard of living that only capitalism, with its unique ability to foster economic efficiency enhancing technical change, was capable of delivering. This point was, unfortunately for Russia, lost on the Bolsheviks in 1917 when they hijacked a "populist uprising by peasants and their soldier sons" for their own purposes (van der Post, 1994, p 137).

Collectivisation was introduced to facilitate the extension of a command "economy" and tight social control across an immense geography, to accelerate the "development" of a medieval agriculture (Fitzpatrick, 1994, p 25) and extract surplus value generated by the rural economy to fund a programme of rapid industrialisation. The devastating impact of forced collectivisation on Soviet agriculture is now well known: Stalin allegedly confided to Churchill that collectivisation was even more devastating than the War (van der Post, 1994, p 135).

As a consequence of collectivisation, agricultural workers were deprived of their responsibilities as stewards of agricultural resources, renounced their own knowledge and experience base in favour of an industrial agriculture foisted upon them by distant bureaucrats, lost any sense of pride in their craft work and were made subservient to scientifically trained "specialists." Peasants were always considered economically and politically retarded, perennially susceptible to bourgeois capitalism, and therefore distrusted. They were "the least among equals" in highly class-conscious Soviet society.

The inadequacies of agriculture under Stalin figured prominently in the "Secret Speech" in which the political accountability argument was used to advantage by Khrushchev in his bid for power. Khrushchev made a rod for his own back with promises to improve the material well-being of consumers and both he and his successor Brezhnev borrowed agricultural technology abroad. His celebrated campaign to introduce widespread corn production into Soviet agriculture was inspired by his visit to the Iowa farm of Roswell Garst. (If Roswell Garst was not on the CIA's payroll, he should have been.) Khrushchev also addressed the question of the country's food grain supply: his campaign to extend agriculture into the Virgin Lands of northern Kazakhstan and Western Siberia was a success insofar as it met the nation's bread grain requirements and enabled Russia to again become a net grain exporter, albeit briefly.

Brezhnev was less successful in his attempts to raise the quality of the Soviet diet by increasing meat supplies. Broiler production technology was imported and the principle of "industrial style" production complexes was extended to other types of livestock and applied on a massive and counterproductive scale. Rural out-migration reached epidemic proportions during the 1960s, precipitating a series of crises which culminated in bread riots in some cities. These difficulties, which still loom large in the collective memory, forced an administrative policy switch from the "stick" to the "carrot." Fortunately, as a result of the oil price "shocks" of the early 1970s, the State found itself in a position to alleviate the economic plight of the rural population by manipulating agricultural input and output prices. It is important to note, however, that these relative improvements were not a consequence of economic **development**: increased agricultural investment was rewarded by sharply diminished returns (inevitably, as will be explained later) throughout the later decades of the Soviet period (Nikolsky, 1996). Nor were the much vaunted improvements in wages reflected in a higher standard of living: although rural workers were better off financially, the perpetual shortages of consumer goods which the Soviet economy entailed—especially in the countryside—meant very limited opportunities to spend their new found wealth. The impact on the morale of those in agriculture who felt they were working in enterprises which were demonstrably more "prosperous" than they had been a few decades before, and had savings accumulating in the bank, should not, however, be underestimated.

Agriculture in Russia was totally unprepared for Perestroika. Although Perestroika was widely accepted among cynical Muscovites as inevitable, "Moscow is not Russia." The majority of those active in the rural economy still believed that they were working toward the "bright future," the mission statement of Soviet ideology, when Perestroika shattered their world. The **illusion** that the rural economy had "developed" dramatically according to the criteria adopted under the Soviet system made the let-down that much more devastating when it was revealed that those criteria were wholly artificial. Savings disappeared quickly in the post-Perestroika inflation. It is no wonder, therefore, that those involved in Russian agriculture feel bewildered and betrayed by post-Perestroika events.

2.2 The agro-technical legacy of Soviet socialism

Readers will no doubt be quick to point out that rural-out migration (mentioned above) is, in market economy contexts, not necessarily disruptive of agricultural production: a smoothly functioning technical change mechanism would instigate the adoption of labour-saving devices and practices. This begs the question why similar adjustments did not occur under Socialism. In his landmark paper, Rosenberg (1991) (summarised in the next few paragraphs) explains why the contrast between a market economy and a centrally planned economy is nowhere more apparent than in the field of technical change:

In a market economy, technical change is driven both by the significant opportunities for economic gain from doing things somewhat differently and from the substantial risks of failing to innovate in an environment containing competitors who are likely to do so. Decentralisation of decision-making among substantial numbers of economic agents who lack the economic or political power to prevent independent assessment of the merits of their "way of doing things"[2] relative to those of others is perhaps the most distinctive feature of a market economy.

2 Boulding (1969) coined this comprehensive definition of technical change which serves the purpose well.

A command and control economy, on the other hand, is distinguished by a built-in aversion to the adoption of new technologies. The negligible freedom of action to determine "the way things are done" accorded to enterprise managers in the Soviet period was one of the consequences. The Soviet economy was strongly oriented to short term, growth oriented goals. Changes in "the way things are done" inevitably impede growth because they entail a high cost in terms of disruption of production, re-tooling, re-training and (in the Soviet system, the very difficult task of) reorganising the supply of necessary inputs. Therefore changes in technology were introduced wholesale across the sector when a decision was made centrally to do so, not autonomously by individual economic agents acting independently.

This is not to say that the Soviet Union was unable to import or develop new technology: it did both and its research efforts at the primary end of the R&D spectrum were internationally respected. Difficulties arose in the translation of the technical know-how into products and practices which had **economic merit**. As Soviet socialism depended on smoke and mirrors on a gigantic scale in economic matters, increased awareness in the West of the profoundly **economic** character of the technical change mechanism goes a long way toward explaining these difficulties in the Soviet context.

While the technical change mechanism in general differs between market and centrally planned economies, the operation of this mechanism in their respective agricultural sectors provides an extreme example. In market economies, the devolution of decision-making among large numbers of agricultural producers, generally in the position of "price takers," biases technical change heavily toward economic efficiency: individual producers who have little or no control over the prices they receive for their output can maintain profitability only by successively lowering their costs per unit of output—in essence by "doing more with less." Under these circumstances the technology mix, and hence the intensity of production, is conditioned by spatial and temporal variations in the economic signals received. Communication and feedback between producers and suppliers of inputs on the one hand, and producers and consumers on the other—conducted in the language of economics—theoretically ensures that the intensity of production is economically appropriate at discrete points in space and time.[3] This is a **necessary** condition for true economic development, characterised by efficiency-enhancing innovation.

In a market economy then, the efficiency with which adjustment of "the way things are done" occurs depends primarily on the communication of economic information to decision-makers with a minimum of distortion and the ability of economic agents to make qualitative assessments of the consequences. In the face of competition, the induced innovation mechanism ensures that the way things are done is adjusted solely according to economic criteria. The pace of technical change has therefore accelerated in most western industries as increased economic **efficiency** has been sought in response to heightened competition.

The Soviet economy, on the other hand, was strongly biased in favour of **growth**-enhancing rather than **efficiency**-enhancing objectives. A growth-oriented economy is characterised by efforts to mobilise resources—human and natural—in the economic process. A growth orientation is feasible so long as the necessary resources are readily available. Access to the resources of the New World and the exploitation of coal and labour to transform them was a feature of the industrial revolution which fascinated Marx. The rapid *growth* of the Soviet Union was a cause of considerable disquiet in the West early in the Soviet period (e g Zavalani, 1951 & Duncan, 1956). Paul Krugman (1996, Chapter 11) has recently questioned the sustainability of the rapid growth in East Asian economies on the basis that it, too, is **quantitative** growth rather than qualitative "growth" or **development**.

In a Socialist economy, state control over resources and prices facilitates the pursuit of growth-oriented objectives. The natural resource wealth of the Soviet Union was undoubtedly a key factor in its longevity. Additionally, one of the major criticisms of the Soviet economy was the lack of incentives

3   The work of von Thunen is the basis for a great deal of this theory in the West. The influence of labour availability on the economics of farm size—namely the greater the availability of labour, the smaller the size of the farm and vice versa—is developed in Curry (1971)

for firms to change the way things were done and indeed, the penalties they incurred if they did (Rosenberg, 1991, p 23). The perpetual sellers market, the lack of competition, the scale of Soviet industrial enterprises, the concentrated pattern of investment decision-making and the fact that the economic process was "top-down" rather than "bottom-up" were all factors. The net consequence was that, despite world-class primary research in many fields, it was almost impossible to implement the theoretical strides made by the Soviet scientific establishment in practical applications which met economic, efficiency-enhancing, objectives.

Under Soviet socialism, technological decision-making was concentrated at the apex of the command and control pyramid and the state also tended to absorb transportation costs for both inputs and outputs. Hence there were reasons on both the supply side and the demand side why agricultural practices tended to be the same across the country irrespective of local conditions. Yet in order for agriculture to play its assigned role in socialist society all enterprises **had** to be "profitable" and in the absence of inter-enterprise competition the only way to guarantee this outcome was wholesale application of "cost-plus" pricing complemented as necessary with subsidies. There was no effective feedback mechanism operating between the suppliers and users of agricultural technology, nor between agricultural producers and the consumers of agricultural output.

Nor was it generally possible, given the way the Soviet economy functioned, to spontaneously induce the adoption of know-how developed elsewhere in the same practical way. This avenue, which most other nations have historically used to short-cut the arduous and inefficient process of reinventing everything themselves, was to some extent closed-off by ideology alone. In a market economy, those enterprises which are able to capitalise on acquired technology are those receptive to new ideas in the first place and possess a highly innovative corporate culture which modifies and improves the new product or technique in order to leap-frog the originators of the technology in the market place. In the Soviet case just the opposite situation obtained: acquisition of the latest (or more likely, slightly obsolete) technology almost guaranteed that it would be applied widely and with much less effect, and that it would not be "obsoleted" in the Soviet context for a considerable period of time. The fact that agriculture was one sector in which technology imports **were made** on a substantial scale is also significant: it suggests a degree of desperation on the part of those in power when it came to agricultural matters.

The Soviet economy intentionally constrained competition, and the implications of this fact for the technical change, which **did** occur in the Soviet context, are important. As in other sectors, agricultural technology during the Soviet period was not allowed to evolve on the basis of large numbers of independent experiments in productivity improvement. In the absence of any operating feedback mechanism, the question what Russian agriculture **needed** was rarely asked. Agriculture was allocated copious quantities of what the state **believed** it required. Nor was there any mechanism for the rigorous and dispassionate means of evaluating the economic merits of the particular style of technical change foisted on the sector from above.

Each year agricultural enterprises **had** to be able to consume the impressive volumes of industrial output faithfully recorded in *Narodnoe khozaistvo*, the compendium of Soviet statistics, whether they needed them or not. Little effort was expended attempting to supply equipment differentiated according to the conditions prevailing at particular locations across the country: scale economies dictated that it was preferable to produce large amounts of a small range of models. In the Soviet context, there was no (independent) price mechanism to measure the relative demand for slightly differentiated products. Quantity generally took precedence over quality and, as in the west, "what gets measured, gets done." The tendency to measure units and weight would therefore naturally predispose the Soviet tractor industry to produce large, heavy, but under-powered units (low power-to-weight ratio) although the tractor industry in the rest of the world evolved in exactly the opposite direction. Durability was similarly a liability: large amounts of new equipment had to be delivered each year, and all enterprises had to take their share.

The industrial structure supporting agriculture also had to be profitable and agriculture therefore had to be in a position to pay for its "requirements." Fortunately, as the state controlled the prices of everything, this could be arranged. Agriculture, too, had to be seen to be profitable, and the pricing of output was therefore based on production costs plus an appropriate profit margin. Thus, in addition to the direct subsidisation of inputs, agricultural output was purchased at high prices to accommodate this "cost plus" approach, and then resold to a captive domestic market at much lower prices to prevent unmanageable discontent among the urban populace.

Insofar as fiddling input and commodity prices did not work, demand could be sustained on the strength of soft credits allocated to agriculture with little hope of repayment. The expectations that new equipment and other inputs would be provided one way or another each growing season eliminated the need for any asset stewardship ethic: if it broke, it could be replaced; if it was wasted, more could be obtained. The ready availability of soft credits naturally stimulated demand in the required fashion: the more nominal the cost of credit the greater the demand for new "toys" and hence the greater the addiction to soft credits.

During the summer of 1995, the administration made a concerted effort to bring inflation under control in an effort to stabilise the economy, attract further foreign financial assistance, and pave the way for victory by reformist elements in the forthcoming elections. Agriculture bore the brunt of this lurch toward fiscal rectitude as the flow of state funds to the countryside finally dried up. A "payables" credit program was substituted under which a modest array of agricultural inputs (fuel, seed and fertiliser) could be obtained on the basis of forward commodity contracts deliverable at the end of the growing season. The high implicit cost of this form of credit was reminiscent of the Soviet era efforts to extract surpluses from the countryside. Yet, in the absence of any alternatives, many enterprises were forced to obtain a payables credit without any expectation that they would be in a position to fulfil the obligations assumed. As the "payables'" credit initiative was announced in conjunction with other schemes for debt restructuring—including interest forgiveness and postponed repayment—the traditional attitude to apparently "soft" credits was reinforced.

Ironically, concerted efforts to emulate the modern industrial mode of production which Soviet planners believed lay behind the superior productivity of western agriculture is one of the main reasons that Russian agriculture came to superficially resemble the "mechanically elaborate" but "agronomically primitive" agriculture which developed on the North American prairies and plains (Joravsky, 1967, p 157). In the process, of course, Russian agricultural enterprises became as dependent as their North American counterparts on purchased inputs. Another, complementary, objective of Russian agriculture was massive consumption of the output of an industrial complex installed to match and surpass that of the "competition," most notably the United States.

Industries supplying agricultural inputs in Russia in effect loosely co-evolved with those elsewhere. Yet while the foreign technology was developed to enhance the market competitiveness of the firm selling it—and the efficiency-enhancing objectives of those purchasing it—when it was transferred into the Eastern Bloc it was mass-produced in order to meet growth-oriented criteria against which the "success" of the Soviet economy was measured. From an economic perspective, a great deal was lost in the translation.

To cite just one example: Massey-Ferguson combine harvesters used to "disappear" regularly following agricultural exhibitions in the Soviet Union (e g Duncan, 1956, p 29 and personal communication with Allan Neal, former Chief Combine Engineer, and Arnott Neals, former Export Sales Director). Soviet industry may well have been able to reproduce all the components, but there is a considerable element of "black art" involved in putting the bits together so that they work properly. In the West, the main criteria farmers use when buying a combine is grain loss from the back of the unit. In the Soviet Union, the objective was to produce the largest possible number of combine-like machines which cut grain. Grain loss was not a relevant criteria in the Soviet system, and hence the "black-art" element was irrelevant.

Although introduction of a market economy by executive *fiat* implies a switch to appropriate success criteria such as grain loss, replacing the entire equipment park of Russian agriculture is not a simple matter. Vast numbers of similar examples illustrate why an economic system which has gone down one path for so long cannot easily or quickly respond to privatisation and competition. In other words, not only is a different direction implied, but a different path completely —one to which the technological legacy of the Soviet period prevents direct access.

The Soviet economy was also characterised by an almost complete absence of down-side risk, a very significant spur to innovation in market economies. Although farm managers were of course replaced or reassigned, farms were never closed down, everybody was guaranteed a job and recourse to private subsidiary agricultural ("private plot") production mitigated the incentive to work diligently in the collective sphere.

The most important implication of all this is simply that *the embodied technology of post-Soviet agriculture was created to meet criteria which were independent from and had little or nothing to do with the **development** of the agricultural economy*. Instead the system was optimised to attain growth-oriented objectives which encouraged the maximal mobilisation of resources, not their efficient utilisation.

In a market economy, agricultural producers have to concentrate on those commodities it is profitable to produce, and produce only those quantities which are profitable. The quantity of output of a particular commodity produced depends on the manner in which it is produced, or the intensity of production. By definition, intensive production means expensive production, involving a considerable expenditure of labour and/or purchased inputs. Intensive production and the high production costs it entails is warranted only if the prices received for the end product are sufficiently high to generate a profit.

Intensity of agricultural production at a particular point in space and time is, in effect, the bundle of techniques or ways of doing things applied. One shorthand way for comparing intensity of agricultural practices involves an assessment of the inputs required to produce a particular amount of output. At the "extensive" end of the spectrum, natural processes account for the bulk of the energy flow (Boserup, 1968, p 104). As more intensive use is made of available natural resources, the amount of man-made inputs increases. Greater effort—whether direct effort in the form of human labour or indirect effort embodied in commodities such as fertiliser, fuel and agricultural chemicals—drives the intensification effort. In the effort to increase production by more intensive use of available resources, diminishing returns are inevitable: each successive increase in energy, money or labour expended generates on average a smaller corresponding output. Depending on the relative prices of the respective factors, the process of feedback and adjustment inherent in induced innovation alters the mix in order to maximise the viability of the enterprise.

Although there is a link between agricultural development and the intensity of agricultural production in the minds of many, the linkage is not a direct one. Intensity of agricultural production is an absolute measure of the resources expended in production, whereas development measures the efficiency with which those resources are employed. It is therefore just as possible to have an extensive agricultural system which is highly developed as it is to have an intensive mode of agricultural production which is underdeveloped. Due to the unique and insulated circumstances in which it evolved, agricultural production in Russia at the end of the Soviet period was uniformly **intensive** yet **underdeveloped**.

The manner in which technical change was imposed "from the top" and the inherent lack of flexibility or "robustness" which the Soviet system required contributed both to agriculture's "under-development" and the persistence of that under-development in the post-Perestroika period. It is to the persistence of the "under-development" in the post-Perestroika period, and the role of public sector infrastructure as a contributing factor to which we now turn.

Perestroika marked the end of autarkic policies and opened the country to imports. The fortunes of Russians have diverged considerably as a consequence of Perestroika: many families find themselves much better off in relative terms than they did during the Soviet period; many others have been economically disadvantaged by the post-Perestroika changes. Both facets of this divergence have negative implications for domestic agriculture: those who are better off have rising expectations both in terms of the quality and variety of the food they eat and the financial means to gratify those expectations. At present this group is forced to satisfy its requirements primarily with imported foodstuffs. Those who find themselves worse off are increasingly reliant on the personal production of private and *dacha* plots and the informal mechanisms of exchange which integrate these sources of supply into the economy. Between these two extremes, the vast majority of Russians now take advantage of access to high quality imported foodstuffs to the extent that their circumstances allow. This ranges from an occasional treat—a banana purchased from street vendors or a visit to a western style restaurant—to regular purchases of imported foods in local shops and kiosks. Perestroika placed Russian agriculture, which had favoured high cost production of low-quality products, in direct competition with agriculture elsewhere which had evolved favouring high-quality, low-cost output. The results were predictable. In the context of Russian agriculture the post-1986 shift toward political and economic liberalisation is justifiably referred to as "catastroika."

When an inefficient (i e underdeveloped), but intensive (i e inherently high production cost) agricultural system spanning eight time zones loses a substantial share of its previously captive market, the results are bound to be devastating. However, it is the loss of transportation subsidies and the lack of alternative employment outside agriculture, coupled with the aversion to being too far removed from food which Russian history has inculcated in the inhabitants, which underlies the shift to locally oriented subsistence agriculture across much of the country. Rural poverty, uncertainty about the future, and the tax system—addressed in the next section—contribute to making low-risk, subsistence agriculture the desirable option.

Perestroika also forced the state to relinquish much of its price manipulation and subsidy role. Perestroika thus marked the end of a "static" operating environment in which changes were instigated only after considerable study and debate among upper echelon *apparatchiks*. As a consequence of Perestroika, the economic environment became dynamic and, initially at least, highly unstable as market forces working from the bottom up began to exert their influence. The whole concept of an economy as a self-organising structure is very difficult for Russians to grasp, and this is perhaps the greatest single impediment to market-oriented reforms. Yet such an attitude is understandable in the light of a political history featuring autocratic rule by edicts (*ykazi*) "from the top." Soviet socialism extended the "top down" process into the economy with a vengeance.

The main symptom of the current problem is the manner in which Russian agricultural enterprises have responded to the sharp deterioration in their terms of trade. A sharp decline in output is the obvious, and anticipated, response. Indeed the collapse of Russia's agricultural production in the post-Perestroika period, which is much lamented in the Russian corridors of power and in the press by those who don't appreciate a fine example of induced innovation in action, **should** be hailed as evidence that Russian agricultural workers, like their counterparts elsewhere in the world do not engage in their vocation simply for the good of their health.[4]

Perestroika abruptly rendered growth-oriented "success indicators" obsolete, along with the state infrastructure which facilitated this orientation. Efficiency-enhancing development objectives were substituted, but the sector proved unable to respond to the new stimuli. The decline in production has been precipitous because enterprises are incapable of altering their "way of doing things." It is locked into a high-cost mode of production, but can no longer afford the inputs such a mode of production entails. Post-Perestroika changes have rendered Soviet-style production economically obsolete and efforts to continue the intensive yet underdeveloped production regime of the Soviet period, without access to the inputs on which such a mode of production depends, makes failure relative to the new criteria inevitable.

---

4   Farmers everywhere are under constant and sometimes subtle pressure from urban-inspired cheap (retail) food policies, often implemented in the form of expensive subsidies. Reed (1995) discusses how these tax-funded subsidies are appropriated by the middlemen. Georgescu-Roegen (1960) explored the role of urban bias in the formulation of various generations of economic theory, and especially as it relates to Marxism and its descendants. (Summarised in Georgescu-Roegen 1965.)

The technological strait-jacket in which Russian agricultural enterprises find themselves is symptomatic of their "under-development." The causes of this technological paralysis include the following:

One of the chief legacies of the Soviet period is an inherently high-cost production **mentality** in the agricultural sector. The intensive and industrial mode of production favoured in the Soviet system was characterised by a highly specialised labour force at the farm enterprise level, very heavy reliance on industrial inputs, large-scale confinement livestock production complexes, the allocation of considerable resources to fodder production and a large-scale, highly mechanised and chemically dependent approach to field crop production. **This mode of production, uniformly applied across the USSR, was sustained solely by the artificial pricing regime which prevailed during the Soviet period.**

Pre-Perestroika agriculture had a built-in ideological bias in favour of large-scale and intensive production methods. This bias was sustained by the strong growth-orientation of Soviet "economics" including the lavish subsidisation of the sector, cost-plus pricing and unlimited demand for the output of the sector as a consequence of protectionism and the perpetual sellers market engendered by the Soviet system. Transportation costs tended to be absorbed by the state and outputs and inputs were priced uniformly "at the farm gate" irrespective of location. In many respects, including centralised decision-making, the minimisation of the friction of distance effect on the inputs supplied to the sector and the output delivered to the state and the lack of inter-enterprise competition, *Soviet agriculture could be thought of as one big farm.*

In a market economy where a wide range of agricultural technologies **are** available to produce a particular commodity, and where the intensity of production is dictated by the location and the specific economic circumstances of the farm enterprise, the product/technology mix is almost infinitely adjustable. Yet the Soviet system not only imposed a specified technology and product mix on agricultural enterprises through a hierarchical system of command and control, it also actively discriminated against alternative "ways of doing things." As a consequence, although the whole system may have been viable under the peculiar rules of the game under which it operated during the Soviet period, **it was completely dependent on the continued application of precisely those same rules.** The whole system evolved to suit a static economic environment dominated by centralised decision-making.

Intensive, high-cost production was, unfortunately, the only sanctioned mode of production mandated across the entire sector. Alternative, lower cost ways of doing things were not developed in parallel, and if such alternatives had been practised prior to collectivisation, much of the know-how was lost during the Soviet period. This fact made the entire system exceptionally vulnerable to changes in the *status quo.*

It is worth speculating whether the process of technical change evident in agriculture during the Soviet period can be characterised as "induced innovation" in any meaningful sense. Schumpeter, after all, took a very broad view of the ability of a capitalist "habit of mind" to influence aspects of life (such as hospitals) not normally subject to profit-maximising behaviour (Rosenberg, 1993, p 10). The "capitalist habit of mind" conjures up a willingness to adopt efficiency enhancing innovations without it being "induced" by profit-maximising behaviour. Yet an evolutionary perspective on economic activity substitutes the more comprehensive notion of enterprise viability for the neo-classical "profitability" success criteria (see Section 3.1, below): in an environment in which public expenditure is being curbed, efficiency-enhancing innovations are indeed "induced" in the public sector. In the socialist context, characterised by "imposed" innovation, unlimited demand, guaranteed profitability, total absence of meaningful inter-enterprise competition for markets, and no feedback mechanism, the "capitalist habit of mind" was exercised mainly in those few activities, including private plot agriculture, not part of the state structure. The contrast in Russian agriculture between the development achieved in the private plot sector and the under-development of the state sector underscores the central role of a bottom-up induced innovation process in economic development. In terms of technical change at least, it is therefore misleading to think of Soviet socialism as "State Capitalism:"

the distinguishing role of public sector institutions in "Capitalism" is the devolution of economic decision-making.

There is currently a great deal of speculation as to whether Russian peasants are in some way fundamentally different from other people: Do they in fact have this "capitalist habit of mind" after 70 or so years of Soviet socialism which drained initiative and intelligence from the countryside and left the rural population disproportionately elderly and debilitated by alcoholism? Those arguing in favour of a negative answer to this question inevitably conclude that the process of agricultural reconstruction in Russia will be exceptionally protracted.

One source of optimism on this issue is the considerable ingenuity workers and managers can bring to bear to circumvent any "system" imposed on them. Russian agriculture is no exception. It is indeed probable that the institutional constraints imposed on this "capitalist habit of mind" during the Soviet period stimulated its development.[5] The blossoming of the *"mafiya"* and the incredible wealth of the so-called New Russians who allegedly now monopolise the most expensive hotel rooms in London, New York, Paris and Geneva corroborates this view. Unfortunately, however, agriculture is a very public activity—it is difficult to hide the factors of production from nosy neighbours, an intrusive bureaucracy and, ultimately, from a punitive tax regime. As such agriculture itself

5   The ingenuity brought to bear by Russian agricultural workers getting around the system is both encouraging and frustrating. One year I was sceptical when one of the enterprises I was working with started to report a sharp increase in milk yields to the local authorities. After some time I discovered that although all the cows were being milked, a number had been designated as "culls" and were being excluded from the yield calculation. The point, of course, is that in a market economy, these sort of games make absolutely no sense; in the Soviet period they were part of the process by which the "mice buried the cat" or the little people undermined the Party bosses (Fitzpatrick, 1994 esp Ch 11).

On the same farm, one of the new leaders acquired a field of autumn-sown crops only to discover at harvest time that the field had only been sown around the edges: much of the fuel and seed allocated to it in the spring had presumably been diverted to other uses. Schumpeter's observation that "the peasant sells his calf just as cunningly and egotistically as the stock exchange member his portfolio of shares" (quoted by Georgescu-Roegen, 1965, p 199) suggests that he too would expect "the capitalist habit of mind" to be particularly robust in the Russian countryside.

remains immune to the "mafiya," a distinction which is both a blessing and an indictment.

Of course the problem of motivation is not unique to Russian agricultural enterprises. In any organisation—whether big business, big government or big farms—motivation of the work force is a major problem. Where it has been able to solve this problem, collective agriculture—in the form of Hutterite colonies—has proved very competitive in Canada. Private farming also remains successful where the small number of individuals directly involved are motivated and there are a broad array of external support services available, each of which is provided on a competitive basis. Although there is considerable stigma attached to "corporate" agriculture in some quarters, its economic success is self-evident where either the motivational challenge has been met and/or where it is actively abetted by government policy, notwithstanding the fact that employees are not owners.

2.3 Current dilemmas

Organisations involved in technical assistance efforts are interventionist by definition and frequently paternalistic by inclination: In the case of eastern Europe this is particularly dangerous because there is a natural affinity between the purveyors of "technical assistance" and those elements of the bureaucracy which are most reactionary. One of the important lessons of an evolutionary approach to economics is that efficiency improvements derive from a bottom-up process—individual decision-makers responding independently to economic signals as they deem appropriate according to their unique circumstances. Yet "development" in the minds of many western "specialists" also seems to be something that must be imposed from the top.

In most countries where "development" is considered desirable, the existing technology **is** the product of the prevailing economics. In these circumstances, well-intentioned foreign assistance efforts designed to convince the decision-makers that other people in **different** economic circumstances know better are almost invariably doomed to failure. The lesson of induced innovation theory for those in the technical assistance business is therefore usually a painful one.

In Russia in the post-Perestroika period, however, just the opposite situation exists: radical changes in the economic rules of the game have rendered the entrenched technology non-viable. The systemic bias against technical change, distortions in the economic signals and lack of awareness of alternative production strategies combine to impede the adjustments in "the way things are done" which are now urgently required by the dramatic adverse post-Perestroika shift in the sector's terms of trade.

The evident need for a shift toward a more highly developed, but extensive mode of agricultural production outlined above is therefore frustrated by the lack of the know-how required to sharply reduce the production costs. Faced as it is with a dearth of capital (and who can be expected to invest under the current circumstances?) Russia's agricultural sector needs to substitute labour and know-how for capital. The aversion of Russian agricultural workers to physical labour is well entrenched. This is the legacy of decades spent attempting to emulate their urban proletarian colleagues to the maximum extent possible. The standard reaction of Russian agricultural workers who visit farms elsewhere is surprise at the amount of physical work entailed. After decades of concerted effort to eliminate local initiative and remove decision-making capability from the countryside, it is difficult to reverse these trends. Hence while the need for technical innovation to reduce the production cost base and improve the quality of output is acute, the potential to do so is, in the short term, exceptionally low.

More widespread awareness of lower-cost production strategies is now urgently required in the Russian context. Unfortunately, foreign agribusiness concerns are (naturally enough) only interested in selling high-cost solutions to production problems and therefore risk repeating some of the longer-term sociological and "technological treadmill" problems which arose from the application of "Green Revolution" technology in other contexts. Pride makes the old guard bureaucrats allies for such interests because they are (again, naturally enough) reluctant to admit that the push toward "high tech," industrial agriculture during the Soviet period, was part of the problem, not the solution.

The potential for profitable production is a necessary stimulus for innovations which reduce the cost of production and increase the quality and quantity of available food by a process of specialisation, rationalisation and geographical redistribution of production. In the Soviet period, the institutionalised discrimination against innovation and experimentation at the enterprise level prevented this from happening. The lack of inter-enterprise competition, a captive domestic market and an ideologically motivated desperation to "succeed" in agriculture caused the state to pay high prices for low-quality agricultural output. In doing so they sanctioned low quality, increased the cost of production and provided a rationale for a vast array of subsidies on purchase prices, subsidies in the form of soft credits, a vast bureaucracy to administer an artificial system of fixed prices and the subsidies which attempted to counter-balance its adverse impacts.

In the post-Perestroika period the possibility of profitable production appears remote to those who now—and for the first time—find themselves cast in the role of decision-makers by the privatisation process which is imposed by the State and abetted by well-meaning trans-national institutions which (incidentally) also operate outside the framework of market economics. Demand has dwindled in the face of imports. The lack of reform in domestic "upstream" agricultural input supply and "downstream" food-processing and distribution means that agriculture is expected to continue to pay high input prices and receive low output prices to cover inefficiencies in these ancillary sectors. Without the potential for profit from agricultural production there is naturally a reluctance to invest in the sector.

Another major impediment to providing economic incentives to Russian agricultural enterprises is the tax system within which they operate. Notwithstanding the sharp deterioration in its terms of trade, the agricultural sector remains the subject of a vast array of punitive taxes. Laws and decrees designed to mitigate these burdens are on the books, but largely ignored. The prevailing attitude to the agricultural sector remains much as it was during the Soviet period: one way or another the urban-based bureaucracy remains bent on confiscating the surplus economic value generated by the sector. In addition to the high absolute level of taxation, the complexity of the system and the uneven manner in which it is enforced compounds the marked disincentive to economic exertion (outside the private plot sector) inherent in the tax regime.

There are considerable differences in tax burden according to the type of agricultural enterprise. The tax system has, unfortunately, been used as a carrot to encourage certain forms of organisational change in Russian agriculture. This is counter-productive because it opens the methodology which has been granted privileged status to the valid criticism that is benefiting from preferential treatment. Such preferential treatment hinders efforts to argue the case for reform on its economic merits. All enterprises, and certainly all agricultural enterprises, should be treated equally under the tax laws.

One of the arguments for privatisation of agricultural land is that ownership is a necessary condition for land stewardship and the implementation of sustainable agricultural practices. Once again this tends to be an external view, derived from oft-quoted sentiments regarding the superiority of ownership over tenancy. Arthur Young (1741–1820) who wrote "Give a man the secure possession of a bleak rock and he will turn it into a garden; give him a nine year lease on a garden and he will turn it into a desert" (Hardin, 1993, p 216) is a typical example.

Sustainability of agricultural systems is frequently thought of in terms of the relationship between production practices and the productive potential of the underlying physical resources. Practices which impair the productive potential of the physical resources on which agriculture depend therefore tend to be termed "unsustainable" while those which maintain or enhance the productive potential of the environment are labelled "sustainable."

This view is, however, a dangerous oversimplification: in a subsistence economy where the producers are indefinitely dependent solely on the long-term productivity of local resources, subsistence exploitation of those resources occurs irrespective of the form of ownership. Subsistence agriculture is almost by definition sustainable because the survival of the community involved depends on maintaining the long-term productive potential of the resource base.

Private ownership of land in the absence of external economic incentives to produce a surplus would therefore be expected to precipitate a widespread regression to "sustainable" subsistence agriculture, and this seems to be occurring in Russia on a wide scale.

Problems of "sustainability" arise when there is pressure or incentive to produce a surplus from outside the enterprise. In the Soviet period when "surplus value" was "snatched away by a repressive regime" state ownership of land did not produce the desired results in terms of the stewardship of agricultural resources.[6] In a market economy where there are economic incentives to produce a surplus sustainability is a concept which has no meaning outside economics (Reed, 1993b). Agricultural producers are not interested in "environmentally appropriate" practices advocated by those espousing sustainability for moral or ethical reasons. Absent influences to the contrary, an owner would always tend to adopt those practices which are economically viable and sufficiently replenish the productive potential of the resource base to permit future viability. This is true because the economic self-interest of the producer is best served by optimising both current and future economic viability: insofar as the economic value of agricultural land is the net present value of future cash flow generated by that resource, it is in his interest to maintain or enhance its value as well as realising a return on an annual basis.[7]

6 Viktor Shevelukha, a Communist deputy in the State Duma, described the predecessor regime in these terms, admitting this particular failing of the Soviet system an article on agricultural issues in *The Moscow Times* (Shevelukha, 1995).

7 Widespread misconceptions among Russians about the constraints imposed on agricultural land use by a market economy context, never mind the considerable rights (taxation, expropriation etc) retained by the State, is unfortunate but symptomatic of the tendency to miss-communication between Russians and foreigners on these often emotional issues. If the whole privatisation process would refer to usufruct rights which were tradable, instead of land ownership rights which are—at least in the short term—generally not tradable, both sides might be satisfied.

Whether or not a particular bundle of production practices increases or decreases sustainability is, at the time it is selected, a function of the decision-maker's appreciation of the long- and short-term economic costs of the option chosen and his weighting of short vs long-term objectives. The trouble is, of course, that to implement sustainable land management practices tomorrow one has to survive economically today: this is why producer poverty is the enemy of sustainable land use in all contexts, including Russian agriculture.

One of the key features of any discussion of sustainability in the context of a market economy agriculture needs to be the extent to which government intervention leads producers to favour the short term over the long term in their economic decisions. In the post-Perestroika case, insufficient economic incentive and short-time horizons are likely to overwhelm any positive influence of ownership in determining whether sustainable agricultural practices will be adopted outside the subsistence-oriented rural economy.

In China, where agricultural reforms have **not** extended to private ownership of land, but **have** facilitated decollectivisation, food production has soared as market-derived incentives have replaced local self-sufficiency as the primary motivating factor. Here state-owned but household "managed" private plots are being effectively farmed under the household responsibility system. These plots have much in common with the private and *dacha* plots which are a feature of the Russian landscape. Russia too could feed itself on the basis of the land currently operated "privately" if it had no other choices and if the economic incentives—the prices paid by consumers—were sufficiently high. However, there are alternatives, including imports and more effective utilisation of land currently controlled by the state.

Attempts to push technical decision-making down to the individual agricultural enterprise level creates a need for the widespread dissemination of information about alternatives from which the appropriate choices can be made. The need to provide a *smorgasbord* of options and allow "self-service" on the part of the individual enterprise when it comes to making decisions whether to adopt a particular alternative cannot be emphasised enough. Naturally this is a radical departure from recent practice and it therefore encounters considerable resistance among those responsible for transforming the public infrastructure.

Resistance to the provision of the information on which to base well-informed choices can be expected because throughout the Soviet period the powerful and liberating potential of information was fully appreciated and its dissemination was tightly controlled as a consequence. Choices between technologies were taken centrally and the implementation of these choices was left to an array of specialists at the individual enterprise level. Perhaps more surprisingly, it is also resisted by potential users who are unaccustomed to the responsibilities associated with making their own decisions.

As the current generation of farm enterprise managers have been brought up in a cost-plus pricing environment, the potential for profitability via cost reduction is something of a revelation. Once this conceptual barrier has been broken, it is **relatively** simple to start introducing enterprise managers to lower-cost production strategies. Unfortunately the enterprises often have exceptionally limited resources and this dictates a low-technology approach emphasising know-how and community wide mobilisation. This goes very much against the grain of the Soviet, high-technology, "everybody's a specialist" style.

Ultimately, there is a great deal of merit in a low or appropriate technology focus: there are tremendous opportunities for improvements in productivity and efficiency via the implementation of minimal or low-cost changes in "the way things are done." Ultimately this is beneficial for the enterprise as a whole because it fosters self-reliance and discourages shifting the dependence of the farm sector from the local administration to various well-meaning foreign organisations offering high-tech "solutions." The nominal cost of "credit" and a complete absence of project cost-benefit analysis during the Soviet period makes farm enterprise managers very susceptible to capital investment, but much less adept at changing more mundane work practices, notwithstanding the fact that the latter are likely to have a much greater impact on the true economic well-being of the enterprise. There is, unfortunately, generally a bias in foreign-sponsored technical assistance efforts towards the "hardware" or the physical manifestations of "development" that can be photographed and used to justify the "good works" which are being undertaken rather than the "software" or the know-how which is less tangible but considerably more valuable.

A stable policy environment is a crucial element in fostering co-operation and investment in all sectors of the economy. The nature of agricultural production makes a degree of stability in policy particularly important. Agricultural production is reliant on natural processes, and natural processes take time. Gestation periods and growing seasons mean that production cannot be readily or rapidly adjusted in response to changes in economic signals. The slow dissemination of information in Russia regarding government initiatives in the agricultural sector and the frequent changes in those initiatives increases aversion to taking the risks always inherent in agricultural production.

The stability of the policy environment is also a prerequisite for sustainable agricultural practices: the absence of some assurance that the rights to develop a particular piece of land will be respected in the medium and longer term is a major impediment to resource stewardship. Initiatives to privatise land are less than enthusiastically received when the entitlement holders see no opportunity to utilise it because they lack assets and capital, see no opportunity to profit from their own efforts, are concerned that their initiative might cause an adverse reaction in the community in the short term, and recognise that the political will to continue the reform in the medium term is doubtful.

Agriculture has been the victim of shifting political winds in Russia for as long as anybody currently active in the sector can remember. In advance of the 1996 presidential elections there was probably a higher level of uncertainty than ever regarding the future policy direction. This was a huge disincentive to the planting of crops and reinforced the retreat of the rural economy to a subsistence footing based on private and *dacha* plot (allotment-style) production for personal consumption.

I was initially very puzzled by the almost total absence of co-operation among individuals or groups in the Russian agriculture in the post-Perestroika period. It puzzled me because immigrants from eastern Europe played a prominent role in the development of the agriculture economy of western Canada where I grew up. There, the high degree of co-operative effort and the widespread development of co-operative institutions established to address problems remarkably similar to those now faced by the agricultural sector in Russia has traditionally been attributed to the positive influence of the immigrants from eastern Europe.

The marked aversion to co-operation and altruism in the agricultural sector is understandable in the light of its current economic circumstances. There is no economic justification for closer community-wide collaboration when the pressure towards an "every-man for himself" subsistence existence is so strong, when privatisation efforts designed to institutionalise the separation of the economic and social spheres are underway, when the policy environment is so uncertain and when personal time horizons are exceptionally short-term. As the collective sector has collapsed, farm residents have been forced to devote the bulk of their energy to their own private plot production. Undoubtedly this preoccupation with private sector production has increased pilfering from the collective sector, contributing to the latter's downward spiral and exacerbating the breakdown in community cohesion.[8]

The psychological damage inflicted on Russian agriculture by Perestroika manifests itself in the negative repercussions of envy in the rural population. Everyone seems content to be

8   This is one area where evolutionary economics potentially sheds considerable light on the economic process. The study of altruism in biology has improved the understanding of the role of *Time* (see note 10 below) in decision-making. The Prisoners Dilemma is a classic example (See Cronin, 1994, especially pp 256–69).

There is also a growing literature in psychiatry suggesting that criminality is marked by a tendency to give "inadequate" weight to future (possible) punishments relative to the (more obvious) temptation of immediate gain. Students of poverty also often call attention to the fact that their subjects, as a group, seem to be deficient in their ability to defer the gratification of their desires to a distant (and hence somewhat uncertain) future. Modern civilised life demands a stronger future orientation than many seem to possess (Hardin, 1987, p 115). Fukuyama (1995) explores this theme in some detail, arguing that for a society to prosper it must engender a high level of interpersonal trust. This is the antithesis of the current situation in the Russian countryside.

Georgescu-Roegen (1965, p 207 ff) discusses the tendency towards altruism which he regards (incorrectly, I believe) as an inverse function of population pressure in an agrarian context.

miserable as long as everyone is miserable to the same extent. Those who rise above the norm risk being the victims of the reprisals to which rural residents are particularly vulnerable: arson, theft, and vandalism. There is no spirit of friendly competition or "keeping up with the Jones's" in the Russian countryside: rural fairs and agricultural exhibitions which give considerable impetus to innovation and improvement in the rural economy elsewhere are conspicuously absent.

If Schumpeter were to view a snap-shot of Russia's agricultural economy today, he would identify with the fact that "entrepreneurs" **are** considered social deviants and that the term is used disparagingly: the whole "mafiya" phenomenon is an extension of this societal view, but with the ironic twist that many of those formerly in power are now active both in the current "Hobbsian" proto-market economy and in their opposition to further reforms which might increase competition and reassert the rule of law (Handelman, 1995).

3. The implications of Soviet and post-Soviet experience for induced innovation, evolutionary economics and economic development

In the previous section, the objective was to explain why the infrastructure of post-Soviet agriculture is superficially similar to that installed in market economy contexts, but yet is almost totally inadequate to performing an **economic** role in the transitional economy which has emerged in Russia since Pereestroika.

The thesis of this section may be summarised as follows: although the problems of post-Soviet eastern Europe in general and its agricultural sector in particular are usually viewed as the unique legacy of Soviet socialism, they are frequently just exaggerated examples of the same problems evident in western market economies.

3.1 The need for appropriate and comprehensive success criteria

The chief benefit derived by economics from recourse to ecological and evolutionary theory stems from their holistic systems approach: the context is comprehensive to the point of being irrelevant and the externalities problem is thereby neatly dispensed with. The temporal and spatial dimensions of interaction are explicitly addressed; the adaptation of a species or firm over time is the product of an intra-specific process of mutation or innovation and an external, conservative, process of selection for desirable characteristics in the context of the relevant and ever changing operating environment.

Within an evolutionary economic framework, the operating environment in which the external selection process operates is the market place and the comprehensive measure of a firm's "fitness" for that environment is its shareholder value: the fitness of the firm relative to its competitive environment is continuously assessed by potential customers and investors.

For both the species (in biology) and the firm (in economics) long-term viability is the ultimate objective. Success depends on adaptation in the face of a dynamic operating environment. Changes in the behaviour of the entity are judged externally and either increase or decrease the probability for success. Survival is the long-term overriding objective, and the struggle for survival is unrelenting.

The Soviet economy was widely criticised for adopting inappropriately narrow "success criteria."[9] Yet it also used to be fashionable among western businesses to optimise business performance according to the particular short-term success measures in vogue at the time. Inevitably these campaigns are frustrated because optimisation of a single objective causes dysfunctional consequences in other dimensions. As an example, price wars between competitors are usually mutually destructive, and rare as a consequence.

Western businesses, too, have been struggling with the "success indicator" problem in recent decades. The substitution of more comprehensive and longer term success criteria

9 The considerable literature on this subject in the Soviet context originated with Nove (1958).

such as "shareholder value" or "economic value added" for traditional accounting measures has been a step in the right direction. Many companies, however, use all the jargon but then fail to link these measures to executive compensation, defeating the purpose.

It is important to notice that these more comprehensive measures are continuous in "Time" while the traditional accounting measures, which when individually optimised can do a great deal of damage to the long-run health of the business in question are "time" constructs.[10] When the latter are used, temporal discontinuities occur in the way financial results are reported: failure to "make budget" frequently results in a management decision to "take a hit" in a particular quarter for the benefit of "success" in subsequent quarters: the balance sheet is cleaned up, deliveries postponed, receivables extended, payables brought up to date, work-in-process inventory expanded and so on. Clearly the medium-term prospects of a business—and hence its value to the shareholders—do not change quickly, and management which report roller coaster results from one quarter to the next are fooling no one but themselves (Reed, 1993a, p 487).

Because "what gets measured gets done," adoption of appropriate and comprehensive "success indicators" is the first step toward ensuring that technical change is **development-oriented** rather than **growth-oriented**. In the West, increased sophistication in all relevant constituencies—consumers, voters, investors and the work force—is helping to redefine the success indicator criteria against which "efficiency" is measured.

3.2 Growth vs development

The second implication of an evolutionary perspective applied in economics involves growth and development. Induced innovation plays a crucial role in the distinction between (quantitative) growth and development (or qualitative growth) in economics. "Development" can usefully be

10 "Time" is used in the sense of continuous, irreversible, evolutionary time designated "T" by Nicholas Georgescu-Roegen (1971, p 135) to distinguish it from mechanical time "t."

214

thought of in terms of the efficiency with which resources are used, whereas "growth" simply reflects the amount of resources mobilised in the economic process. In other words, doing less with more achieves growth-oriented objectives; doing more with less is necessary for development. By implication, "development" takes place in Time, whereas growth occurs in "time."

A growth-oriented economy is characterised by efforts to mobilise resources—human and natural—in the economic process. A growth orientation is feasible as long as the necessary resources are readily available. The Soviet economy was frequently criticised because the control of **all** (natural and human) resources by the state facilitated the pursuit of growth-oriented objectives. Yet in "market" economies, the public sector is frequently co-opted by private firms to reduce **their** costs of acquiring appropriate resources. Private firms thereby capture the short-term benefits and externalise the long-term costs on society as a whole.

In an economy in which demand is growing rapidly it is also possible to pursue growth-oriented objectives because it is possible to pass the inherent inefficiencies along to the consumers in the form of "cost-plus" pricing. This factor provided a major impetus to growth in many economies during the post-war period[11]. Thus while growth is comforting to politicians and others with short-term time horizons, society as a whole would be better served in the long run by public policies which foster development.[12]

11 Hence the "Staple Theory of Economic Growth" developed by Harold Innis based on his studies of the sequential exploitation of Canada's natural resources is aptly named as it has little or nothing to do with economic **development**. This same theme has been elaborated more recently by Sachs & Warner (1995), based primarily on the experience of oil-rich nations. As Watkins (1963) pointed out in his commentary on Innis' work, when growth is strong there is no incentive for development; when growth slows, the incentive for development increases but the where-with-all to implement development-oriented policies is impaired. This observation applies in spades to the current situation in Russian agriculture.

War, the ultimate example of dysfunctional human behaviour, is itself an interesting example of government intervention with considerable growth enhancing potential. It however involves "destructive destruction" rather than "creative destruction". (See also Reed 1993a, pp 495–6.)

12 I was very interested yet somewhat surprised by the furore sparked by Paul Krugman recently on the same theme (Krugman, 1996, Ch 11 and *The*

In market economies, the pursuit of "development" objectives by a broadly distributed array of entrepreneurs generates growth via a process of successive specialisation and market niche exploitation. Competition and feedback of market needs to suppliers stimulates this process and results in the choice—of technologies, of consumer products, and of services—the absence of which characterised Soviet socialism. It was the lack of entrepreneurs, competition, risk and feedback in the Soviet command economy which ensured that the pursuit of "growth" objectives precluded "development." In the following sections, it is argued that limitations on competition, risk and feedback always adversely affect achievement of development objectives, even in market economy contexts where economic decision-making is broadly distributed.

3.3 The Importance of Feedback

The integration of technical change into economic theory was one of the great leaps forward recently achieved by the discipline. Traditionally it was very hard for classical economics to explain why the "way things were done" changed over time and varied over space. Induced innovation theory provided the understanding necessary to integrate technical change into the economic process. Ultimately, the induced innovation mechanism is a feedback loop from consumers to producers which results in successive modifications of the "way in which things are done."

Technical change therefore has three main components: the first is the experimentation which introduces novelty into the system, a component which Schumpeter recognised as not wholly rational (Rosenberg 1993 p 6); the second is the process of innovation whereby the preference for one "technology" over another is "induced" **by the user's appreciation** of the extent to which it will maintain or enhance economic viability; the third is the selection mechanism which determines whether the innovation withstands the continuous assessment by potential customers and investors. The Soviet Union

Economist, December 15, 1995).

216

perverted this process by monopolising the process of generating or importing novelty into the system, appointed itself the sole arbiter of which new ways of doing things were to be adopted wholesale across entire industries, and dispensed entirely with the feedback mechanism which normally directs the technical change process (Rosenberg, 1969).

In market economies, the effectiveness with which the adjustment of "the way things are done" occurs depends primarily on the communication of economic information to the decision-makers with a minimum of distortion and the ability of economic agents to respond. Hence a bias towards growth-oriented success measures implies some combination of restraint of inter-enterprise competition, interference with the economic signals received by the decision-makers, or exceptionally buoyant demand. The fact that the Soviet system actively manipulated the "economic" signals, suppressed inter-enterprise competition and (unintentionally) created perpetual shortages of consumer goods contributed to the impressive growth recorded by the "economy" of the USSR.

State control over all resources and their prices facilitated resource mobilisation efforts during the Soviet period. It should come as no surprise therefore that under Soviet socialism, both agricultural labour *and* the physical environment on which agriculture depends were ruthlessly and unsustainably exploited (Reed, 1995).

Evolution has been described as "chaos with feedback." Certainly, in the absence of an evolutionary perspective the circumstances in which Russian agriculture is currently embroiled might well be dismissed as chaotic. The economic cost of maintaining order in a social system devoid of integral feedback mechanisms was debilitating in the Soviet case. Perestroika jump-started the feedback mechanism, but one of the legacies of the Soviet system was a seriously impaired ability to respond. As a consequence, the agricultural sector has thus far been able to respond in only one way to the new circumstances: by retreating toward a local subsistence orientation, poorly integrated into the economy as a whole.

The structure of the Soviet economy prevented the feedback of the information required to prompt development-oriented technical change. As a result it collapsed. The fact that market economies **do** involve a feedback mechanism is an important advantage but hardly a cause for self-congratulation. In too many cases the mechanism is interfered with, and the inevitable adverse consequences sooner or later manifest themselves.

3.4 The role of competition and risk

The case has been made above for the havoc wrecked when competition and risk are absent from the economic arena: the Soviet Union was a prime example. Yet if a closer look is taken, it quickly becomes apparent that a great deal of public policy in the West also acts to constrain competition and reduce risk.

Neo-classical economic models tend to make broad assumptions about the virtues of competition and risk which are difficult to appreciate in practical terms. An evolutionary approach to economics with technical change as an endogenous component suggests that the adverse social and environmental consequences of market capitalism are not ascribable to a competitive mechanism which rewards efficiency *per se*, but to exogenous biases and lack of competition which make such consequences "economic" (Reed, 1993a, p 497).

"Golden parachutes" and other creative forms of compensation for management and directors are a prime example. Institutionalised looting along the lines discussed by Akerlof and Romer (1994) in the case of the U S Savings and Loan scandals, the Chilean financial crisis and the junk bonds debacle are another. In both cases the inherent inefficiencies are disguised because the cost is transferred to shareholders or lenders in the former example, and to tax payers (via bailouts) and investors (via lower interest or dividend rates) in the latter. The excesses of the European Union's (EU) Common Agricultural Policy (CAP) not too long ago threatened the viability of the EU, notwithstanding the considerable wealth of the member states. Part of the problem was the high cost of disposing of the excess production prompted by the *reduced* risks producers faced under CAP.

3.5 The role of the state

Under Soviet socialism, the involvement of the state in the political economy of the empire was explicit: in the sphere of technical change, Soviet socialism eliminated economic experimentation and independent assessment from the process of technical change and simply imposed new, untested ways of doing things wholesale across sectors of the economy.

It therefore became fashionable in the West to attribute the problems evident in the Soviet economy in general and in the agricultural sector in particular to the direct involvement of the state. This is, however, a dangerous over-simplification: in the West agriculture is also a perennial problem but government intervention is more subtle. The fact that the short-term consequences of the resulting inefficiencies are less dire in the West than those evident in the Soviet context makes them less obvious, but does not necessarily mean that they are any less serious.

Implicit in Perestroika was an acknowledgement from the top that fundamental changes were required in Soviet socialism. No less momentous changes have also been occurring in the way the operation of a market economy is understood in the West. The economic theories which underpinned corporate strategy and public policy formulation for decades are being discarded. Economics is increasingly being recognised as an evolutionary science and the comforting, mechanistic models which held out the hope that future implications of current or planned actions could be accurately predicted are being discredited.

One of the implications of the revolution in economic thinking in the West which is relevant to the current discussion involves the role of government. Increased understanding of the sensitivity and sophistication of the market mechanism goes a long way toward explaining why government intervention in a market economy frequently results in unanticipated responses from economic agents. The insights of an evolutionary economics permit fuller appreciation of the negative implications of government intervention. The scope for effective and desirable government intervention is being more narrowly defined as a consequence.

These changes in understanding of economic theory and practice have taken place in the West with much less fanfare than those associated with Perestroika in the former Soviet Union. From a Russian perspective one possible explanation might be that these changes have not yet been acknowledged "at the top" and adopted as official policy. However, the lack of widespread publicity is due to the fact that a market-oriented approach does not require official sanction: widespread adoption of a new perspective or a new way of doing something by independent firms or individuals depends only on its ability to improve viability. As such the market mechanism itself automatically selects new ideas and new ways of doing things which successfully aid the achievement of economic objectives. In a market economy, practice leads theory; in socialist economies, theories led practice.

The pervasive "top down" attitude which one encounters in eastern Europe is a major stumbling-block to market-oriented reforms. Russian agricultural bureaucrats will complain vociferously about the fact that high-quality New Zealand "Anchor" butter is widely available and in great demand across Russia, but just don't want to know about "Rogernomics," the process under which New Zealand dismantled subsidies and increased the international competitiveness of its economy.

Policy-makers in market economies are frequently surprised by the reaction of entrepreneurs to intervention. The inevitable reaction is a treadmill mechanism which generates additional policy solutions to mitigate the unanticipated consequences of the previous generation of intervention. The cumulative cost inherent in such inefficiencies may be borne for a substantial period by free-spending governments. Ultimately, however, as was the case with spending on the EU's Common Agricultural Policy, a political or economic feedback mechanism does assert itself and a correction is effected. When resources are scarce the unsupportability of such inefficiencies is immediately self-evident.

The basic danger inherent in government intervention in the economy is the inevitable distortion of the price signals received by economic agents. Recent improvements in understanding the dynamics of economic activity emphasise that its efficient evolution depends on decentralised decision-making. Market-oriented agriculture generates product differentiation. Yet state intervention in the evolutionary process involving countless independent entrepreneurs limits differentiation and is the source of the chronic over-production problems for the commodities targeted. State control of a national agriculture which operated as a single enterprise during the Soviet period caused both insufficiency and an undifferentiated product range.

3.6 Labour relations in the information age

While the alienation of the workers in Soviet agriculture as a consequence of the sector's turbulent relationship with its Communist Party masters may be an extreme case, it is by no means unique. I worked for a long time in the automotive components industry in Europe and North America. This industry has undergone far-reaching changes in the past 15 years, mostly stimulated by the threat to the established order by competition from Japanese firms. At the beginning of this period most workers felt a lot like Charlie Chaplin in the film "Modern Times," a cog in a process on which they had little impact and over which they had absolutely no control.

This adversarial role was tolerable if not efficient in a market place in which the consumers were not that sophisticated, competition was restrained (to put it politely), and capital could be readily substituted for labour. "Taylorism" or "scientific management" was a product of this era which downplayed the role of the individual employee. Taylorism, incidentally, was a "way of doing things" greatly admired by Lenin (Cooley, 1987, pp 35, 93). The information age has changed the rules of the game significantly in the West, increasing consumer sophistication and competition, and reducing the extent to which capital can be substituted for know-how. The role of the employees in the economic process has changed dramatically as a consequence.

In any enterprise, improvements in efficiency stem directly from more effective deployment of resources. More effective deployment of human resources lies at the heart of the substantial improvements in the competitiveness of western firms during the last two decades. All sorts of jargon such as "re-engineering," "empowerment" and "right sizing" have been invented to say this in a more obscure way.

Workers respond well to greater responsibility, appreciate and take advantage of opportunities to increase their range of skills, respond more to the example of successful peers than the demands of superiors and officials, need to feel appreciated and respected (again primarily by their peers), and have the greatest interest in, and capacity for, adopting "new ways of doing things" which enhance effectiveness. Conversely stress levels are highest among employees who feel that they have no say in their deployment (See, for example, Drucker, 1994 and Cooley, 1987).

The longevity of the Soviet system owed a great deal to the long-term objectives it was able to conjure up for the populace, and its ability to motivate the majority of its citizenry in pursuit of those objectives. To the extent that Soviet agriculture operated as "one big farm," the term "State Capitalism" (Duncan, 1956, p 2) may be considered appropriate: however, while the Soviet "management" recognised the importance of employee motivation, like managers in many other contexts they found it difficult to do so effectively.

However, one of the legacies of the Soviet period is a labour force which prided itself on its degree of functional specialisation. In a system where the **compensation** differentials among the jobs were for the most part inconsequential, the **status** of the individual derived primarily from his or her specialisation.

However, extreme functional specialisation anywhere means that there is always someone to blame if things do not turn out properly. Extreme functional specialisation also alienates workers from their tasks by eliminating any sense of responsibility for the final product. Specialisation also goes a long way toward turning part-time work into full-time work. This is counterproductive for a number of reasons: there are few things more onerous than boredom: the time goes by very slowly, productivity is low, there is a great temptation to get into mischief and a complete absence of job satisfaction. Part-time and ineffective work creates a demand for more labour—and labour shortages are a frequent complaint of Russian agricultural enterprise managers. High-quality agricultural labour is increasingly scarce, but most of the shortfall is artificial.

Successful enterprises everywhere have recognised the importance of the individual and acted to harness individual potential for the achievement of enterprise objectives. In western market economies there is a concerted effort underway to have the employees act as though they are owners. Incentive compensation of employees tied to the shareholder value of the enterprise in which they work is one means of achieving this end. In the case of publicly held companies, this sometimes involves an ownership stake in the form of shares. Among the chief benefits of this ownership ethos is the reduced need for supervision and hence a reduction in X-inefficiency[13].

3.7 Evolutionary economics as a bottom-up process

I have argued elsewhere (Reed, 1995) that Tolstoy was probably a much better role model for economic theory—in Russia and elsewhere—than Marx, and it is unfortunate that the Bolsheviks chose to import rather than use the home-grown variant. In *War and peace*, Tolstoy observed that for all his activity, Napoleon was very like a child, sitting in a carriage, pulling on the straps in the belief that he is moving it along. The point was, of course, that he wasn't moving it along at all. The outcome of the great events of 1812 was determined not so much by the grand stratagems of the leaders as by the discrete decisions made by thousands of individuals, life and death decisions about whether to fight or run away, decisions which no one—not even the protagonists themselves—could predict until they occurred. Tolstoy's point, of course, was that the Russian commander Kutuzov was more aware of his limita-

13 Company decision-makers are able to choose "the way things should be done" or the technical efficiency of the firm. X-efficiency theory explicitly recognises the importance of human resources as the ultimate determinant of the way things are actually done, and focuses particular attention on the "Time" element. Both technical change in the broad sense and shareholder value are concerned with the "way things are actually done."

tions as a leader than Napoleon and hence made fewer mistakes (Dyson, 1993, pp 67–68, 278–81).

Tolstoy understood that society is the aggregate expression of countless individual decisions, and that the exact course of its evolution is therefore unpredictable. Marx was the antithesis of Tolstoy, believing that dialectic materialism was the key determinant of both the past and the future. Schumpeter was among the first to recognise that economic history does not march to a predictable tune as both Marx and neo-classical economists believed.

Kenneth Boulding pointed out long ago that it was the shift in the relative prices of labour and raw materials which "made the exploitation of nature so attractive that the exploitation of labour became obsolete" and induced the technical changes we retrospectively label the industrial revolution (1964, p 113). In the information age, it is now feasible to make the feedback of economic information so efficient that the exploitation of nature is no longer economically attractive (Reed 1993a, p 498). Yet the current predicament of Russian agriculture illustrates that this inherent potential can only be realised under circumstances in which decision-making is broadly distributed both among and within "economic" enterprises.

3.8 Temporal discontinuities

The durability of the Soviet pseudo-economy was something to marvel at. The relative stability of the Soviet system and its insulation from outside influences was fundamental to its longevity. The pervasive role of the state and the static nature of an economic system in which the state held all the strings severely constrained the manner in which the "capitalist habit of mind" could express itself. Experimentation with alternative "ways of doing things" and innovation at the grassroots level was both unthinkable and unnecessary in the context of the *one big farm* which comprised agriculture in the Soviet period. When the static framework within which this "one big farm" evolved and operated was swept away, its collapse was swift and complete.

Government intervention in any economic system attempts to introduce static controls or constraints into a system which is inherently dynamic. Yet individual enterprises which due to their capitalist frame of mind **are** responsive to economic feedback can and do adapt to changing circumstances irrespective of whether those changes are a result of market forces or government intervention. Changing the basis of competition—endogenous change introduced by a participant in the economic ecology—is a strategy favoured by successful companies for building competitive advantage. In a market economy, the multifaceted nature of competition to which the companies are subject severely constrains their ability to introduce changes in "the way things are (actually) done" which devastate the opposition (see Reed, 1993a, p 496 for the biological parallels). Government intervention which is exogenous to the economy system is not traditionally so constrained, and thus often has a devastating effect on one branch of the economy or another.

In the West, agricultural producers themselves often lobby for government intervention which biases their technical change decisions in favour of the short-term and discriminates against the long-term sustainability of the economic system on which they depend. Rigidities introduced into the system are perceived as preferable to the series of adjustments which would inevitably be required to maintain competitiveness where economic evolution allowed to take its course. This phenomenon has become known as the "transitional gains trap." The costs incurred breaking out of this trap when the underlying economics assert themselves are generally greater than the sum of the costs associated with the alternative—a series of evolutionary adjustments. The current predicament of Canada's supply-managed agricultural commodities in the wake of the GATT is a case in point (Reed, 1994). Frequently, of course, the state is called on to intervene and mitigate the down-side consequences of what ultimately prove to be "unsound" policies initially installed because they were requested by those who end up seeking compensation.

In many respects, the Soviet period constitutes a classic illustration of the "transitional gains trap." After successfully postponing the inevitable adjustment, Perestroika finally sprung the "trap."

To the extent that state intervention—whether piecemeal as in the West or wholesale as in the Soviet period—overrides evolutionary change, the cost of the inherent inefficiencies will ultimately have to be paid. Everywhere increased efficiency of government, labour, management and capital or product markets depends largely on **more** information, **more** competition and **more** accountability and hence on more sophisticated consumers, investors and employees.

3.9 Summary

It is easy to disparage Soviet socialism as more of a religion than a bungled attempt to sustain a utopia on the basis of a wholly artificial economic system. Garrett Hardin points out that Marx's dictum "From each according to his abilities to each according to his needs!" (ironically) owes a great deal to religion in general and Christianity in particular, but makes for very poor (neo-classical) economics. In essence, a Marxist-based economy allows an individual to privatise his needs while "commonising" his abilities. Hardin regards it as inevitable, therefore, that the former are exaggerated and the latter minimised. On the basis of this argument it is a logical consequence, rather than a joke, that during the Soviet period the populace "pretended to work" while the state was able only to "pretend to pay them."

However the purely selfish human behaviour traditionally extolled by neo-classical economists is increasingly found wanting. Almost any popular management book one picks up these days is replete with religious metaphors and sentiment. Rigorous rational self-interest in the short term is frequently counter-productive in the medium and longer term as the Prisoner's Dilemma (see note 9) suggests. Following Japanese examples, many western companies are beginning to embrace a kinder, gentler capitalism than the Hobbsian (nasty, brutish, etc) proto-Capitalism currently evident in the Former Soviet Union.

The Soviet experience discussed here lies at one extreme of the argument in favour of an evolutionary economics by graphically illustrating what happens when the evolution of the economy is thwarted. Are there then positive examples of cases where economic **development** has occurred under circumstances of heightened inter-enterprise competition, absence of governmental or other distortion of price signals, an effectively-operating feedback mechanism between the technocrats (the creators of innovation), the practitioners (those adopting the innovations) and customers, and where the success criteria are comprehensive and long-term? Such examples might be expected to exhibit strong spatial concentration, a strong market orientation, and high-quality, excellent value-for-money products. Although it takes Michael Porter nearly 800 pages to do so, his *Competitive advantage of nations* (1990) provides some excellent illustrations.

4. Conclusions

Evolutionary economics in the Schumpeterian tradition makes it possible to discern some of the reasons behind the current chaos that is Russian agriculture. An evolutionary economics which emphasises the need for comprehensive success criteria, respects the crucial role of technical change, underlines the need for accurate feedback of economic signals to a large number of independent decision-makers, recognises the limitations inherent in government intervention in the sector and highlights the positive role of competition can assist in the definition of a policy environment conducive to the **development** of Russia's agriculture. It can also contribute to the more difficult step of determining how that policy objective can best be reached from the current predicament.

Such a perspective suggests that Russian agricultural enterprises require the following in order for the sector to play a positive role in the Russian economy instead of being a perennial black hole into which scarce state resources are poured:

- Economic incentives

- Access to appropriate know-how

- An ability to make decisions independently

- A stable policy environment

- A re-definition of the role of the agricultural bureaucracy

- Recourse to legal protection

At present, these requirements are either totally absent or woefully inadequate.

The potential currently exists in Russia to create the conditions for a level of agricultural **development** as yet unattained in many western market economies. In the West, institutional curbs on innovation and adaptation are often introduced at the behest of agricultural producers and in the mistaken belief that a market economy which emphasises pursuit of economic efficiency is—left to its own devices—biased against practices which are socially desirable in the longer term.

Ideally the desperate situation in which Russian agriculture now finds itself should be translated into feedback which forces policy-makers to learn from the mistakes made elsewhere and tackle the underlying problems head-on.

Eliasson (1997) draws attention to the fact that some transitional economies in eastern Europe are putting in place the enabling institutional infrastructure to facilitate rapid transition to more efficient economies, exploiting the opportunity which exists while the democratic process—and the attendant resistance to change—remains incompletely developed. Russia is, unfortunately, lagging behind in creating this enabling institutional infrastructure. This is, however, only partly because "democratic" opposition to the as yet intangible benefits of reform is well orchestrated: the primary cause is entrenched interests, nominally given the status of economic agents, but which lack the incentives for innovative behaviour which derive from a competitive operating environment.

In the Russian case, and in agriculture in particular, reform-minded politicians play into the hands of the opposition by creating "Potemkin village" privatisation, and then allying themselves with traditional interests resisting the introduction of competitive markets. In the process, the real benefits of a market economy are denied the majority of the population, a situation reminiscent of that prevailing prior to the "feedback" historically known as the Bolshevik revolution.

Only when Russian policy-makers appreciate and seize the opportunity which history has dealt them—and for which the country has paid so dearly—although the path taken might well be mocked as "the most painful of all possible roads from capitalism to capitalism" those involved in Russian agriculture could have the last, and therefore longest, laugh.

Bibliography

Akerlof, G A & Romer, P (1994), *Looting : the underworld of bankruptcy for profit.* Toronto: Canadian Institute for Advanced Research Program in Economic Growth and Policy. Reprint Series—Paper Number 7.

Boserup, E (1969), *The conditions of agricultural growth.* Chicago: Aldine Press.

Boulding, K E (1969), "Technology and the changing social order," in *The urban industrial frontier,* David Popenoe (ed). New Brunswick, NJ: Rutgers University Press.
– (1964), *The meaning of the twentieth century.* New York: Harper and Row.

Bray, F (1994), *The rice economies : technology and development in Asian societies.* Berkeley, Los Angeles and London: University of California Press.

Cooley, M (1987), *Architect or bee : the human price of technology.* London: Hogarth Press.

Cronin, H (1994), *The ant and the peacock.* Cambridge: Cambridge University Press.

Curry, L (1971), "Geographical specialisation and trade," in *Urban and regional planning,* Wilson, A G (ed). London: Pion Press, pp 85–95.

Dovring, F (1979), "Under-employment, slow motion and x-efficiency," in *Economic Development and Cultural Change,* Vol 27, No 3 (April), pp 485–490.

Drucker, P (1994), *Post capitalist society.* New York: HarperCollins Publishers.

Duncan, J S (1956), *Russia's bid for world supremacy : a challenge to western thinking.* Toronto: Massey-Harris-Ferguson Ltd.

Dyson, F (1993), *From eros to gaia.* Harmondsworth: Penguin Books Ltd.

Eliasson, G (1977), "From plan to market," in *Journal of Economic Behaviour and Organization,* Vol 34, pp 1–20.

Fitzpatrick, S (1994), *Stalin's peasants : resistance and survival in the Russian village after collectivisation.* New York: Oxford University Press.

Fukuyama, F (1995), *Trust : the social virtues and the creation of prosperity.* New York: Free Press.

Georgescu-Roegen, N (1971), *The entropy law and the economic process.* Cambridge, MA: Harvard University Press.

– (1965), "The institutional aspects of peasant communities : an analytical view." Chapter 8 in *Energy and economic myths.* New York: Pergamon Press, 1976.

– (1960), "Economic theory and agrarian economics," in *Oxford Economic Papers,* Vol XII, pp 1–40. (Chapter 6 in *Energy and economic myths.* New York: Pergamon Press, 1976.)

Handelman, S (1995), *Comrade criminal : Russia's new mafiya.* New Haven and London: Yale University Press.

Hardin, G (1987), *Living within limits.* New York: Oxford University Press.

– (1968), "The tragedy of the commons," in *Science,* Vol 162, pp 1243–1248.

Hinterberger, F (1993), "A note on sociobiology : Schumpeter, Georgescu-Roegen and beyond," in *Entropy and bioeconomics,* Dragan, J C, Seifert, E K & Demetrescu, M C (eds). (Proceedings of the First International Conference of the European Association for Bioeconomic Studies held in Rome, November 28–30, 1991.) Milan: Nagard Press, pp 282–310.

Joravsky, D (1967), "Ideology and progress in crop rotation," in *Soviet and east European agriculture,* Karcz, J (ed). Berkeley and Los Angeles: University of California Press, pp 156–172.

Krugman, P (1996), *Pop internationalism.* (A collection of previously published essays.) Cambridge, MA & London: MIT Press.

Medvedev, R A & Medvedev Z A (1967), *Khrushchev : the years in power.* (Translated by A R Durkin.) London: Oxford University Press.

Nelson, R R & Winter, S G (1982), *An evolutionary theory of economic change*. Cambridge, MA: The Belknap Press of Harvard University.

Nove, A (1958), "The problem of success indicators in Soviet industry," in *Economics* (February), reprinted in *Readings in the Soviet economy*, Holzman, F D(ed). Chicago: Rand McNally Co, 1962.

Nikolsky, S (1996), "Contemporary agrarian reform in Russia : blueprints, implementation and alternative perspectives." Contribution to the electronic conference *Privatisation and agrarian reform* sponsored by the Foundation for Agrarian Economic Development and UNDP, Moscow State University (March-May).

Porter, M (1990), *The competitive advantage of nations*. New York: The Free Press.

Rosenberg, N (1993), *Joseph Schumpeter : radical economist*. Toronto: Canadian Institute for Advanced Research, Program in Economic Growth and Policy—Working Paper No 10.

– (1991), *Economic experiments*. Toronto: Canadian Institute for Advanced Research, Program in Economic Growth and Policy—Working Paper No 1.

– (1969), "The direction of technical change : inducement mechanisms and focusing devices," in *Economic Development and Cultural Change*, Vol 18, pp 1–24.

Reed, A (1996), "Privatisation and agrarian reform in Russia." Paper contributed to the electronic conference *Privatisation and agrarian reform*, sponsored by the Foundation for Agrarian Economic Development Research and UNDP, Moscow State University (March-May).

– (1995), "A role for western experience in a 'made in Russia' agricultural policy?" Remarks for a presentation at the International Conference *Peasants and Power* at the State Duma, Moscow, November 4–5 (in English and Russian).

– (1994), "A system that milks consumers," in *The Globe and Mail* (Middle Kingdom Page), January 11.

– (1993a), "The concept of shareholder value and evolutionary analogue economics," in *Entropy and bioeconomics*, Dragan, J C, Seifert, E K & Demetrescu, M C (eds). (Proceedings of the first International Conference of the European Association for Bioeconomic Studies, held in Rome, November 28–30, 1991.) Milan: Nagard Press, pp 484–500.

– (1993b), "Sustainable land management : looking through the wrong end of the telescope?" Toronto (mimeo). An abridged version was published in *AgriScience*, Ottawa, February 1994.

Sachs, J & Warner, A (1995), *Natural resource abundance and economic growth*. Cambridge, MA: Harvard Institute for Economic Development (October) and *The Economist*, Dec 23rd 1995–Jan 5th 1996 (double issue), pp 87–89.

Shevelukha, V (1995), "The case for state farms," in *The Moscow Times*, June 5.

van der Post, L (1995), *Feather fall*. Harmondsworth: Penguin Books (an anthology—relevant excerpts are from *Journey Into Russia*, 1964).

Watkins, M H (1963), "A staple theory of economic growth," in *Canadian Journal of Economics and Political Science*, Vol 29, pp 141–58.

Zavalani, T (1951), *How strong is Russia?* London: Jarrold & Sons Ltd.

Chapter VII

Private and Public Expenditures and the Faeroese Business Cycle

Valuable comments by professor Michael Møller, Inst of Finance, Copenhagen Business School, are gratefully acknowledged.

Erik Gørtz

"A system—any system, economic or other—that at every given point of time fully utilizes its possibilities to the best advantage may yet in the long run be inferior to a system that does so at no given point of time, because the latter's failure to do so may be a condition for the level or speed of long-run performance."

Joseph A Schumpeter in "Capitalism, socialism and democracy". First published 1942 by New York and London: Harper & brothers. This reference from London: Allen & Unwin, 1961, p 83.

Abstract

The paper treats the Faeroese industrial policy during the eighties. The policy was characterized by heavy subsidization of both investment and current expenditures which increased the level of activity and implied demand-induced growth rates of around 10% per year. Furthermore, investment projects were generously guaranteed.

Finally, there was immense investment activity in the public sector—harbors, tunnels, roads—with low social rates of return. For several years the investments amounted to 40–50% of GDP. Besides low rates of return on the investment (in periods even negative marginal real profit rates), the activity implied a high-risk level. As a by-effect, the high investment level in the fishing sector implied sharp reductions in the stock of fish around the Faeroe Islands.

Since the investments ended up being worth very little, the public guarantees were activated, and the public debt reached a level close to 3 times GDP in the beginning of the nineties. The level of unemployment reached approximately 25%, and around 10% of the population emigrated in the years around 1990. Even though it is difficult to define such a concept, one is inclined to argue that this must be rather close to what might be called state bankruptcy.

The development naturally implied a collapse of the financial system including the banks. In the end, the authorities took over the two important banks, thereby increasing the total public debt by another 3 billion DKr (i e by one more year's GDP).

One of the important lessons to be drawn from the Faeroese events is that while economic policy matters, it does not always improve the economy. Competence on the part of the policy-makers to do only what they can and stay away from tasks where they lack competence appears lacking. Another lesson is that distorted signals in a market economy may very easily imply disastrous consequences. There was plenty of creative thinking, but at least as much destruction. And in the end it all resulted in an enormous public debt, i e debt of taxpayers.

1 The Faeroese Economy

The Faeroe Islands is a group of small islands in the Atlantic Ocean. They are rocky and best suitable for sheepfarming. The population was around 50 000 inhabitants in 1988, but in the last seven years about 15 percent of the population has emigrated due to the economic crises.

Denmark, the Faeroe Islands, and Greenland form a joint kingdom. The Faeroe Islands were in many years more or less a Danish colony, and the Danes have not been particularly popular. A referendum on the independence question after World War II did not change the constitutional situation. A relatively large subsidy from Denmark is still given to the Faeroe Islands. For all other practical purposes the islands govern themselves. The tax policy is decided locally as the population doesn't pay taxes to the Danish authorities.

The Faeroe Islands ran into a serious economic crisis at the end of the 1980s. This crisis resulted in a heated debate about who were responsible. In general the Faeroese felt that the Danish State, the Danish Financial Sector and the Danish Financial Supervisory Authorities had a very large responsibility for the crises.

After the rise and fall of the Faeroese economy many asked, and for good reasons: "What went wrong, now that everybody believed that the boom would continue for ever?"

The first answer was: "We need an unprejudiced investigation." And a couple of more or less successful reports were written, describing the spinal IMF-recommendation: "By Jove, now we must save." Other analyses treated the collapse of the fishery. They were more solidly founded, but without much effect, as well.

After a' long row of pleas, rumors and mutual accusations, the Governments of Denmark and the Faeroe Islands appointed a commission of independent economists. The author of this chapter had the honor of serving as Chairman of the commission.

It is not easy to decide what an independent economist really means. Perhaps it means a person who has never participated in any earlier inquiry of, or debate, on Faeroese problems.

The most important criterion for becoming a member of the commission was also that the candidate was ignorant of the Faeroese economy, because knowledge as regards the subject was considered a sign of a candidate's prejudism, at least by one of the appointing parties.

2 Faeroese Crisis

The Faeroese economy is a small and open economy with only two important "sectors:"

a) Net transfers from the Danish State, amounting to around 1 billion DKr, i e around 4 000 dollars per inhabitant per year

b) Fishery and related industries

Export values peaked in 1991 (cf figure 3), when the export of fish was close to 2.5 billion DKr. The only two other export articles worth mentioning were ships (200–300 million DKr) and stamps (28 million DKr). Other products amounted to as little as 6 million DKr.

The ship export consisted mainly of previously imported ships—soon to be sold because of lack of fish, due to overfishing, and at a significant loss.

In many ways, the situation of the Faeroese economy is similar to that of many developing countries with only one export commodity. The prices of fish do not fluctuate as much as the prices of many raw materials, but the yearly catches of fish vary much more than the production of minerals etc. Experts tend to agree that overfishing has been a significant problem and has caused huge fluctuations in catches.

Finally, the balance of payments on the current account contains a large income component consisting of a subsidy from Denmark. This transfer was originally dependent upon public investments, social sector expenditure etc. From 1988, the transfer was made more or less fixed relative to the Danish GDP, i e rather stable in amount. The purpose was to avoid conflicts of interests when one authority pays and another authority decides. However, the result was that the Faeroese GNI per inhabitant in some years at the end of the 1980s was larger than that of Denmark. Since the subsidy relative to the Danish GDP remained stable, however, through the Faeroese slumps during the 1990s, the Faeroese GNI per inhabitant is now at least 30–40% less than that of Denmark.

The exogenous export and politically induced changes in public and semi-public expenditures had immense effects on the total business cycle. Figure 1 shows that private investment and public expenditures were leading the boom, but also the slump. Private consumption was much more stable. Figure 2 shows that although the savings rate was large compared to international standards, the level of investment was overwhelmingly large until 1989. This implied balance of payments deficits and accordingly debt creation. Although the value of exports increased considerably until the end of the 1980s, imports grew faster and created balance of payments deficits, as savings lacked far behind investments. Private consumption propensity was, however, relatively stable, and the consumers can hardly be blamed for the instabilities created.

When export volumes decreased from 1984/85 to 1993 by approximately 50% (cf figure 3), and exports prices dropped by close to 10% after 1991—implying that the prices in the 1990s were only 20% above those in the 1980s (cf figure 4)—the total value of exports decreased by approximately 40% during the decade after the middle of the 1980s. The Faeroese GDP consequently collapsed. No economy could have adjusted well to such a disturbance.

The boom before 1988 implied endogenously determined and very large public incomes. This again tempted the politicians to indulge in excessive expenditure increases (cf columns 2 and 3 in table 1).

3 Analysis of the Policies

The income increases were erroneously interpreted as signs of a healthy economy. This proves that the effects of built-in-stabilizers do not always work as believed by New Classical Economic Theory. The increases in public debt from 1988 and onwards were not interpreted as serious warning signals. Although warnings were published, e g from the permanent committee of advisors, little was done to correct the situation and, when done, much too late.

The presented figures and tables were cornerstones for the analysis of the special committee.

The 1994 critical indicators were:

- The rate of unemployment: 20 percent

- The total foreign debt (net): 6–7 billion DKr or 120–140 percent of GDP

- The total public debt to foreigners (net): 8–9 billion DKr or 160–180 percent of GDP

Besides the analysis, it was necessary to talk to many participants in the game—both in Denmark and the Faeroe Islands—before the first documents were produced. Due to the immense political interest, the analysis had to be carried out before September 1st (general elections in both countries). The report was available ultimo August 1994.

The members of the Committee were not surprised to "observe" that the report raised an uproarious silence. Politicians, lobbyists and public opinion creators were busy guessing the political results of the campaigns.

The members of the committee were, however, pleased that the report was well received by colleagues and students. Some of these called it *the* book on that period of Faeroese history. The members were convinced that there were already visible signs of stabilization of the population and the economy, albeit at a lower level.

a) Bad risk management when fiscal and monetary policy decisions were taken. Subsidization, wrong price-signaling, and the creation of wrong stimuli both in the investment and the production phases implied too large and too risky investments.

b) This, furthermore, contributed to the "downfishing" and consequent depletion of the stock of fish. The decisions were against the advice of fishery biologists and other experts.

c) The extremely expansive public expenditures on e g harbors, tunnels, and roads seriously destabilized the macro economy.

d) Strong local political influence and regional competition implied immense expansionary local economic policy stimuli.

e) Not all negotiation possibilities had been considered before a political solution of the refinancing of the Faeroese economy was chosen. When a solution had finally been agreed upon, it was difficult to decide which part was to blame: the authorities in Denmark or the Faeroe Islands. Private persons having reached mutually binding juridical results can hardly be blamed for having safeguarded their own interests, but political authorities cannot be judged by such yardsticks.

Industrial policy interventions are often referred to as the most erroneously used policy measures because they place the highest demands or competence on the policy-makers. This time heavy subsidization explained the main part of the boom in unprofitable private investments. The public and semi-public (via subsidization) investments plus public consumption expenditures amounted to approximately half of the Faeroese GDP at the top of the demand-generated boom in 1988, i e to approximately 3 billion DKr.

The savings deficit, hence, amounted to one fourth of GDP that year. If the subsidy from Denmark is taken into account, the deficit amounted to one sixth.

Some would have called this an admirable and normally unheard effort, as investments were running at more than twice the level of savings, and as large as one fourth of GDP. The implied increase in debt could easily have been served, IF the investments had produced a real rate of profits only somewhat above the real rate of interest. That was *not* the case, however, on the contrary, most of the projects went, or nearly, went bankrupt:

- Cargo ships meant for transportation of chemicals

- Huge trawlers (some of which intended for whiting fishery)

- Several shipyards

- Open-sea fish farms

- At least four fifths of the filleting stations

242

- Another airline company, besides the old private airline company, etc

To summarize: The large investments turned out to be worth close to nothing. Only the debt was left. There was no contribution to the real rate of profits. The real value of the capital in fact decreased.

One might argue that this was not a burden of industry, since large parts of the debt were guaranteed by the Faeroese Government. But that is obviously a debt of the tax payers of the islands with depressive effects on their net available future income.

Probably the situation in the beginning of the 1990s was as close as one could get to a state of state bankruptcy. In Denmark one must go as far back as to 1340 to find a similar situation. And the result in 1340 was that a Danish squire killed a German, a so-called bald-headed count ("Den kullede greve" in Danish). Will the result be different in the Faeroese case?

If one reflects more deeply on the situation, the German bald-headed count did nothing but inspect the value of his mortgage on real property. It has always been part of Danish jurisprudence to give such a privilege to the creditor.

4 Why Such a Policy Debacle?

"Why did the fiscal policy-makers not react in a more responsible manner to the described changes?" Unfortunately, this question is easier to ask than to answer.

Three reasons stand out:

a) The Faeroe Islands consist of no less than 50 municipalities, many of which have taken up large loans to finance infrastructure investments in a—desperate—attempt to lower emigration.

b) The Faeroese Government favored a system with many semi-independent "funds;" their accounts were not consolidated within the government budgets. There were as many as 100 such funds, and mutual lending between the funds was legal.

c) The government on the Faeroe Islands was very much involved with the private sector. As a matter of fact, there was no real private sector, everybody being dependent on government subsidies and guarantees. The real costs of (especially) the guarantees emerge with a time-lag. Therefore, the official budgets gave a much too favorable impression of the state of the public finances. On top of that, there was a built-in destabilization in the policy model chosen. If the government tried to cut down on expenditures, the private sector would be hit to the extent that many of the guarantees would become effective.

Anyhow, the official figures show a small surplus on the public budget in the growth years up to 1988 (cf table 1). In the later years the situation deteriorated rapidly year by year. In 1992–93 the government had to bail out the banks at huge costs. Although these events and changes are difficult to interpret in fiscal policy terms, it must be concluded that the Faeroese public expenditure policy has been extremely procyclical. This is evident now that the total result of the policy emerges clearly and can be studied by means of more refined analytical methods.

But as mentioned above, the largest and most disastrous errors were what we might call microeconomic mistakes:

1) Fish is a limited resource and subject to "the tragedy of the commons." The optimal policy is to limit fishing through quotas, sold to the highest bidders. But the Faeroese Government instead decided to subsidize fishing in a lot of different ways: minimum prices for fish, cheap financing and loan guarantees, salary support for fishermen etc, etc (cf table 2). This led to a huge boom in investment activity. But the mistake was mainly of a microeconomic nature. It meant not only a bad timing of investment, but much more seriously that the investments as such turned out worth nothing. Ships were bought and factories built, but there was no use for them. The Faeroese population got absolutely no benefit of the investments. And on top of that the policy meant a depletion of the stock of fish around the Faeroe Islands.

2) A very large part of the public investments were of the same character as the private investments, i e giving very little "value for money." Tunnels were built at enormous costs just to please very small communities. One island was called "the

244

flute," due to the number of tunnels through it. Roads were built in a vain attempt to keep the population settled in very small villages. But the roads were used by the population to move to the main islands.

In the 1980s, labor and capital resources were attracted to the Faeroe Islands from all over the world, especially Europe (East as well as West, but especially from Denmark).

From 1990 there was an outflow of labor. Many had lost most of their capital, but some got a rebate via government guarantees.

This development implied that private debt was transformed into public debt, i e into tax payer debt (cf figure 5). Accordingly, much creative thinking was followed by a lot of destruction. Earlier in history this has happened after wars etc. Today the total foreign debt is 4.5 billion DKr, and the public foreign debt is 7.3 billion DKr.

It is interesting to note that the Faeroese fishing economy had a similar bad experience after World War II. After a risky, but lucrative transportation of fish during the war to the British market (where a national dish is "fish and chips"), the Faeroese entrepreneurs invested huge amounts to expand their industry. Shortly after 1950 Sjovinnubankin collapsed. History seems to repeat itself with intervals of around 30–40 years.

The events raised all kinds of responsibility questions and questions about how to distribute the enormous losses. These questions are political and almost impossible to sort out in a neutral and fair way. These questions should therefore be postponed and perhaps forgotten.

5 Conclusions

To sum up:

a) The Faeroese economy is by nature a cyclical economy and difficult to stabilize.

b) Animosity and mutual mistrust have excluded the simplest and easiest way of stabilization, namely to let the Danish transfers to the Faeroe Islands be dependent on the Faeroese unemployment and GDP. Instead the choice was to stabilize transfers vis-à-vis the Danish GDP.

c) The main reasons for the disasters on the Faeroe Islands, hence, were that huge amounts of resources were completely wasted—and more than wasted, since the investments led to overfishing and the destruction of a natural resource.

d) A perfect macroeconomic planner which had distributed the public and private expenditures contracyclically over time might have been able to *diminish* the disaster, but the disaster would have *occured anyway*. The policies should not have been directed toward macro stabilization.

e) The optimal policy concerns the microeconomic situation and is much easier to understand, define and implement than any macroeconomic policy. It essentially involves taking the policy design down to the market and linking resources, responsibilities and consequences at the level where they belong, with the decision-makers in the market. This policy would have been much easier to enact, had it been understood, than pursuing less important macroeconomic stabilization policies.

Figures

Figure 1. Various components of Faeroese GDP

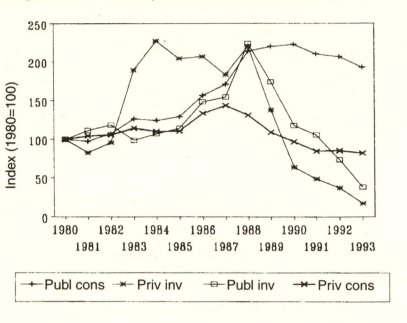

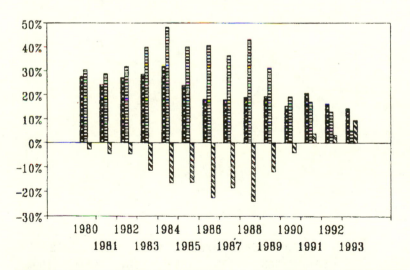

Figure 2. Saving, investment balance, percent of GDP

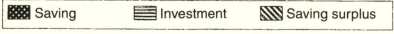

Figure 3. The Faeroese fish export

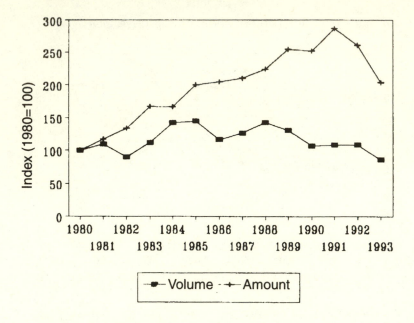

Figure 4. Price level of Faeroese fish export

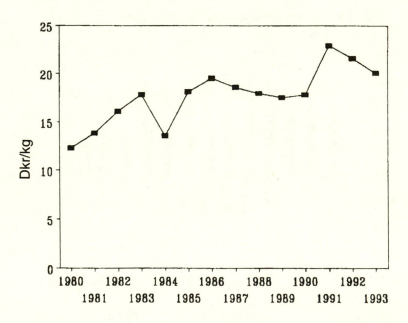

Figure 5. Public and total debt (both net debt)

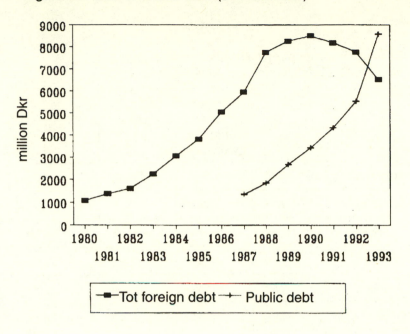

Tables

Table 1. Faeroese public budget (million Dkr)
Source: Det Rådgivende Udvalgs beretning.

	Income	Investment and current expenditures	Net debt creation[1]	Total
1980/81	717	729	40	-52
1981/82	871	867	39	-35
1982/83	1042	951	24	67
1983/84	1219	1103	21	95
1984/85	1442	1374	46	22
1985[2]	1221	1112	49	60
1986	1857	1474	69	314
1987	2234	1671	36	527
1988[3]	3086	3022	200	-136
1989	3010	3342	185	-517
1990	2698	3138	80	-520
1991	2563	3135	0	-572
1992	2477	2939	0	-462
1993[4]	2428	2853	0	-425
1994[5]	2476	2724	0	-262

1 Net debt creation before 1988 includes the loans to the fish fleet only. From 1988 the budget principles are changed.
2 April 1th to December 31th, only.
3 Since 1988 the subsidies from the Danish state are included in the budget. In 1988 this amounted to approximately 670 million Dkr.
4 Estimated.
5 Budget.

Table 2. Various subsidies to the fishery
Source: Det Rådgivende Udvalgs beretning.

	1980/81	1983/84	1986	1989	1992[1]
Minimum wage	6.0	9.5	12.2	43.5	
Subsidy to cost fishery	5.9	7.4	22.1	26.2	
Landing subsidy	5.6	14.3	22.1	23.9	
Subsidy to industrial fishery	6.5	9.8	19.3	2.7	
Oil subsidy	31.0	36.3	3.8	0.0	
Subsidy to Raw Fish Fund	67.7	88.3	85.7	232.0	
Bait subsidy	5.2	10.8	4.7	0.0	
Current subsidies	29.3	62.1	87.0	94.8	
Other subsidies	6.3	24.0	33.6	39.9	
Total, excl loans	**163.5**	**252.1**	**294.4**	**462.8**	**242.2**
Loans	47.3	21.2	69.0	117.4	19.6

1 The subsidies to the fishery were rearranged 1990/91 and are since 1989 reduced each year.

Chapter VIII

Problems in Assisting New Business Start-ups in Germany

I would like to thank Stephan O Hornig and Sandra Waller for their assistance.

Karl Heinrich Oppenländer

Abstract

Market entry conditions are major factors in deciding on establishing a business. High initial investments are usually required. But especially young entrepreneurs frequently have insufficient equity resources of their own, and access to the necessary additional funds from external sources is often extremely limited. Lack of venture capital in particular delays or hinders investments (Oppenländer 1988), notably of potential business start-ups. The main reason is asymmetric information between enterprise and capital providers, the enterprise being better informed about the opportunities and risks of its project than potential financiers, a fact which leads to adverse selection effects. The questions are: how can the problems that result from asymmetric information be solved at the micro-level in such a way that positive results are obtained for overall economic growth? How can capital assistance programs be organised such that they fit the framework of a free market system? Is government intervention as a second-best strategy for assisting business start-ups advisable?

There are two direct effects of business start-ups: the business founder (1) offers additional goods and (2) creates a demand for investment and labour; both contribute to expansion (multiplier effects). But business founders can also force competitors out of the market (crowding-out effects). To assess the overall impact from these effects and from the costs of government intervention we use the LFS model developed by the Ifo Institute to simulate the long-term total impact of the macroeconomic adjustment process in the German economy.

Calculations using this model show that between 1987 and 1992, GDP increased to an annual average of DM 4 billion higher when new business start-ups were included, i e ca 1.5 times the start-up investments. Moreover, between 54 000 and 93 000 new jobs were created.

254

1 Problems and discussion in Germany

In Germany the debate has never stopped about how to help business start-ups and why—in an international comparison—relatively few technology-based new businesses have been founded. This is not the time or place to revive this discussion or expand on it. A discussion would have to start with the lack of supply on the German stock market, the aversion of the German investor to shares, reflected in a preference for simple forms of saving (savings accounts), all the way to the lending practices of German banks which—according to Schumpeter—are supposed to promote creative destruction via the granting of credit and the creation of loan capital (see Oppenländer 1988, pp 254 ff). Instead they prefer to make loans to the government or to the states, which is easier (in terms of the sums involved) and possibly also less risky.

2 Why are there programmes for assisting business start-ups?

For young and often innovative firms, the particularities of the market entry conditions are among the most important factors in the decision to start up a new business. The free accessibility of a market is a basic prerequisite for competition. The founding of new firms, as a rule, requires high initial investments. Young companies, in particular, are frequently starved for capital, however, and finding the necessary financing via external funding is extremely difficult. Time and again the thesis has been advanced that insufficient funds are available for innovations and other risky investments (see German Council of Economic Advisors 1994, para 441). Especially the lack of risk capital is said to delay or prevent innovations and business start-ups (Oppenländer 1988). This description refers to the situation in Germany.

Competitive capital markets, which are characterised by complete information, automatically achieve an efficient allocation of resources (see Modigliani & Miller 1958). A variety of factors prevents a smooth functioning of capital markets, however. One major reason is the problem of asymmetric information between companies and owners of financial capital (see Stiglitz & Weiss 1981): The firm is better informed about the chances and risks of its projects than are potential financiers, a fact that results in adverse selection effects. Furthermore, capital owners cannot control where their funds actually flow. This provides incentives for the companies not to behave in the interest of the financiers, but to undertake riskier activities (moral hazard).

The problems of the information mentioned, which play a role in raising equity capital as well as loan capital, may lead to a situation in which—in contrast to the case of perfect information—start-ups in particular cannot get enough capital (for a survey see Hillier & Ibrahimo 1993). Insufficient funding may result in an inefficiently low level of investment in the economy at large[1] and—in the case of new businesses—may prevent market entry. In such circumstances, economic measures to assist and promote new business start-ups may be helpful.

Allow me to make some additional remarks about asymmetric information on capital markets. Because of asymmetric information between the potential business founder and the investor, the external funding of new start-ups does not function smoothly. The founder as an insider is better informed about the chances and risks of his business idea than are his financiers as outsiders.

Asymmetric information can exist in raising equity as well as loan capital. Furthermore, potential investors may be ignorant of important facts about the firm (hidden knowledge) or may not be able to control the behaviour of the firm or may do so only by incurring information costs (hidden actions).

The influence of asymmetric information in raising external equity capital is explained by Akerlof's (1970) "lemons" problem (Myers & Majluf 1984). Accordingly, in contrast to the managers, the investors have insufficient information about the true value of the firm's assets and its business prospects. They value the shares of an individual company with an aver-

---

1   De Meza &Webb (1988) have shown that theoretically the obverse cannot be excluded either, i e that, compared to a macroeconomically efficient solution, too many (too many bad) projects are being funded—there is excess investment.

256

age price. This implies that the shares of "good" companies must be issued at too low a price in order to offset the investors' losses from "lemons," and this may limit the amount of equity capital raised.

In addition, there are conflicts of interest between the investors and the managers of a firm, who in connection with equity capital cannot be controlled as well as in the case of loan capital (Stiglitz 1985). When loan capital is raised, the control of the firm is concentrated in the hands of a single financial intermediary, which is specialised in this task. In the case of equity capital, however, this task must be managed by each individual investor. Because of the problems of control, companies may find their access to equity capital barred or at least limited. Taking recourse to loan capital, for example in the form of bank credit, is not necessarily a viable alternative, however, because here, too, serious information problems exist.

As for resolving problems of asymmetric information, financial intermediaries are much better suited than anonymous capital markets.[2] One economic explanation is that financial intermediaries can avoid any duplication of effort (Williamson 1986, p 161). If every borrower were to raise part of the required loan from several investors, each investor would have to incur costs and effort in order to acquire information on the credit risk of the borrower and to control his actions. At the same time a free-rider problem arises: If one financier uses up resources in order to control the entrepreneur, all others profit from this because of the public-good character of the control. On the other hand, if the potential investors deposit their savings with a financial intermediary which re-lends these funds as business credit, the latter is the only one to acquire information and exert control. Another advantage of financial intermediaries is the diversification of the investors' risk as the financial intermediary simultaneously invests in many projects and thus reduces the total risk of its portfolio. Although concentration of control in one financial intermediary may minimise the costs of control, it cannot eliminate the

2 See Diamond (1984) and Williamson (1986) for the advantages of banks as financial intermediaries.

problems of asymmetric information (adverse selection and moral hazard).

The effects of adverse selection and moral hazard imply that an increase in interest rates will cause less risky investments to be postponed while riskier projects are increasingly undertaken. The banks, being aware of these effects, do not respond to a high demand for loans by raising interest rates but by credit rationing. The result is underinvestment.

Firms may reduce the asymmetry of information, which can lead to credit rationing, in several ways. Thus they can signal their creditworthiness by offering collateral (Bester 1985a, Chan & Kantas 1985, Besanko & Thakor 1987a) or by the size of the desired loan (Bester 1985b, Besanko & Thakor 1987b, Milde & Riley 1988). Young companies, as a rule, are not able to offer sufficient collateral. Information problems may also be reduced by firms gaining a reputation based on long-term relationships with financial intermediaries (Stiglitz & Weiss 1983, Diamond 1989). This possibility is also unavailable to business start-ups.

For young companies, therefore, information asymmetries form an especially serious barrier to the acquisition of external funds.

3 When is government assistance to business start-ups justified?

If the capital markets were to finance all projects whose rate of return exceeds the relevant rate of interest, they would guarantee an efficient allocation of scarce financial resources. With well-functioning capital markets, therefore, there would be no need for government assistance to start-up firms. After all, it should not be easier for the government than for professional investors to select the profitable start-ups. Given a perfect capital market, intervention in the market mechanism would lead to welfare losses.

Government intervention for the promotion of business start-ups as a second-best strategy may be considered reasonable if it results in a positive effect on welfare. Government assistance to facilitate the acquisition of equity and loan capital not only provides for the additional funding of profitable projects, but also attracts potential lossmakers. Government assistance will be welfare-enhancing if the additional expected profits are higher than the additional expected losses including the state assistance funds. Which of the two effects will prevail cannot be deduced from theoretical considerations alone; it also requires empirical analysis of the individual programmes.

In Germany—as in most industrialised countries—there is a multitude of financial assistance to business start-ups. In addition to government loans there are state guarantees, subsidies (interest subsidies and premiums) as well as the promotion of equity participation. Aside from this specific start-up assistance, business start-ups can avail themselves of assistance programmes which have other primary goals (e g research and development). The financial assistance granted by the federal and state governments, increasingly also by local governments, may as a rule be combined. In contrast to the great number of programmes for loan capital assistance, the availability of equity capital assistance is limited.

In Germany, government loans are the most important instrument of start-up assistance. Here government offices grant financial assistance at terms which are more favourable than those of regular bank loans. The equity capital assistance programme makes loan capital available to new business start-ups. Because of the special terms of the contract, however, the loan capital has the character of equity capital.

4 The equity capital assistance programme of the Federal Republic of Germany

4.1 Description

In the following I shall report about the findings of a study by the Ifo Institute, contracted by the Federal Economics Ministry. This study discusses and evaluates the equity capital assistance programme of the German Government for the period from 1987 to 1992 (Breitenacher et al 1994a, 1994b).

In its annual report of 1977/78 the German Council of Economic Advisors (1977, para 436–458) stated that in a market economy the problem of business start-ups does not warrant the granting of interest subsidies and other assistance for the purpose of facilitating the founding of new businesses which may later require permanent subsidies. Business start-ups require additions to their own limited equity capital in the form of equity-type loans which will later be repaid out of profits, as well as long-term loan capital. As a consequence, the federal government created the equity capital assistance programme in 1979, which was originally terminated for the west German Länder on December 31, 1991.[3]

The most important characteristic of this programme, as compared with other programmes with the same purpose, is the delayed drain on company liquidity through interest payments and debt repayments which has a stabilising effect on the business. This gives the equity assistance funds a true equity function during this time, permitting the borrowing of additional loan capital and also providing a risk buffer. During the first two years of the programme, the equity assistance is interest-free,[4] after which interest rates gradually rise. After ten redemption-free years the equity assistance must be repaid in 20 equal half-yearly instalments. Thus the maximum life of the loan is 20 years.

The equity capital assistance programme is targeted at private individuals in the small and medium-size company sector and at professionals who want to found a company, buy an existing firm or want to undertake additional investment within three years of the initial receipt of funds from the eq-

3 Originally the equity capital assistance programme was terminated for the western German Länder on December 31, 1991 and for the eastern Länder on December 31, 1993. The programme had been prolonged for the eastern Länder until December 31, 1995. Within the framework of the governmental programme for growth and employment it was re-established in the western Länder in 1994, but with a stronger accent on the funding of the eastern Länder. Since the beginning of 1997, the financing of the equity capital assistance programme has been covered by the special assets of the European Recovery Programme (ERP) of the Federal Government and is therefore independent of fluctuations in the federal budget. The new official name is ERP equity capital assistance programme.

4 During the period under investigation (1987–1992), the first three years of the programme were interest-free in the eastern Länder.

uity capital assistance programme. These individuals may apply for a loan to add to their own equity capital, with the government guaranteeing the credit risk. The equity assistance funds are granted by the Deutsche Ausgleichsbank upon the request of a housebank without the usual security required by the banks; the federal government assumes responsibility for the interest subsidies and postponed repayments. As a rule, the applicant is required to put up 15% of the basic assessment. The equity assistance increases the equity up to 40% of the basic assessment, with a maximum funding of DM 1 000 000[5] per applicant. The project must be expected to be fully viable and the applicant must prove to be technically and commercially qualified.

Following its creation, the equity capital assistance programme attracted increasing interest; since 1984 the number of businesses so promoted has stabilised at between 9 000 and 10 000 (in the western Länder).[6] In general, only a relatively small part of all business start-ups participated in the equity capital assistance programme—the share may have been below 5%, which was primarily due to the strict lending criteria. Because of the required proof of technical and commercial qualification, the trades accounted for an above average share.

4.2 Macroeconomic effects of the equity capital assistance programme

The more dynamic an economy and the greater the number of business start-ups, the easier it is to manage the problems of structural change. Lack of capital, however, often stands in the way of starting up innovative and employment-intensive small firms, in particular. A government programme for overcoming these problems should only be created, however, if it

5 Since January 1, 1997. During the period under investigation, the maximum funding was DM 300 000 per applicant. The minimum funding of DM 10 000 has been discontinued.

6 In the eastern Länder the number of business start-ups enjoying equity assistance loans has been considerably higher, at 48 300 in 1991 and 34 700 in 1992, which may be traced to the start-up boom in the private sector following German reunification.

is efficient from a macroeconomic point of view, i e if it raises national income or at least does not have a negative impact. At the same time it must not result in a displacement of the existing companies by equally efficient, government assisted start-ups. An efficiency analysis of the equity capital assistance programme was conducted with the help of the LFS model developed by the Ifo Institute for the simulation and long-term projection of macroeconomic adjustment processes in Germany (see Breitenacher et al 1994a, 1994b, Ch H).[7]

The equity capital assistance programme is to create the conditions for those business start-ups which would not have been undertaken without assistance by expanding the equity capital of the founder in order to allow him to get a bigger credit line from his housebank. The effects of a business start-up are of a quantitative (additional supply of goods and services, additional demand for investment and labour) and of a qualitative nature (new, more sophisticated goods and services). The additional demand of the new firm and its employees triggers a multiplier effect.

At the same time, there are displacement effects, like:

- The additional demand may raise the price of the resources which may also have negative effects on other branches

- Depending on the form in which the government finances its business start-up assistance, interest rates may rise, crowding out private investment

- The expansion of output and capacity utilisation may result in the displacement of existing firms

The total effect of business start-ups and their promotion by the equity capital assistance programme, which consists of a multitude of—in part contrary—subeffects, was estimated with the above-mentioned LFS model. Two scenarios were contrasted: One variant took account of the equity capital assistance programme and the other did not. As for the first scenario (taking the support programme into consideration), the net number of assisted firms was derived from the figures of the Deutsche Ausgleichsbank on the number of assisted start-ups, deducting the number of failures as well as the cases

7 For a description of the LFS model see Langmantel (1993).

of free-riders. In a survey, 20.4% of the respondents stated that they would also have fully founded their company without the equity capital assistance programme, 45.3% of the cases would not have started, and 36.6% would only have done so after some delay or to a lesser extent (see Breitenacher et al 1994a, p 32). This leads to the conclusion that about one fifth of the start-ups were free-riders. This share appears small in comparison to other subsidy programmes. The total investment figure was then derived by multiplying this number by the average investment per start-up. The costs to the federal budget (interest subsidies, postponed repayments) were also taken into consideration (see Table 1).

Table 1: The Equity Capital Assistance Programme

Data of the equity capital assistance programme						
	1987	1988	1989	1990	1991	1992
Number of start-ups	8,983	9,162	4,924	8,655	9,919	4,521
Surviving firms (cumulated)	8,983	18,136	22,979	31,493	41,260	45,304
Surviving firms excluding free riders (cumulated)	7,120	14,480	18,400	25,200	32,960	36,240
Investment per start-up ('000 DM)	228.4	234.0	203.4	223.5	227.5	301.7
Total investment (bn DM)	1.64	1.71	0.80	1.54	1.81	1.09
Delayed repayments, interest subsidies (bn DM)	0.17	0.18	0.19	0.18	0.19	0.20
Macroeconomic effects of equity assistance via the equity capital assistance programme (deviations from the base level excluding assistance)						
	1987	1988	1989	1990	1991	1992
Billion DM, in 1985 prices						
Gross national product	3.2	3.7	2.5	4.5	5.6	5.0
Private consumption	1.2	2.2	2.5	3.6	4.8	5.6
Public consumption	0.3	0.5	0.6	0.9	1.3	1.5
Change in inventories	0.4	0.1	-0.2	0.2	0.2	-0.1
Gross fixed investment	2.9	3.0	1.5	3.0	3.5	2.4
Exports	-0.8	-1.2	-1.3	-2.0	-2.7	-3.0
Imports	0.8	0.9	0.6	1.2	1.5	1.4
Billion DM, current prices						
Government budget balance	1.9	2.6	2.1	3.4	4.4	4.1
In % of the base level						
GNP deflator	0.3	0.4	0.7	0.9	1.0	1.1
Thousand persons						
Employees (cumulated)	54	64	43	75	93	80

Source: Deutsche Ausgleichsbank, LFS model, Ifo calculations; based on Breitenacher et al (1994a, pp 25, 27).

Including the equity capital assistance programme, the gross national product was higher than without the programme by around DM 4 billion annually during the period 1987 to 1992, exceeding the start-up investment by one half. These DM 4 billion arose primarily from investment and private consumption, corresponding to the composition of the start-ups which focused on household-related services and the trades. At the same time the price level rose, leading to a deterioration of international competitiveness and a decline in exports. The intensified start-up activities yielded additional government revenues (e g taxes due to a larger number of employees and firms) and reduced government expenditures (e g social insurance benefits), leading to an improvement of the fiscal balance by about DM 3 billion annually. This implies—formulated cautiously because of the simplifications of the model—that on balance the equity capital assistance programme has not cost the government anything.

5 Conclusions

The phenomenon of asymmetric information on credit markets leads to moral hazard and adverse selection effects. These have especially negative consequences for start-up activities and young firms. Given these facts, the government faces the question as to how it can contribute to resolving these problems in financing business start-ups and innovations at the micro level in a way that will result in positive consequences for economic growth.

The equity capital assistance programme of the German Government has proven to be valuable in achieving this end. Because those founders wishing to participate in the programme must fulfil certain requirements and provide information about themselves and the planned project, the asymmetry of information is reduced and thereby also the risk for the lender/investor.

A special advantage of the equity capital assistance programme is the protection of liquidity of the new firms due to the postponement of interest payments and debt repayments. This gives the start-up a better chance to withstand the risks of late payment or default and prevents the frequently occurring liquidity bottlenecks which may result from the need to pre-pay personnel and materials. The delayed payments of interest and principal raise the level of available equity capital, improving access to additional equity and loan capital on the financial markets. Firms supported by equity assistance are shown to be able to replace assistance funds with equity funds relatively quickly, precluding long-term dependence on government subsidies.

Furthermore, firms supported by the equity capital assistance programme have a smaller failure rate, at 9.9%, within the first seven years than unsupported firms at 15% (Breitenacher et al 1994b, p 88). In general, equity assistance facilitates more full-fledged start-ups which—independent of any assistance—have a better survival rate. In addition, a suboptimal start-up size caused by lack of capital may be avoided more easily, again raising the firm's chances of long-term survival.

On the whole we can say that the equity capital assistance programme has been able to make a contribution to the growth of output and employment. Another positive element is the fact that the government suffered no financial costs, even though—as with any kind of subsidy—free-rider effects cannot be precluded. Because government intervention may be justified by the imperfect nature of the capital markets, the equity capital assistance programme cannot be criticised for being anti-competitive. Rather it can contribute to a better allocation of resources and can support the necessary structural change.

Bibliography

Akerlof, G (1970), "The market for lemons : qualitative uncertainty and the market mechanism," in *Quarterly Journal of Economics*, Vol 84, pp 488–500.

Besanko, D & Thakor, A V (1987a), "Collateral and rationing in monopolistic and competitive credit markets," in *International Economic Review*, Vol 28, pp 671–689.

Besanko, D & Thakor, A V (1987b), "Competitive equilibrium in the credit market under asymmetric information," in *Journal of Economic Theory*, Vol 42, pp 167–182.

Bester, H (1985a), "Screening vs rationing in markets with imperfect information," in *American Economic Review*, Vol 75, pp 850–855.

Bester, H (1985b), "The level of investment in credit markets with imperfect information," in *Zeitschrift für die gesamte Staatswissenschaft*, Vol 142, pp 503–515.

Breitenacher, M et al (1994), "Gesamtwirtschaftliche Wirkungen der Existenzgründungspolitik sowie Entwicklungen der mit öffentlichen Mitteln—insbesondere Eigenkapitalhilfe—geförderten Unternehmensgründungen." Abschlußbericht zum Forschungsprojekt. Munich: Ifo-Institut für Wirtschaftsforschung. (Ifo-Studien zur Finanzpolitik 56.)

Chan, Y & Kanatas, G (1985), "Asymmetric valuation and the role of collateral in loan agreements," in *Journal of Money, Credit and Banking*, Vol 17, pp 84–95.

De Meza, D & Webb, D (1987), "Too much investment : a problem of asymmetric information," in Quarterly Journal of Economics, Vol 102, pp 364–378.

Diamond, D W (1989), "Reputation acquisition in debt markets," in Journal of Political Economy, Vol 97, pp 828–862.

German Council of Economic Advisors (1977) [Sachverständigenrat zur Begutachtung der gesamtwirtschaftlichen Entwicklung: Jahresgutachten 1977/78. Bonn. Bundestagsdrucksache 8/1221.].

266

German Council of Economic Advisors (1994) [Sachverstän-digenrat zur Begutachtung der gesamtwirtschaftlichen Entwicklung: Jahresgutachten 1994/95. Bonn. Bundestags-drucksache 1037/94.].

Hillier, B & Ibrahimo, M V (1993), "Asymmetric information and models of credit rationing," in Bulletin of Economic Research, Vol 45, pp 271–304.

Langmantel, E (1993), "LFS.MOD. Ein makroökonomisches Modell zur Analyse der deutschen Wirtschaft." Munich: Ifo-Institut für Wirtschaftsforschung. (Ifo Discussion Papers No 12.)

Milde, H & Riley, J G (1988), "Signalling in credit markets," in Quarterly Journal of Economics, Vol 103, pp 101–129.

Modigliani, F & Miller, M (1958), "The cost of capital, corporation finance and the theory of investmen," in The American Economic Review, Vol 48, pp 261–297.

Myers, S C & Majluf, N S (1984), "Corporate financing and investment decisions when firms have information that investors do not have," in Journal of Financial Economics, Vol 13, pp 187–221.

Oppenländer, K H (1988), Wachstumstheorie und Wachstumspolitik. Munich: F Vahlen.

Stiglitz, J E (1985), "Credit markets and the control of capital," in Journal of Money, Credit and Banking, Vol 17, pp 133–152.

Stiglitz, J E & Weiss, A (1981), "Credit rationing in markets with mperfect information," in American Economic Review, Vol 71, pp 187–221.

Stiglitz, J E & Weiss, A (1983), "Incentive effects of termination : applications to the credit and labor markets," in American Economic Review, Vol 73, pp 912–927.

Williamson, S D (1986), "Costly monitoring, financial intermediation and equilibrium credit rationing," in Journal of Monetary Economics, Vol 18, pp 159–179.

Chapter IX

Do Public Capital Subsidies to Firms Increase Employment?

The author would like to thank Niclas Berggren, Magnus Blomström, Gunnar Eliasson, and Dan Johansson, participants at the applied economics seminar at the Stockholm School of Economics. He would also like to thank seminar participants at the Sixth Conference of the International Joseph A Schumpeter Society in 1996 for comments on an earlier version. Financial support from Margret and Axel Ax:son Johnson Foundation is gratefully acknowledged.

Fredrik Bergström

"The popularity of the market-failure approach has caused many programs to be justified in terms of market failures. But this may simply be the rhetoric. There is often a significant difference between the stated objective of a program (to remedy some market failure) and the design of the program ... One may gain more insight into the political forces at work and the true objectives of the programs by looking at how the programs are designed and implemented than by looking at the stated objectives of the legislation."

Joseph E Stiglitz, "Economics of the Public Sector" (1988, p 83).

Abstract

I ask whether the Swedish Government, using capital subsidies, to the business sector has reached its objective to increase the total employment. To empirically examine the employment effects panel data for supported and a random sample of non-supported manufacturing firms located in the same area are compared. The study reveals no significant differences between the two samples of firms. Both groups follow the general development of the whole manufacturing industry.

1 Introduction

In many countries the government has subsidised the business sector to increase employment in regions which are lagging behind. Such supports have become increasingly popular in the EU as well.[1] To motivate the supports market-failure arguments are often used and a common theme of these arguments is that the politicians and the bureaucracy have to soften the problems caused by the market forces. It is then implied that the State has the intention, and all the information and competence needed, to solve the same problems.

This view has, however, been criticised. One critique states that politicians use market-failure arguments to motivate the decisions while the "true" intentions are to gain votes and/or to favour politically influential groups[2]. A consequence of this view is that suboptimal decisions might be taken, e g, projects which are extremely costly might be realised if the projects are politically attractive. It has also been argued that even if market failures exist and even if the State is interested in correcting them it is not certain that the State has sufficient information or competence to solve the same problems. Efficient policy decisions require knowledge about locally dispersed and changing information. Typically, however, relevant information about local conditions is missed, ignored, extremely costly to collect or potentially false and misleading.[3] Firms which apply for a support, for instance, may not reveal all information of relevance.[4] Politicians and bureaucrats, furthermore, lack the relevant competence to understand and implement many decisions efficiently. He or she normally lacks the

1 Until the creation of the European Regional Development Fund in 1975 regional policy was relatively unimportant in the EU. Since then the role of regional policy within the Union has become much more important and in 1994 the EU granted 26 Billion ECU via the structural funds; see EU (1995a) and Jones (1996). In addition to this, the European Commission reports that in twelve European countries in 1992 about 94 Billion ECU were transferred nationally to the industry; see EU (1995b). These supports can to a large extent be considered as regional policy aid.

2 For a discussion about political decision-making; see e g Peltzman (1976).

3 For a discussion about the importance of efficient use of locally dispersed information; see e g Hayek (1948), Burton (1983) and Lavoie (1985).

4 See Milgrom & Roberts (1992) for a discussion about asymmetric information.

competence to assess which firms will perform well and which firms are more likely to become losers.[5] A final problem is that politicians and bureaucrats are not working under the "laws of profit and loss," i e they do not have the competence to pick "winners" and they lack the incentives of private investors to avoid "losers."[6] Ambition to correct perceived market failure, hence, might easily turn into a Government failure.

In addition to this general critique of the State's competence to successfully intervene in the market process, there are several other reasons why politicians and bureaucrats might fail to create new jobs by using different types of subsidies. At the macro level, subsidisation of some firms' crowd-out jobs in other unsubsidised firms and if resources are transferred to declining industries lock-in effects might occur. By granting subsidies to declining industries the government can only uphold the level of employment as long as they continue to grant subsidies and the potential unemployment effects are only postponed to a later date, see Carlsson (1981) and Carlsson et al (1983). Lock-in effects might also affect growth negatively, or as Olson (1982, pp 63) argues: "Special-interest groups also slow growth by reducing the rate at which resources are reallocated from one activity or industry to another in response to new technologies or conditions. One obvious way in which they do so is by lobbying for bail-outs of failing firms, thereby delaying or preventing the shift of resources to areas where they would have a greater productivity." [7]Since the regional supports examined in this study are predominantly investment subsidies, it may be of interest to recall Eliasson & Lindberg's (1981) observation for simulation experiments of various Government support programs: The macro economy can absorb fairly significant investment mistakes at the micro firm level, the large macroeconomic effects occur when production

5   According to Eliasson (1997) the lack of relevant competence is one important reason why the government should not carry out ambitious industrial policy programs.

6   See Burton (1983).

7   See Beason & Weinstein (1996) and Lee (1996) for two empirical studies which show that the industrial policy of Japan and Korea primarily has targeted low productivity industries and consequently has not affected long-run growth positively.

is carried on, supported by subsidies, in the failed investments, tying in scarce resources, notably labour.

At the firm level the outcome is also less clear. First, even if the firm must promise to hire new workers to get a subsidy this does not necessarily mean that new jobs will be created. The support-granting authorities do not know whether the employer would have hired a new worker irrespective of the support. Second, because the support-granting authorities cannot force the firm to uphold a certain level of employment over time, the firm can, after a while, reduce the number of employees. Finally, if the recipient uses the subsidy in order to lower the prices then unsubsidised firms might be outcompeted and forced to reduce the number of employees.

Empirically, a number of government evaluations have reported that different types of producer subsidies have given rise to relatively large employment effects. For example, in the 8th Annual report on the Structural funds of the EU it is estimated that the result of Objective 2 assistance (the conversion of regions in industrial decline) is that more than 870 000 gross jobs will be either created, saved or redistributed as a result of the assistance over the 1997–99 period. A problem with this study is that it does not take the problems with subsidisation discussed above into account. While other studies, on the other hand, that try to take these problems into account often report that the employment effects of various industrial policy supports are small or non-existent. An example of the latter type of studies are Carlsson (1981) and Carlsson et al (1983), who examines the large selective supports that were granted to firms with severe economic problems in the Swedish basic industries at the end of the 1970s and in the early 1980s using a dynamic, firm-based simulation model of the entire Swedish economy. The studies, which are very critical to the use of selective subsidies to solve employment problems in declining industries, come up with several conclusions. In the short run unemployment was lowered, but to the cost of delayed reorganisation of the industry. In the long run the effects of the supports to the industry were negative because the unemployment problems were postponed until the day the support programs ended. Another effect was that non-supported firms were negatively affected because lower unemployment led to higher wages which increased the labour costs and consequently hindered the expansion of these firms. On the whole the Swedish industrial subsidies program of the 1970s amounted to granting enormous subsidies to the most mismanaged and hopeless firms. Carlsson (1981) and Carlsson et al (1983) therefore simulates different allocations of support money, holding the Government budget approximately unchanged, and distributing the subsidies, for instance, evenly on all as a general reduction in the payroll tax, or allocates the subsidies to the most profitable firms with the fastest growing exports. In that comparison, except for a temporary period of about 3–5 years where the failing firms lay off labour, the subsidy program significantly lowers growth and long term employment.

Another type of studies compare the employment development for supported firms with a control group of non-supported firms. The control group is assumed to represent what would have happened if the supported firms had not been granted any supports. Although these studies do not take into account indirect effects, e g the effects of the financing of the supports, these studies often report that the job creation effects of subsidies are relatively small. One such study is Bohm & Lind (1988, 1989). They report that in 1984–1986 a general reduction of the employer fees in the north of Sweden had no direct effects on the level of employment. See also Hart & Scott (1994) and Krmenec (1990) for two similar studies of employment effects of assistance programs in Northern Ireland and in the USA respectively.

Because different types of job-creating support programs are high on the political agenda in several countries (and especially in the EU and in the Member States of the EU) and because it is far from clear that politicians successfully can intervene in the market process the purpose of this paper is to evaluate the employment effects of two Swedish regional policy supports granted to firms (the localisation support and the investment support). The supports are primarily granted (selectively) to firms which are located in areas with economic problems, notably unemployment. The support programs are discussed in more detail in section 2.

To examine the employment effects of the supports one would have liked to know what would have happened if no supports had been granted. Because this counterfactual problem is impossible to answer, if you don't have a complete and appropriately defined simulation model of the Swedish economy (cf the studies by Carlsson 1981 and Carlsson et al 1983), a different approach has been chosen. The employment effects of the subsidies are studied by comparing the development of employment for a large number of similar supported and non-supported manufacturing firms located in the same area during the period 1988 to 1993. A limitation of our study is that only the partial effects of the subsidies are studied and that we do not take into account several of the indirect effects on the macro level which were discussed above. However, some of them are discussed at the end of the paper.

The paper is organised as follows. In section 2 the subsidies that are examined are shortly described and the data-set is presented. In section 3 an econometric model and the results of the estimations are presented. The paper ends with some concluding remarks.

2 Data

Since regional policy was introduced in Sweden at the end of the 1960s, the main objectives have been to uphold and increase employment and growth in the northern regions and especially in the so-called support areas.[8][9] To reach these objectives of regional policy different types of subsidies have been granted to firms in the support areas. Basically two types of supports have been granted: the general ones (e g lowered employer fees and employment support) which are granted to all firms that belong to the support areas, and the selective ones (e g localisation subsidies and loans, different types of development support, support to sparsely populated areas and loans to investment firms), which the firms must apply

8 This section is based primarily on SOU 1984:74, SOU 1996:69, SFS 1990:642 and NUTEK 1993:43 and 44.

9 See NUTEK 1993:43 for a description of the support areas.

for.[10] Totally about 2 billion SEK have been granted annually in the 1980s and early 1990s.[11]

In this study only the selective subsidies are examined. The selective subsidies constitute about half of all subsidies (see NUTEK 1993:43). The selective supports are largely capital supports because the total capital cost for the investment is subsidised by up to 40%. To be eligible for the support some general requirements are that the supports are to be used primarily for investments in machinery and buildings, that the firms are relatively profitable and that they promise to increase their number of employees. The supports are administrated primarily by local officials. Larger supports are granted either by NUTEK (Swedish Industrial Board for Industrial and Technical Development), which is the support-granting authority that monitors the supports, or the government.

To examine the employment effects a data-set which consists of supported and non-supported manufacturing firms has been constructed. Information from NUTEK, which is one of the authorities that administrates the support, has helped us to identify a large number of firms which received their first support in 1988. From UC AB, a credit-report firm that collects annual reports from every Swedish firm, financial as well as some non-financial information for both the supported and non-supported firms between 1988 and 1993 have been collected. To compare the development of the supported firms with a control group of non-supported firms, the firms in the control groups have been randomly collected from the whole population of firms and have not received any support between 1980 and 1995.[12]

10 See SOU 1996:69 and NUTEK 1993:43 for more detailed descriptions of the different types of supports that are granted to the industry in the support areas.

11 These supports constitute a minor part of all supports to the corporate sec-Taking into account other types of supports Barkman & Fölster (1995) have calculated that about 50 to 80 billion SEK, 1994 prices, have been transferred annually in the 1980s and 1990s to the business sector.

12 Note that both supported and non-supported firms might have received other supports. Unfortunately, data do not allow us to control for this problem.

Several selection criteria have been used. Because the capital subsidy primarily is granted to the manufacturing industry, only data for manufacturing firms are used; see Table 1.

Table 1. Distribution of the support between 1983–1994. 1994 prices.

ISIC	1	2	3	4	5	6	7	8	9	Total support
Share of support, %	<1	5	52	<1	<1	9	3	22	7	11 B.SEK

Note 1. ISIC is ISIC 68 which is called SNI 69 in Sweden. 1 = Agriculture, forestry, hunting and fishing; 2 = Mining and quarrying; 3 = Manufacturing industry; 4 = Electricity and water service; 5 = Construction; 6 = Wholesale and retail trade, restaurants and hotels; 7 = Transport and communication; 8 = Finance, insurance, real estate and business services; 9 = Community, social and personal services.
Note 2. Total support: 1994 prices.
Source: NUTEK, Statistics Sweden and own calculations.

To exclude geographical factors that might affect the development of employment only firms which are located in the so-called support areas are studied.[13] Two other criteria are that all firms have between 1 and 75 employees and that none of the firms had an operating income of zero in 1988. These criteria were used to remove small and inactive firms and large firms. Another selection criteria is that only joint-stock companies are included in the study. Due to data limitations, a problem which we have not been able to control for is the historical performance of the examined firms. If the supported firms prior to the year when the supports were granted had various economic problems and performed less well, then the employment effects of the subsidies might be underestimated, and vice versa.[14]

The first group consists of 136 non-supported firms (NS-firms), which had 1067 employees in 1988. The second group consists of 81 firms which received a subsidy in 1988 (S-firms), and which had 1392 workers employed in 1988; see Table 2. Several of the supported firms received additional supports after the first one (53%). Between 1988 and 1993 175 million SEK were transferred to the supported firms (average support

13 Most of them are in the north of Sweden; see SOU 1996:69 for a detailed description of the support areas.

14 However, a study by Bergström (1998), who uses a similar data-set, indicates that the supported firms do not differ, from a financial point of view, from randomly chosen firms.

278

per firm was 2.2 million SEK).[15] This corresponds to 234 thousands SEK per employee. Both groups have a similar distribution among the industries too; see Table 3.

Table 2. Size of samples and support, 1994 prices.

	Non-supported	Supported
Total no. of employees	1067	1392
No. of firms	136	81
Total support 1988-1993, M.SEK	0	175
Avg. supp./firm in 1988, M.SEK	0	2.2
Avg. supp./employee, T.SEK	0	234
% of all firms which received more than 1 supp 1988-1993.	0	53%

The supported firms are larger than the non-supported in the sense that they have more employees and a greater turnover per firm; see Table 4. The supported firms pay higher wages, which might indicate that they have more skilled workers than the non-supported firms. They are also established slightly later than the non-supported firms. No significant differences could be found for capital intensity (= total assets/no of employees), labour productivity (= value added/no of employees) and level of profit (= (value added - total wages)/total assets)).

15 In February, 1997, 100 SEK = $13.50.

Table 3. Distribution among industries in 1988.

| | Non-supported | | Supported | |
ISIC	Count	%	Count	%
31	9	6.6	5	6.2
32	8	5.9	6	7.4
33	22	16.2	24	29.6
34	12	8.8	2	2.5
35	14	10.3	6	7.4
36	7	5.1	1	1.2
37	1	0.7	3	3.7
38	60	44.1	32	39.5
39	3	2.2	2	2.5
Total	136	100	81	100

Note. ISIC is ISIC 68 which corresponds to SNI 69 in Sweden. 31 = Manufacture of food, beverages and tobacco; 32 = Textile, wearing apparel and leather industries; 33 = Manufacture of wood and wood products; 34 = Manufacture of paper and paper products, printing and publishing; 35 = Manufactures of chemicals, petroleum, coal, rubber and plastic products; 36 = Manufacture of non-metallic mineral products; 37 = Basic metal industries; 38 = Manufacture of fabricated metal products, machinery and equipment. 39 = Other manufacturing industries.

To conclude, most subsidies are granted to the manufacturing industry, an industry which has performed less well since the 1970s. Moreover, it seems as if the supported firms are larger, established slightly later and pay out higher wages than the non-supported ones. The situation is thus a mini-variation on the famous shipyard subsidy debacle of Sweden in the 1970s (see Carlsson et al 1981 and section 2) which generated two dimensional negative dynamics; (i) through the diversification of resources to inferior performers and (ii) through pegging wages at new recruitment to a higher level than would have been the case if these low-performing high-wage producers would have laid off people. In both ways investment and growth in other industries would have been lowered, to judge from the Carlson et al results. These indirect effects are important to keep in mind in the following section because the statistical model that is used is linear and dynamic and cumulative allocation effects, notably negative side-effects, are not taken into account. That is to say, the result underestimates the employment effects of the subsidies.

Table 4. Descriptive statistics for the whole period, 1994 prices.

	Non-supported		Supported		
	Mean	Std D.	Mean	Std D.	T-test
Capital intensity, T.SEK	589	1469	706	607	-1.56
Profit, %	0	88	5	12	-1.12
Labour productivity, T.SEK	184	197	200	117	-1.46
Wage, T.SEK	151	66	164	39	-3.52ᵃ
Age[1]	1972	14	1974	12	-3.21ᵃ
Turnover, T.SEK	7153	14064	18244	21283	-10.62ᵃ
Avg. No. of employees.	8	9	18	16	-14.35ᵃ

Note. a indicates significance at 1 percent, using a two-tailed test.
[1] Average year firms were founded

3 Employment effects of the subsidies

The development of the total employment between 1988 and 1993 shows that the supported firms seem to have had a slightly better development; see Table 5. On an aggregated level (ISIC = 3) the total number of jobs fell with 35% for the non-supported firms and with 28% for the supported firms. The supported firms had a better development in the beginning of the studied period. However, from 1989 employment dropped slightly more in the supported firms, about 34% compared with 30% for the non-supported ones.

At the two-digit level there were large differences between the industries. In industry 38 (Manufactures of fabricated metal products, machinery and equipment), which received most of the support, the supported firms performed worse than the non-supported. While in industry 33 (Manufactures of wood and wood products), which was the second largest recipient of subsidies, the supported ones had a better development than the non-supported ones. Both types of firms also experienced about the same proportion of bankruptcies; see Table 6.

Table 5. Total number of employees. 1988–1993.

		1988	1989	1990	1991	1992	1993	Change 1988-93, %
Index for the whole Industry (ISIC=3)		100	99	103	95	85	77	-23
3	NS	1067	983	1009	880	782	690	-35
	S	1392	1518	1377	1261	1083	1005	-28
31	NS	55	58	60	61	58	64	16
	S	56	76	73	68	48	49	-13
32	NS	74	66	34	32	12	9	-88
	S	135	112	112	110	102	90	-33
33	NS	268	272	280	253	213	161	-40
	S	447	472	400	398	390	378	-15
34	NS	107	84	95	85	65	66	-38
	S	21	21	20	18	17	17	-19
35	NS	73	72	66	53	50	45	-38
	S	118	162	149	145	171	126	7
36	NS	44	40	48	44	46	52	18
	S	30	30	40	70	-	-	-
37	NS	4	4	-	-	-	-	-
	S	77	81	76	75	66	62	-19
38	NS	433	382	424	348	335	290	-33
	S	489	545	489	363	286	280	-43
39	NS	9	5	2	4	3	3	-67
	S	19	19	18	14	3	3	-84

Note. The employment index for the manufacturing industry was slightly modified in 1989 so the figures before 1989 are not fully comparable with the figures after 1989.

Table 6. Bankruptcies in % of all firms which existed in 1988

	Non-supported		Supported	
Year	Count	%	Count	%
1990	2	1.5	1	1.2
1991	2	1.5	1	1.2
1992	6	4.4	2	2.5
1993	6	4.4	4	4.9
Total	16	11.8	8	9.8

The fall in total employment over the whole period (see first row in Table 5) and the increase of bankruptcies after 1992 suggests that the general economic development is important for the level of employment and that the supports are of marginal value. To test if this observation is correct, and to assess more exactly the effects of the supports, an econometric model, which controls for the general economic development as well as other factors, is presented and estimated below.

3.1 Econometric specification

The change in the level of employment over a period of time in an individual firm can be seen as a function of firm-specific factors, industry-specific factors, political factors and other factors.

To test if political factors matter, i e if the capital subsidies affect the total level of employment between 1988 and 1993, we look at the supported and the non-supported firms on an aggregate level in order to cancel out firm-specific factors. The dependent variable is an index of the development of the total employment of supported and non-supported firms at the ISIC 2-digit level for industries 31–39 between 1988 and 1993 (EMPL). To explain the dependent variable the general development in the whole industry, some control variables and a time-dummy for the supported industries for each year between 1988 and 1993 are included.[16] As a measure for the development in the whole industry an index of the overall development of employment in industry i for industries 31–39 between 1988 and 1993 (IND) is used. The time-dummies take on the value one for supported industries for each year and zero for non-supported industries, (λ). If the supported industries perform better than the non-supported industries then each of the time-dummies should be positive and significant. To test the importance of the supports over the whole period an F-test, which simultaneously test all time-dummies, is calculated. That is to say, the following hypotheses are tested.

$H_0 : \lambda_{t,S} = 0$ for t = 88, …, 93 and

$H_0 : \lambda_{88,S} = … = \lambda_{93,S} = 0$

16 The model we use is a modified version of a fixed effect model; see Judge et al (1985, Ch 13).

A problem when one tries to assess the employment effects of subsidies is the choice of time-span. If one uses too short a period there is a risk that the evaluation misrepresent the success/failure of the program. Having too long a time span might make it difficult to isolate the effects of the support. What is too short and too long is difficult to say. We have chosen six years primarily due to data limitations. However, the inclusion of time-dummies allows us to study if the effect of the support changes over the years.

Looking at the two-digit ISIC level cancel out several firm-specific factors. Some differences might still exist and in order to control for these differences, several variables which pick up different dimensions of the firms have been included. The total assets (book value) per employee (CAPINT) have been included in order to control for differences between the industries in the capital/labour structure. Because the supported industries were, on average, much larger than the non-supported ones the average turnover (SIZE) is included in order to control for differences in size. A value added per employee (LPROD) is included to control for differences in productivity. To control for differences in the skill of the workforce an average wage (SKILL) as a proxy has been used. The variable AGE (= average year firms were founded) is used as a proxy for differences between old and new firms. Finally, to control for differences in profitability the variable PROFIT (= (value added - wages)/total assets)) has been included.

The estimated model is specified as follows:

$$EMPL_{itv} = \bar{\beta_1} + \lambda_{tS} + \beta_2 IND_{itv} + \beta_3 CAPINT_{itv} + \beta_4 PROFIT_{itv} + \beta_5 SIZE_{itv}$$
$$+ \beta_6 LPROD_{itv} + \beta_7 SKILL_{itv} + \beta_8 AGE_{itv} + e_{itv}$$

where:

$i = 31,32,...,39$ (industries at the ISIC 2 - digit level),

$t = 88,...,93$ (year),

$v = NS,S$ (type of firm).

3.2 Results

To be able to calculate the F-test, two models have been estimated. One which does not contain the time-dummies and one in which the time-dummies are included. In the estimated models no problems with heteroskedasticity, non-normality or multicollinearity were found. The Durbin Watson test was in the inconclusive region. In Table 7 the results are presented.

Irrespective of model, the general development (IND) is significant and important. That is to say, both supported and non-supported firms follow the general economic development. The control variables indicate (in both models) that industries which consist of larger firms and firms that pay out higher wages have a higher employment level, i e employment does not fall as much in these industries. Other variables are insignificant.

Do the subsidies significantly increase employment? The tests of the hypotheses indicate that this has not been the case. The F-test is insignificant, i e no additional information is added when the time-dummies for the supported industries are included. The individual time-dummies are insignificant, too. That is to say, it seems as if the capital subsidies do not affect the total employment in the supported firms.

Table 7. Employment in supported and non-supported industries, 1988–1993.

Variable	Coeff.	t-value	Coeff.	t-value
CONST	-23.78	-0.82	-6.64	-0.20
IND	0.76	5.03[a]	0.69	3.65[a]
CAPINT	-4.02E-07	-0.06	-5.24E-06	-0.62
PROFIT	20.22	0.47	3.76	0.08
SIZE	1.65E-06	6.24[a]	1.96E-06	4.92[a]
LPROD	-5.12E-05	-1.14	-4.23E-05	-0.92
SKILL	2.58E-04	3.08[a]	2.57E-04	2.99[a]
AGE	-0.16	-0.52	-0.27	-0.86
$\lambda_{88,S}$			-6.72	-0.83
$\lambda_{89,S}$			-7.44	-0.86
$\lambda_{90,S}$			-7.37	-0.83
$\lambda_{91,S}$			3.76	0.44
$\lambda_{92,S}$			-13.78	-1.56
$\lambda_{93,S}$			-10.82	-1.16
N	102		102	
Adj. R Square	0.59		0.58	
SS Residual	35624		33550	
DW Test	1.62		1.61	
F-test of the time dummies.	$0.90 < F_{95\%, 14, 88} \approx 1.80$			

Note. a indicates significance at 1 percent, using a two-tailed test.

4 Concluding remarks

To create jobs, governments grant subsidies to the business sector, and to justify the subsidies they often refer to different types of market failures. However, because government intervention in the market process is not unproblematic there is a possibility that subsidisation of firms destroys more jobs than it creates. Moreover subsidisation can, if the subsidies are granted to an inferior producer, give rise to lock-in effects which affect both growth and long-term employment negatively. To study whether subsidisation of firms creates any new jobs, this paper has examined the direct employment effects in Sweden of two selective capital subsidies to the business sector.

By comparing supported and randomly chosen non-supported manufacturing firms located in the same area between 1988 and 1993 it was found that the supported ones had a better development of employment in the first year. But, after the first year the development was worse than in the non-supported firms. The proportions of bankruptcies were about the same for both types of firms. Because the two groups differed in different respects, a model, which controlled for different factors and which isolated the employment effects of the support, was estimated. The estimation showed that no differences in the development of employment could be found between supported and non-supported firms, and that both types of firms to a large extent followed the general development of the whole industry.

Although the firms must promise to hire new workers to be eligible for a support, the results of the study are not especially surprising. One reason is that the supports are capital subsidies, which give the firms an incentive to substitute labour for capital. Another reason is that the support-granting authorities cannot force the supported firms to uphold the level of employment over time. Due to the severe economic crisis the Swedish industry experienced in the beginning of the 1990s, both the supported and non-supported firms seem to have been forced to lower the number of employees or to become liquidated.

So far, the indirect employment effects of the supports have not been discussed. Perhaps the most important is the financing of supports. Resources have been withdrawn from other uses, resources which could have been used to e g start new or expand existing firms.[17] A second effect is that the supports might have led to unfair competition. The supported firms might have been able to lower their prices and outcompete non-supported firms, firms which might have been forced to fire several workers. How many jobs the financing of the sup-

17 These and other more "dynamic" welfare losses of taxes have also been discussed by e g Kirzner (1985, Ch 5–6). He argues e g that taxes (and regulations) destroy the entrepreneurial discovery process which is an important characteristic of a well-functioning competitive market process.

ports destroy and whether non-supported firms have been outcompeted by supported firms are two interesting questions for further research.

In the introduction we referred to the 8th Annual report on the Structural funds of the EU, which reports that the expected result of Objective 2 assistance is that about 870 000 gross jobs will be either created, saved or redistributed as a result of the assistance over the 1997–99 period. A policy implication of our study is that using gross jobs to assess whether a support program has been or will be successful is insufficient. Policy-makers, who wish to make good decisions and who wish to evaluate different types of support programs correctly, must take into account several other factors. In addition to the ones that have been discussed above, two more are worth mentioning. First, because it might be profitable to lobby for a subsidy it is important to take into account the costs related to lobbying and the risk that the entrepreneurs become more interested in unproductive support-seeking activities than in other more productive activities. If the entrepreneurs become less interested in productive activities, then long-run growth might be negatively affected, or as Baumol (1990, p 909) argues: "The allocation of entrepreneurship between productive and unproductive activities, though by no means the only pertinent influence, can have a profound effect on the innovativeness of the economy and the degree of dissemination of its technological discoveries." Second, government evaluations of supports to the business sector should to a larger extent examine productivity effects rather than the number of jobs created, because productivity is much more important for welfare and competitiveness in the long run.

Bibliography

Baumol, W J (1990), "Entrepreneurship : productive, unproductive, and destructive," in *Journal of Political Economy*, Vol 98, No 5, pp 893–921.

Beason, R & Weinstein, D E (1996), "Growth, economies of scale, and targeting in Japan (1955–1990)," in *The Review of Economics and Statistics*, Vol 78, No 2, May, pp 286–295.

Bergström, F (1998), "Characteristics of publicly supported firms." Unpublished paper. Stockholm School of Economics, Dept of Economics.

Bohm, P & Lind, H (1988), "Sysselsättningseffekter av sänkt arbetsgivaravgift i Norrbotten 1984–1986." Research Papers in Economics 1988:1 RS. University of Stockholm, Dept of Economics.

– (1989), "Regionala arbetskraftssubventioner – har de någon effekt?" in *Ekonomisk Debatt*, No 5, pp 342–350.

Burton, J (1983), *Picking losers ... ? : the political economy of industrial policy*. Hobart paper 99. London: Institute of Economic Affairs.

Carlsson, B, et al (1981), "Industristödspolitiken och dess inverkan på samhällsekonomin." Stockholm: IUI (The Industrial Institute for Economic and Social Research).

Carlsson, B (1983), "Industrial subsidies in Sweden : simulations on a micro-to-macro model." Ch 6 in Eliasson, G & Fries, H (ed), (1983), *Microeconometrics*. Stockholm: IUI Yearbook 1982-1983.

Eliasson, G & Lindberg, T (1981), "Allocation and growth effects of corporate income taxes." In Eliasson, G & Södersten, J (eds), *Business taxation, finance and firm behaviour*. Stockholm: IUI Conference Reports 1981:1.

Eliasson, G (1998), "Competence blocs and industrial policy in the knowledge-based economy." Forthcoming in *Science Technology Industry (STI) Review*. Paris: OECD.

EU (1995a), *Europeiska unionens stöd och lån : vägledning till gemenskapens finansiering.* Brussels: EUR-OP (the official publisher of the institutions of the European Union).

EU (1995b), *Fjärde översikten från kommissionen av statliga stöd i Europeiska Gemenskapen inom tillverkningsindustrin och vissa andra sektorer.* Brussels: KOM (95) 365.

Hart, M & Scott, R (1994), "Measuring the effectiveness of small firm policy : some lessons from Northern Ireland," in *Regional Studies,* Vol 28, No 8, pp 849–858.

Hayek, F A (1948), "The use of knowledge in society." Reprinted in Ch 14 in Ebeling, R M (ed) (1991), *Austrian economics : a reader.* Hillsdale: Hillsdale College Press.

Jones, R (1996), *The politics and economics of the European Union.* Cheltenham: Edward Elgar.

Judge, G G, et al (1985), *The theory and practice of econometrics,* 2nd ed. New York: John Wiley and Sons.

Kirzner, I M (1985), *Discovery and the capitalist process.* Chicago: University of Chicago Press.

Krmnec, A J (1990), "The employment impacts of an investment incentive : differential efficiency of the Industrial Revenue Board," in *Regional Studies,* Vol 24, No 2, pp 95–107.

Lavoie, D (1985), *National economic planning : what is left?* Cambridge, MA: Ballinger Publishing Company.

Lee, J-W (1996), "Government interventions and productivity growth," in *Journal of Economic Growth,* Vol 1, September, pp 391–414.

NUTEK R 1993:43, *Värdet av regionalpolitiken.* Stockholm: NUTEK.

NUTEK 1993:44, *Regionalpolitiskt företagsstöd : effekter på regional och nationell omvandling 1975–1991.* Stockholm: NUTEK.

NUTEK (1994), *Finansieringsmöjligheter i Sverige.* Stockholm: NUTEK.

Olson, M (1982), *The rise and decline of nations : economic growth, stagflation, and social rigidities.* New Haven: Yale University Press.

Peltzman, S (1976), "Toward a more general theory of regulation," in *Journal of Law and Economics,* Vol 19, pp 211–240.

SFS 1990:642, *Förordning om regionalpolitiskt företagsstöd.* Stockholm: Fritzes.

SOU 1984:74, *Regional utveckling och mellanregional utjämning.* Betänkande av regionalpolitiska kommittén. Stockholm: Fritzes.

SOU 1996:69, *Kompetens och kapital : om statligt stöd till företag.* Betänkande från Företagsstödutredningen. Stockholm: Fritzes.

The Authors

David Allen, Professor, co-editor of *Information Economics and Policy*, Concord, MA, USA.

Fredrik Bergström, PhD Candidate, Department of Economics, Stockholm School of Economics, Stockholm, Sweden.

Jean-Philippe Bonardi, PhD Candidate in Strategic Management, HEC School of Management, Jouy-en-Josas, France.

Richard H Day, Professor, Department of Economics, University of Southern California, Los Angeles, USA.

Gunnar Eliasson, Professor, Department of Industrial Economics, Royal Institute of Technology, Stockholm, Sweden.

Erik Gørtz, Professor, Institute of Economics, University of Copenhagen, Denmark

Nils Karlson, President, City University of Stockholm, Sweden.

Erik Moberg, Dr, independent scholar, Sweden.

Karl Heinrich Oppenländer, Professor, President of the Ifo Institute for Economic Research, Munich, Germany.

Bertrand Quélin, Professor, HEC School of Management, Jouy-en-Josas, France.

Andrew N Reed, Dr, Project Manager, Agricultural Reform Implementation Support (ARIS) Program, Ministry of Agriculture and Food of the Russian Federation.

Clas Wihlborg, Professor, School of Economics and Commercial Law, Gothenburg School of Economics, Sweden.

Index

295